Effective Grading Practices for Secondary Teachers

*To Kenneth Frank Nagel, my dad, who has taught me that life is only lived when you are **standing inside the fire.***

Effective Grading Practices for Secondary Teachers

Practical Strategies to Prevent Failure, Recover Credits, and Increase Standards-Based/Referenced Grading

Dave Nagel

CORWIN
A SAGE Company

A SAGE Company

FOR INFORMATION:

Corwin

A SAGE Company

2455 Teller Road

Thousand Oaks, California 91320

(800) 233-9936

www.corwin.com

SAGE Publications Ltd.

1 Oliver's Yard

55 City Road

London EC1Y 1SP

United Kingdom

SAGE Publications India Pvt. Ltd.

B 1/I 1 Mohan Cooperative Industrial Area

Mathura Road, New Delhi 110 044

India

SAGE Publications Asia-Pacific Pte. Ltd.

3 Church Street

#10-04 Samsung Hub

Singapore 049483

Acquisitions Editor: Dan Alpert

Associate Editor: Kimberly Greenberg

Editorial Assistant: Cesar Reyes

Project Editor: Veronica Stapleton Hooper

Copy Editor: Sarah J. Duffy

Typesetter: C&M Digitals (P) Ltd.

Proofreader: Jeff Bryant

Indexer: Sheila Bodell

Cover Designer: Gail Buschman

Marketing Manager: Stephanie Trkay

Printed in the United States of America.

A catalog record of this book is available from the Library of Congress.

ISBN: 978-1-4833-1989-6

This book is printed on acid-free paper.

SFI Certified Sourcing
www.sfiprogram.org
SFI-00453

SFI label applies to text stock

15 16 17 18 19 10 9 8 7 6 5 4 3 2 1

Contents

Foreword

In schools, there should be an 11th commandment, "Thou shall not touch my gradebook." Without a doubt, grading is one of the most private, autonomous acts that takes place in a school. Those who venture into conversations about grading need to be well equipped to tackle these practices. There has never been a more critical topic to address than in school today. Once you open the door to grading conversations, you enter into conversations around instruction, assessment, engagement, motivation, and classroom management, to name a few. Leaders need to be prepared to engage colleagues in these conversations.

Many of the current practices result in grades not truly reflecting student achievement; rather, they reflect a hodgepodge of components such as behavior, homework, and participation. The result? Students don't have an accurate picture of what they've mastered in a course. This impacts students not only today but with their future postsecondary plans. The roadblock? It is that tradition is often what stands in the way of true reform. The time is *now* for change.

There are numerous resources about grading and reporting. The hard work is not acknowledging the research, it is putting it into action. Nevertheless, what Dave Nagel has accomplished with his book is taking theory, adding the policy, and turning it into practices that work. When schools do adopt new policies and practices, you cannot overlook the fact that, while districts have many policies on the books, few, if any, impact teachers' daily work. With this seminal work, educators will have the tools in their hands to tackle this 11th Commandment and it will serve as a catalyst for your school to identify your its mission and the purpose of grades. First, Dave tackles the question of why. Most teachers were winners in the traditional grading system and do not see the compelling reason for change. Decisions are based on experience versus evidence. Carefully, Dave helps schools develop their own *why* for change. In this process of transforming practices, teacher voice is needed, and this book provides key questions to gather that voice.

Throughout this book, Dave provides vivid examples of grading scenarios, causing readers to pause and question their own practices—from the effectiveness of homework based on the latest research from John Hattie (2008, 2012) to Rick Stiggins and Jan Chappuis (2011). The examples make the case for schools to develop a clear set of grading parameters so that grades are truthful, reliable, and impartial. These parameters provide the basis for schools to be confident that grades are accurate and that there is a high level of consistency.

Once you've determined your school's mission for grading, Dave provides a framework for reducing failures by turning the tables and having the consequence for not doing the work be simply *doing the work*, perhaps with a stipulated second chance. Again, the theory needs to be put into practice, and Dave provides templates and examples on how schools can have more students learning at higher levels.

The timing of this book is opportune as school are currently implementing new standards. Often, schools become stymied in their reform when they attempt to implement a full-blown standards-based report card rather than using standards-based strategies. As articulated by Dave Nagel, the latter lead to higher levels of accuracy while still maintaining traditional letter grades.

Some may argue that now is not the time for a change, or this can wait until we've perfected our grading plan, or—a common theme—we need to wait for buy-in. However, each day students under traditional, flawed systems are impacted by antiquated and, at times, harmful practices. In this enlightening text, Dave Nagel paves the path for schools to, at last, take action!

Jeffrey A. Erickson

Acknowledgments

Kristin Anderson, director of professional learning at Corwin, has been influential in my journey as a professional developer and now published author. Her knowledge and passion about increasing the quality of education and the lives of children through working effectively with adults and increasing their learning has had a tremendous impact on me. She is by far one of the reasons why this project has come to fruition.

Dr. BR Jones, superintendent of Tate County School District, in Tate County, Mississippi, has been both a colleague and a close personal friend for the past 5 years. His knowledge and drive to become the best learner he can be each and every day has served as a model for me in my path to authorship. He provided me with many quality insights that shaped my thinking for crafting many of the ideas contained in this book.

Dan Alpert, senior acquisitions editor at Corwin, has been an exceptional mentor and friend during the process of becoming a first-time author. The expertise, knowledge, and time that he devotes and shares so unselfishly are an example for everyone. He desires only to help all his authors see their ideas come to light in order to shape the path for more students to be successful. I cannot thank him enough.

Larry Ainsworth, international author, keynoter, and educational thought leader, has shaped virtually every part of my career as a professional developer and now author by example. I describe him as the best teacher I have ever met. He has always been there to help me in forming my thoughts into a message that can be transferred to others that is practical and useful.

Finally, Kristen Nagel—my rock and my wife. For everything you do to support me and Nicholas (10), Zachary (5), and Jacob (3), without ever having to be acknowledged—simply thank you.

PUBLISHER'S ACKNOWLEDGMENTS

Corwin gratefully acknowledges the contributions of the following reviewers:

David G. Daniels
Principal
Susquehanna Valley Senior High School
Conklin, NY

Martin J. Hudacs
Superintendent of Schools
Solanco School District
Quarryville, PA

Darryl L. Williams
Associate Superintendent of Middle Schools
Montgomery County Public Schools
Rockville, MD

About the Author

 **Dave Nagel** is an international educational consultant and researcher. His educational career started as a middle school science and high school biology teacher. His administrative experiences involved being a middle school assistant principal, high school associate principal, and director of extended day and credit recovery programs. In his former district, Dave was instrumental in implementing power standards and performance assessments. He was honored numerous times as a "Senior Choice" winner, with graduating seniors selecting him as someone who dramatically affected their life in a positive way.

His efforts in augmenting and implementing a multifaceted credit recovery model transformed Ben Davis High School (enrollment 3,400, Grades 10–12) from a middle-of-the-road high school in terms of diplomas awarded into a graduation factory. By focusing on differentiated goals for students based on specific proficiency measures, Ben Davis was able to improve its graduation rate 14% in just over 4 years.

Dave has been a national and international presenter and consultant to schools for over 10 years. Using his experience and expertise, he has presented and helped schools, from pre-K through Grade 12, implement effective practices leading to gains in student achievement. His main focus when working with schools has revolved around assessment, instruction, leadership, and effective collaboration. He has worked specifically with schools in implementing the following topics: prioritizing standards, common formative assessments, building authentic performance tasks, effective use of scoring guides, data teams, rigorous curriculum design, and effective grading practices.

In the past few years, Dave has done extensive work with teachers and leaders across the country assisting schools and entire districts through a proven process to identify essential Common Core State Standards and their relationship with state and local assessment results.

Dave has also done extensive work around helping school teams work on critical aspects of effective collaboration. This has significantly impacted student achievement through focusing on intentional adult actions.

Published multiple times in various publications such as *Principal Leadership* and *Educational Leadership*, Dave has also presented at various national conferences such as those hosted by the Association for Supervision and Curriculum Development, National Staff Development Council, National Association of Secondary School Principals, and National School Boards Association.

Dave stays very busy with his beautiful and supportive wife, Kristen, and three boys (ages 10, 5, and 3). Kristen works full time and does most of the raising of the children, and he is extremely grateful for her every day. He acknowledges every day that the Lord guides his actions and is the driving force in his life.

Introduction

I was recently on a long layover and finished with work, so I went looking for something leisurely to read. The shop was sold out of *Sports Illustrated* and *ESPN The Magazine,* my usual go-to choices for easy reading. The *Time* magazine cover caught my attention, so I grabbed it. The lead article was on the economy and conveyed a bleak picture of where the United States was financially:

> The US economy remains almost comatose. The slump already ranks as the longest period of sustained weakness since the Great Depression. The economy is staggering under many structural burdens as opposed to familiar cyclical problems. The structural faults represent once in a lifetime dislocations that will take years to work out. Among them job draught, the debt hangover, the banking collapse, the real estate depressing, and the runaway federal deficit. (Gwynne, 1992)

The quote sent chills down my spine. I am the father of three young children and knee-deep in planning financially and maximizing 529 plans. As I read "once in a lifetime dislocations" and "longest period of sustained weakness since the Great Depression," my heart sank.

I eventually realized that the airport newsstand never throws away old issues because I was actually reading *Time* . . . from September 28, 1992. That was when the quote was published and when the Dow Jones industrial average was 3,276! Yet the quote was still somewhat believable. In over 20 years, very little has changed related to the economy.

GRADING: AN 80-YEAR+ WAR

I have worked with many school districts over the past few years, adjusting or completely revamping existing grading policies and or practices. Many teachers, leaders, and even parents have been open to the idea of looking at grading practices just like they do at instruction or assessment practices; effectiveness and what prevents failure and increases achievement trumps what they like personally or what they have been doing for the past decade.

A few places have been very resistant to change. I found myself particularly frustrated at the lack of progress in one district after two full evenings of discussions and brainstorming sessions. Teachers, parents, community members, and even some alumni had voiced concern and even outrage at some ideas that were being considered related to grading practices as well as how grades would be reported. That night, I came across an article written by someone who seemed to have just walked a mile in my shoes. The following is a quote was from his facilitation of a grading committee meeting that seemed to resemble mine:

> The Committee on Grading was called upon to study grading procedures. At first, the task of investigating the literature seemed to be rather a hopeless one. What a mass and mess it all was! Could order be brought out of such chaos? Could points of agreement among American educators concerning the perplexing grading problem actually be discovered? It was with considerable misgiving and trepidation that the work was finally begun. (Middleton, 1933)

That statement came from a source published more than 80 years ago. Oh, how very little has changed in 80+ years. The world seemed so different then—a dollar could certainly buy you a lot more, as Figure 1 shows. But teachers, administrators, parents, and others were arguing about grading practices much as they do today.

Grading change dialogue and discussions do not have to continue to be painful and feared experiences. Teachers, administrators, and parents

Figure 1   How Much Certain Items Cost in 1933

• Average new house: $5,750	• Pound of hamburger meat: 11 cents
• Average early wages: $1,550	• Silk and rayon stockings: 39 cents
• Gallon of gas: 10 cents	• Plymouth 6 car: $445
• Average monthly rent $18	• Health-building tonic: 89 cents
• Vacuum cleaner: $17.75	• Campbell's vegetable soup: 10 cents
• Loaf of bread: 7 cents	
• Newport Boulevard Ladies Hat: $1.69	• Radio: $52.00
	• Average laborer's weekly wage: $20

Source: Adapted from "The Year 1933 News, Prices and Popular Culture" (http://www.thepeoplehistory.com/1933.html).

all want what's best for students. We all simply must keep a sense of perspective that perhaps our beliefs and experiences might not include examples of evidence that current grading actions are truly impacting learning and achievement. Far too often tradition and opinion have driven grading discussions. The ideas and strategies in this book should help with that.

Disagree but Don't Be Disagreeable

Grading change is a passionate topic. For successful implementation of any changes and potential resolutions to come to fruition, we must agree to not be disagreeable. Far too often debates about grading changes involve anger and indifference. This is usually because we've *all* had grading done to us. Everyone, with rare exception, whether we reside within the confines of the educational world or not, has spent time in schools. We have been administered, given, received, earned, blessed with, rewarded by, or punished with GRADES. This has led to many teachers, parents, and even students having a perception about which grading practices or policies should ring true until the second coming—or the first coming of a Cubs World Series title since 1908. (As a native Chicagoan and die-hard White Sox fan, I sure hope the latter never happens.)

Example

Former Norfolk Superintendent Dr. Stephen Jones was quoted in an article discussing possible tweaks to a grading system (Bowers, 2009). When talking about minimum grading policies implemented from the previous year, he clearly agreed with critics that "the grading change this year wasn't adequately explained" (para. 4). Jones said he wanted to "encourage students to keep trying as well as create consistency and fairness across the grading scale and between schools" (para. 6). He said, "The intent was to give kids a fighting chance if they had a bad day. Saying to them, 'You failed this grade, and you have every opportunity to bring it up'" (para. 7).

Despite Jones's admission that there was some fault in the way the change was implemented and his open invitation for suggestions for improvement, commenters were less rational or helpful and more passionate and irritated. Here are some comments from the online article, each followed with my commentary:

1. "To create consistency and fairness across the grading scale and between schools. The scale that begins at zero has been used since I was in school. That's the one that is 'consistent and fair' and used all around the world. Stick with it."

Here is where we have to ask where our schools would be if we didn't continue to innovate and devise better ways to do things. Technology and specific standards for classroom lessons are just two examples of innovations that are much different than in even the recent past.

2. "I think it should be the teacher's discretion whether the student's lowest grade should be a 61 or a zero. Therefore, no student or parent can complain to an administrator or anyone else if the performance was failing and the student receives a grade less than a 61. This will teach students that they cannot play the system and get away with it."

We must demand consistency and reliability in all classroom practices. Schools can and should provide a proper amount of structured freedom to allow teachers to thrive, but not allow islands of autonomy.

3. "As a certified educator in Virginia Beach, I am outraged that they are going in the same direction. Giving a kid who does nothing a 50 is a lie. What about the kid who tries hard and makes a 50. Why should he bother. Also, he grades are being 'fluffed' up for appearances sake. The kids will suffer when they hit higher education. This is dishonest and wrong!"

We have to be cautious of emotion. This certified teacher forgot the importance of punctuation:

As a certified educator in Virginia Beach, I am outraged that they are going in the same direction. Giving a kid who does nothing a 50 is a lie. ***What about the kid who tries hard and makes a 50?*** Why should he bother?

We have to remember: Missing punctuation can kill!

My message here is simple. The teacher making this comment is passionate, and I would bet my bottom dollar she cares deeply about her students. We all can lose focus when emotion gets the best of us, though. Trust me, I know; just ask my wife!

This is a prime example of how heated grading change discussions can be—not much different from the 1933 example of passion and anger. Many school districts simply choose to avoid making changes rather than face such pushback. Unfortunately, this means they may be stuck using antiquated grading practices that do not benefit students, teachers, or anyone else in the education community.

In this book, I strive to address why grading changes can be so difficult to implement and what school teachers and administrators must consider when attempting to make meaningful changes in school and classroom grading approaches. I also provide examples and actions that can prevent unnecessary failures and increase the honesty in grading at the middle and high school level without decreasing expectations.

Change Not Usually Welcomed

So many things have changed in our lives in the past few decades alone. Can you remember not asking for someone's cell phone number? When was the last time you didn't consider Googling something that you had a question about? Only 25 years ago, Germany was two countries—East Germany and West Germany. The world is a much different place than it used to be.

American secondary schools have changed a great deal in the past two decades as well. Was it always the norm for teachers to focus on a standard in their lessons? Is online learning at least some part of the equation for lesson and instructional planning for students? Don't we now consider the least restrictive environment for students with special education needs? Finally, when was the last time middle and high school administrators used paper and pencil instead of computer programs to assist them in scheduling their staff and students?

These are only a few examples of practices and approaches in middle and high schools that have changed in the past 15 to 20 years alone. Many archaic grading *practices* that predated these and other advances in secondary schools are still well in place regardless of changes in grading *policy*. This book is predicated on the notion that practice trumps policy.

Example

In 2009, Texas state senator Jane Nelson (R-Flower Mound) authored Senate Bill 2033, barring minimum grade policies in schools. This occurred after some teachers had voiced concern that they had been ordered not to assign grades lower than a minimum percentage—usually a 50 on a 100% scale. The legislation was called the "truth in grading" law. The law was created to minimize the ability of schools and districts to put forth policy that mandates minimum grading (Robelen, 2010).

Eleven school districts filed lawsuits to stop the full implementation of the law. They felt the law was unclear and that it should apply only to class assignments and not to progress reports or semester report cards. They cited vague language in the law. The Texas School Alliance, representing the state's large, urban districts, argued that minimum grades provide early failure detection for students at risk of dropping out, so that one blown grade doesn't doom them to failing a semester.

The courts ruled against the schools and stated that the law was not ambiguous and reflected the legislature's intent to protect teachers from having to issue grades to students they felt they did not earn. Some called the policies fundamental grade inflation. Districts in Houston, Dallas, and Fort Worth that had minimum grading policies that were approved and being implemented abolished them. Shortly after the ruling, Linda Bridges, president of the Texas chapter of the American Federation of Teachers (AFT), said, "We believe that any shred of doubt about the meaning of this law has been eliminated and that all school districts must, without further delay, comply fully with the legislative intent to outlaw minimum grades" (quoted in Stutz, 2010, para. 6). She went on to say that the Texas AFT would "be on watch" to make sure all school districts come into compliance with the truth-in-grading law.

In November 2012, Senator Nelson pre-filed SB 132 to clarify the law and its verbiage prohibiting what is considered grade inflation (Texas AFT, 2012).

Sec. 28.0216. DISTRICT GRADING POLICY. A school district shall adopt a grading policy, including provisions for the assignment of grades on class assignments and examinations, before each school year. A district grading policy:

(1) Must require a classroom teacher to assign a grade that reflects the student's relative mastery of an assignment;

(2) May not require a classroom teacher to assign a minimum grade for an assignment without regard to the student's quality of work; and

(3) May allow a student a reasonable opportunity to make up or redo a class assignment or examination for which the student received a failing grade.

Source: Texas Education Code. (2003). Retrieved from http://www.easylawlookup.com/_easylookup .blp?ru_sz=50&data=EDUCAT2&site=EASY&spon=&stype=P&setnewzip=y&sterm=%2B&smode=AND&s exact=ON&pgno=176&par=0&dlevel=0&subject=&topic=&ZipCodeLocation=78232&goaction=Continu e&submit=Go#par_0.

We must fully support the AFT's stance on ensuring schools and districts uphold and abide by all laws. The question becomes, are we then ensuring that all schools are just as much on watch to ensure the quality of classroom instruction related to student achievement is held to the highest standard? The issue here is not easily answered, and people are very passionate about it. This book tackles issues like this by addressing specifically classroom and school grading practices to minimize unnecessary failures and to support student needs when recovering grades and credits.

Standards-Based Grading

The standards movement of the late 1990s and early 2000s sent shockwaves into many high school classrooms where, prior to their conception and implementation, teacher autonomy in terms of what was taught and how it was timed was the norm—as was how anything students turned in was graded.

There was, however, a well-founded belief that students and parents should expect the same standard of classroom instruction in all classrooms in any given school or any given school district. This idea gave birth to the instructional standards revolution of the early 21st century. The thought that some standards would be taught and assessed at a high level in all classrooms regardless of teacher opinion, judgment, and belief was ground-breaking for some and earth-shattering for others. While logically this made sense, it certainly infringed on a common belief among many teachers: "I know what's best for my students." Standards attempted to eliminate the educational lottery, whereby a school's computer-based student information system may assign a student to teacher X versus teacher Y, and thus determine a different set of expectations and ultimately different grades for that course for the same level of proficiency.

Districts nationwide have spent the past decade working on aligning curriculum and assessment practices to match their adopted set of standards. Many states are still attempting to eliminate the same lottery on a nationwide basis with the advent and implementation of national standards like the Common Core. While there has been much commentary about their intent or merit, for the most part weren't they created to ensure that, whether you are a Hoosier, a Buckeye, or from the Show Me State, there is not a different set of standards and objectives for our students? Finally, attempts at standards-based and standards-referenced grading are becoming more and more prevalent in schools and districts. Many are having a hard time implementing standards-based and standards-referenced grading because of the fear of abandoning the letter grades that teachers and parents are comfortable with. This book will address how schools can increase the quantity and quality of standards-based and standards-referenced grades successfully without having to completely abandon traditional letter grades.

Dialogue Not Monologue

Schools must have open and transparent communication with teachers, parents, and other stakeholders about both *how* and *why* any grading changes are taking place. They must start first by sharing what will not change—or what will be the grading givens. Far too many grading change initiatives have failed because of a lack of two-way communication. A lack of listening, most often on the part of the schools, has directly led to these failed attempts at change.

My grandmother told me often, "You have two ears and one mouth for a reason, David Theodore!" We need to apply this lesson to the topic of grading practices as much as anything else. Listening to what is perceived about grades and grading practices may open the door to conversations and dialogue to not only avoid anger but also lead to support for implementation. This book will also address how to better communicate and collaborate on grading decisions with the entire school community.

Emotion and Thought

When any discussion involves passion, there is potential for an absence of reasoning. Fred Kincer, a former colleague of mine, often said, "God gave us two great gifts—emotion and thought, both useful and powerful. The problem is, you can only use one at a time."

We have all been in situations where we may have been arguing or trying to prove a point so much that it's quite possible we forgot what we were trying to argue about. When this happens, with rare exception, it would benefit us greatly to acknowledge we are usually trying to come to some sort of resolution. Will it be safe to say that—based on evidence from arguments 80 years ago, laws being passed in Texas, and a superintendent being blasted for doing his very best to make sure students do not unnecessarily fail—the grading debate quite possibly makes us need to consider Fred's emotion and thought metaphor?

Ownership of discovery can limit emotion. Far too often, secondary teachers have not been involved in many of the grading decisions that directly impact their day-to-day work. In this book I will refer to a gap in the evidence and research related to effective grading practices, where teacher voice is noticeably absent. Allowing, and even demanding, teachers to conduct their own grading action research is essential for emotion to be eliminated from grading practice adjustments and decisions. Finally, this book will focus specifically on how to create and conduct grading action research to better help districts in minimizing emotion and maximizing logical buy-in and benefit for the entire education community.

DO NOT WORRY OVER OUTLIERS

Secondary schools must implement strategies to best prevent failures while increasing overall student success. Teachers and administrators should not dwell on a few students that a particular or nontraditional grading practice may not work for, or worry about students that may attempt to beat the new system—because many are already beating the old one. Middle and high school teachers applying strategies to prevent failure by offering students multiple paths for proficiency can create a clearer picture of which students need specific interventions and which are ready to advance to higher levels. I have strived to share in this book strategies that are evidence based but also practical. I have been fortunate to have witnessed the positive impacts of many of these strategies in schools I have directly worked in.

The average rate of return on the U.S. stock market has been 8% since the late 19th century, but unless adjustments are made, we see huge dips in its success. Every time one of these strategies was reattempted or implemented a second time, adjustments had to be made for its success. There is not any one grading practice that will be equally effective in every classroom; however, there are approaches that provide teachers with a roadmap for increased success with students. Together, we can navigate them.

I thank you for taking the time to read and consider the ideas in this book.

Yours in education,
Dave

PART I

Why Changing Grading at the Secondary Level Is a Tough Sell

Grading

1

Long Perceived as the One Immovable Element in a Constantly Evolving Field

For which situation would you invest more energy: Earn $100 or avoid losing $100 you already have? If you're like most people, and if you answer this question very honestly and don't just say what you think people want to hear or what you want to believe about yourself, you'd work harder to avoid loss. Nobel Memorial Prize in Economics winner Daniel Kahneman talks in his 2011 *New York Times* best-selling book, *Thinking, Fast and Slow,* about his findings related to humans and loss aversion. The pain of loss is often twice as strong as the reward from a gain. That idea resonates with many of us, even though we might not want to admit that because of the fear of being perceived as too conservative and not a go-getter. Yet the evidence is clear that we will fight harder for things we already have.

A 2010 University of Chicago study examined the impact of merit pay, a financial reward for increasing student achievement. Teachers were divided into three groups: Group A teachers received their merit pay, approximately $8,000 up front at the start of the year. If their students met their achievement targets, the teachers would keep the money; if not, they would have to return it. Group B teachers had the same targets for their students for the same merit pay incentive, but they would not receive the financial reward until after students had met the targets. Group C teachers did not have a merit pay incentive. Results? Group A teachers had student improvements that were double those of the other two groups (Fryer, Levitt, List, & Sadoff, 2012). Loss aversion can lead people to engage in greater efforts to maintain what they already possess. For people who have already lost something else, this desire to protect what they have increases and intensifies.

ACCOUNTABILITY DECREASES INDEPENDENCE

In the past, the teaching profession thrived on an input = effective model. Effectiveness of teacher practices was determined by considering what the teachers did, looking at the execution of their actions and their strategies. Effectiveness of teacher actions was not, until recently, judged on the impact those actions had on students, specifically related to how they perform on academic standards. At the turn of the 21st century, two occurrences took place that changed the landscape of schools and classrooms related to increased accountability in U.S. schools:

1. Virtually every state had implemented academic standards in core subjects (reading and math).

2. The No Child Left Behind Act of 2001 was signed into law.

Schools at all levels began to monitor classroom practices for fidelity and effectiveness to ensure students could meet and demonstrate mastery of instructional standards. Teachers being able to just close their door and teach became a thing of the past. This new accountability in schools replaced the words *good* with *effective* and *what I like* with *what works*. At the secondary school level, this change in landscape has been especially profound. Middle and high school classrooms have a long history of being closed off to anyone other than the presiding teacher, where the sentiment was "Let me close my door and teach." Teachers had lost freedom in areas they had never given much thought to owning completely.

Content Freedom

Accountability changed how teachers were able to determine the specific content they taught to their students to address specific standards. Teachers lost a great deal of autonomy in terms of determining topics they focused on in their classrooms. Many had to remove certain units they had taught for years because these were not specifically tied to their school's instructional standards. This was ground-breaking for some and earth-shattering for others. Some, perhaps many, secondary teachers felt this was an infringement of their professional opinion as to what subject matter their students needed to learn. Many teachers felt a sense of loss (#1) in their ability to determine *what* they would be teaching to students.

Teaching Method Freedom

Teachers also saw an increase in accountability around instructional strategies and approaches in their classrooms. The emphasis shifted from what was being *taught* to what was being *learned*. Teacher effectiveness swung from being historically about what they did to being about what their students are able to do. Building and district leaders began to monitor classrooms with increased presence and visibility. Research evidence about which instructional practices had the most impact on student achievement came to the forefront. The filter for how teachers used classroom practices was no longer experience. Instructional approaches many teachers had been accustomed to using with their students might no longer be considered best practices. Teachers were now being asked, recommended, or mandated to use different instructional strategies in their classrooms. Many had not experienced this level of outside influence on the decisions they made once they closed their classroom doors. Teachers perceived this as another loss (#2), especially at the secondary level.

Results Only = Freedom

Finally, the implementation of No Child Left Behind required schools to show consistent increases in student achievement, which added another layer of accountability. Teachers, many for the first time, were being compared to theirs peers based on results, test scores, and student outcomes. Many educators did not embrace this with open arms.

In his 2007 dissertation at the University of Minnesota, Edward Minnema's findings called for teachers to go beyond their perceptions of what they felt was effective to look more at the evidence on student outcomes. One teacher commented, "We have always done it this way and we are the best, so why would we change?" This subtle statement in the middle is telling: "we are the best." It likely originates from one teacher's belief in comparing his school's results to others. This type of statement has been a common response when grading practice changes are mentioned, proposed, or enacted in many secondary schools. The standards movement pushed the sentiment of "I taught it. They just didn't learn it," if not off the table, at least to the very edge. Teachers, in many schools, lost (#3) their ability to rest on the notion that input = output. Teachers have worked and always will work very hard. This loss was that the effort and painstaking work might not be equated with results and, worse, might not get noticed.

Impact of These Losses

While this may seem effective from the outside looking in, for teachers, especially in middle and high schools, this meant change by subtraction—giving up favorite lessons, favorite videos, favorite activities, and more. For many middle and high school educators, including me, this change was perceived as loss. I can remember distinctly being angry that dissecting bullfrogs and squids was eliminated from the ninth-grade biology curriculum in my former district because these activities did not address state science standards. This infuriated me. I remember not being able to connect the dissections to any standards in our curriculum. I enjoyed them because the students thought they were neat and I could use them as a motivator for a week or two prior. I thought, "Who is this person to tell me what I can or cannot do when I close my classroom door?" Although I eventually accepted the change, I distinctly recall feeling a sense of loss.

Many secondary educators have, or perceive to have, lost a great deal in the past 15 years. As we learned from Kahneman, when we lose something, we can easily feel threatened to protect what we still have with more intensity. American middle and high school teachers still had one area of classroom actions that had not been taken away or analyzed for impact to know what practices work or don't. For many teachers, the last thing they perceive they can protect is their grading practices, and they're *not* going down without a fight!

GRADING IN SECONDARY CLASSROOMS—THE BASTION OF AUTONOMY

The last mainstay of control that many middle and high school teachers feel they have is grading practices. Giving these practices up is not something they would want to do anyway. Having lost other classroom practice freedoms, they feel even more strongly that they need to protect themselves against the loss of the practices they use to grade students.

While grading policies in many districts attempt to guide teacher practices to ensure fairness and equality for students, rarely have specific practices been defined that would direct teacher actions. Often the best evidence for how to implement grading practices in middle and high schools is not considered. There are several factors middle and high school teachers and leaders can look at as to why there continue to be challenges to teachers making effective adjustments in grading: ineffective collaboration, experience trumps evidence, and lack of teacher voice related to grading changes.

Ineffective Collaboration

The structure and schedule of most high schools and a large number of middle schools has led to professional isolation. Teachers are often the only adults in their classrooms, and they rarely cross paths with other teachers except in the hall or the teachers lounge. Very often in secondary schools, even with the existence of professional learning communities (PLCs), collaboration focuses on topics other than best practices and their impact on student achievement.

Former superintendent and author Richard DuFour has written a great deal on the potential impact of effective PLCs and has called for schools to *deprivatize* the professional practices of teachers for over a decade. His colleague Robert Eaker (2002) says, "The traditional school often functions as a collection of independent contractors united by a common parking lot" (quoted in Schmoker, 2006, p. 23). Secondary schools that have struggled with the implementation of PLCs have frequently met resistance from teachers who believe in instructional autonomy. Often their defense of grading autonomy is even fiercer.

Blissful Ignorance

Sometimes grading autonomy stems as much from lack of awareness as from lack of following through on agreed-upon practices. Robin Tierney (2011), a professor and researcher from the University of British Columbia, found results similar to Raznov (see below). Tierney surveyed 77 secondary teachers regarding their awareness and implementation of four specific and agreed-upon principles for standards-based grading in their schools. Tierney found that over 30% of the teachers who were not implementing them said they were not even aware of the principles. Ignorance wasn't completely to blame for the lack of consistency, though. Of the 70% who were aware of the standards-based grading principles, only 43% said they "somewhat followed" these practices in their classroom, and 26% said they simply "did not agree" so they did not follow them at all (Tierney, 2011, p. 18).

Going Rogue

Teachers may agree on grading practices in collaborative settings, but when the door closes, autonomy in grading often reigns. In an in-depth University of Pennsylvania study of 70 high school teachers from Philadelphia, looking at the level of fidelity of implementation of agreed-upon grading practices between peers, Gail Brookstein Raznov (1987) found that most teachers eschewed expected marking guidelines and weight percentages for grading. Collaboratively teachers had agreed to implement specific grading practices for tests, class participation, written work, homework, labs, and oral work. Raznov found that most high school teachers tend to regard themselves as experts in their subject because of having acquired master's or doctoral degrees. When teachers were faced with the decision of remaining consistent with their peers in terms of using grading practices or implementing their own specific actions, even if they were different from what the team had agreed on, they chose the latter.

Experience Trumps Evidence

The teaching profession has been referred to as both an art and a science. Sometimes teachers rely too much on the art aspect and miss that the art, or manner in which we do things, allows the science to have a great impact. Dr. Robert Marzano's (2007) book *The Art and Science of Teaching* placed this question in the laps of educators across the country. His book outlines 10 questions teachers should ask during planning to drive effectiveness in their practices and increase achievement (p. 7). The art and science crossed over together, needing both, but for sure needing the science.

Many educational researchers have become well known for their evidence regarding what practices are most effective in increasing student results and achievement in the recent past. Marzano and University of Kansas researcher Jim Knight are considered experts when it comes to effective instruction, and UCLA Professor Emeritus James Popham and researchers and authors Rick Stiggins and Larry Ainsworth are the top names for best practices in designing, implementing, and making meaningful inferences from classroom assessments. Also, giants in our field such as Canadian researcher and author Ken O'Connor and University of Kentucky researcher and author Thomas Guskey have shaped a great deal of what we know to be the best professional practices related to effective grading practices.

Finally, and more recently, in his book *Visible Learning,* New Zealand professor John Hattie (2008) has revealed his findings from over 50 years of meta-analyses about what actions really have had the greatest impact on student achievement. Hattie's evidence has been called "teaching's holy grail" (Mansell, 2009). Unlike other research studies, Hattie conducted meta-analyses of meta-analyses (large-scale studies of large-scale studies) that have included over fifty thousand educators and a quarter billion students (see *Visible Learning* box). Hattie challenges all of us to "know thy impact." He calls for educators to consistently raise questions regarding the actions adults take in schools and the effect they have on student learning and growth.

Hattie (2012) conducted studies comparing the effectiveness of expert versus experienced teachers and notes,

Expert and experienced teachers do not differ in the amount of knowledge they have about curriculum or teaching strategies. . . . Experts can detect and concentrate more on information that has relevance. . . . [T]hey seek negative evidence about their impact . . . and to use it to make adaptations to problem solve. (p. 25)

This insight has begun to tip the scales in terms of emphasizing evidence of what works best versus experience. It is starting to become understood in the education industry that evidence trumps teachers' experiences as a basis for decision making.

Even with that, far too often in middle and high schools, discussions around the effectiveness or potential impact of changes in grading practices involves one part evidence, three parts opinionated debate, and five parts cynicism. While instruction and assessment evidence related to best practices is becoming more accepted by teachers, evidence regarding effectiveness of grading practices often remains "stubbornly focused on experience instead of evidence" (Reeves, 2011, p. 5).

Visible Learning: Looking at Effect Sizes

Professor John Hattie (2008), in his book *Visible Learning: A Synthesis of Over 800 Meta-Analyses Relating to Achievement,* shares his findings from looking at 150 influences on achievement. He compared thousands of studies that looked at impact on achievement related to teacher actions such as feedback, goal setting, and study skills. He also determined the impact on student learning from external influences such as parental involvement, mobility (shifts schools), and the amount of television students watch at home. Hattie focused only on achievement, specifically growth over time.

Why Effect Size?

Schools, districts, states, and countries use different forms of external assessment measures. Indiana has used the Indiana Student Testing for Educational Progress tool (ISTEP+), which has a different measurement matrix from Texas's TEKS and Minnesota's MAP. The MCAS (Massachusetts Comprehensive Assessment System), NAEP (The National Assessment of Educational Progress) and others measure achievement and growth in student learning over time, but they are all different in some manner, so results of NAEP cannot be compared equally to say the international assessment tool PISA (Programme for International Student Assessment).

In compiling his evidence, Hattie needed some method to use for comparison, so he used effect size as his measurement tool. This allowed him to measure growth over time on whatever external measure schools, teachers, and students were measured against.

(Continued)

(Continued)

What Hattie (2008) found, through compiling hundreds of meta-analyses, is that the average affect size for all influences was .4 ($d = .40$). He calls this the "hinge point" (p. 18). He determined that student growth over time that was anything less than .4 is below average. Far too often, teachers and schools measured achievement based on looking at results starting at 0. Hattie's use of effect size allows us to look at what actions result in the type of growth in student learning and performance we should expect. Anything less than .4 is simply not good enough.

Effect	Zone	Description
Less than 0	Negative effects	Impact on achievement goes backward
0.00–0.18	Developmental effects	Effects on achievement that would be expected for students
0.18–0.39	Teacher effects	Typical impact on student achievement (approximately a year's growth in a year's time)
.40 or higher	Desired effects	Above the average of all influences (more than a year's growth in a year's time)

Example of Baramoter

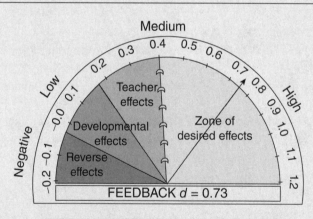

KEY	
Standard error	0.061 (medium)
Rank	10th
Number of meta-analyses	23
Number of studies	1,287
Number of effects	2,050
Number of people (10)	67,931

Evidence Trumping Belief: Minimum Grading

Teachers very often resist implementing new or adjusted practices in grading, due to the belief that these changes will not positively impact achievement and will likely lower standards and expectations for students at the same time. This happens because middle and high school teachers rely not only on their previous years of teaching experience but also on their experience as former middle or high schoolers. This belief persists frequently in secondary schools, even when there is clear evidence that the change in grading practice positively impacts achievement and raises standards for students.

Minimum grading (no-zeros) is a classroom grading practice in which teachers score missing student work with a minimum number, other than a zero, that moderates the mathematical impact on the final grade calculation. Advocates for minimum grading practices believe that when a zero is factored into a student's grade, often for missing assignments, it excessively punishes students. They contend that calculating zeros along with other scores of a student's performance distorts the accuracy of the grade, which then loses its ability to accurately reflect student mastery of academic content. Also, supporters believe the zero is rarely effective in altering student behavior.

Opponents of the practice say that when schools implement minimum grading, they are lowering expectations, allowing grades to become inflated, and ultimately decreasing achievement. Many teachers, and even some parents, feel minimum grading policies are unfair, encourage laziness, and do not prepare students for life after graduation (Hanover Research, 2013, p. 13). In essence, they argue, students pass classes when they don't deserve to in schools that use minimum grading.

This example illustrates how beliefs about grading are often based on experience and not evidence. Most parents share beliefs based on their understanding of how grading was when they attended middle and high school. Unless they became teachers themselves, they haven't logged significant time working with students, other than their own children. They remember their schooling experiences, but they do not truly observe the impact of grading practices on a daily basis. For many teachers, the evidence they follow related to grading changes is often short term. Schools or individual teachers may implement a new strategy and collect a few samples of evidence or even perhaps one to two specific examples or anecdotes. They then determine irreversibly the strategies effectiveness. Teachers must invest in paying attention to results and their impact on grading changes over time.

In 2012, researchers Theodore Carey and James Carifio shared their findings from a 7-year study of a large high school in Massachusetts implementing minimum grading. They note that the practice led to over 900 fewer course failures, and conservative estimates were that this large urban district saved over $1.25 million during that period due to the decreased need for course repeats and remedial interventions for students demonstrating proficiency. Opponents of minimum grading sometimes agree that those *could* be results they would see in their school if they implemented the practice (as if that shouldn't be enough). But they still challenge that minimum grading lowers expectations and teaches student laziness and indifference, that students would be passing classes when they should have failed and their school would just be lowering standards.

Carey and Carifio (2012) note that during the 7-year study, almost 350,000 grades were assigned to almost 11,000 students. Of all the grades assigned, students who passed their courses because of grades including a 50% replacing a 0 represented just 0.3%. "Clearly," they state, "the assigning of minimum grades was not leading to large numbers of courses being passed that would otherwise be failed or anything remotely close to this claim and contention" (p. 204). Carey and Carifio also found that during this time period, the school's Massachusetts Comprehensive Achievement (MCAS) scores for math and language arts went up 17% and 20%, respectively. Also, only incoming freshmen who received the full treatment according to the school's minimum grading practices were included in the MCAS data reported. The theory that the school's minimum grading practice inflated grades, reduced achievement, and promoted laziness and apathy was more than rebuked; it was proven completely false.

Carey and Carifio's evidence related to minimum grading is compelling because it provides an authentic example of the impact of a change in grading practice, but it has been questioned in terms of its merit and potential to affect achievement over a long-term implementation period. The debate about using minimum grading has led to picket signs and changes in state laws. Some people have the opinion that minimum grading is simply a desperate ploy to keep lazy students from failing or to prolong the inevitable. They argue, without evidence, that it lowers academic standards and removes student responsibility by making students' grades stay just above water. This sentiment persists, even though researchers have noted the disproportionate impact on student grades when a score like a zero, unrelated to achievement, greatly distorts its accuracy and in essence renders the grade meaningless (Guskey & Bailey, 2000, 2010; Marzano, 2007; O'Connor, 2009, 2010; Reeves, 2009; Wormelli, 2006). Middle and high schools have struggled and will continue to struggle with effective grading changes if experience and opinion are allowed to trump evidence.

Minimum Grade Policy Disasters

In July 2013, Hanover Research published findings from a study examining secondary schools that had implemented no-zero grading policies that were virtually identical to the Massachusetts school Carey and Carifio (2012) studied. Hanover noted examples in which the no-zero policy was implemented successfully and is still in place today. More important, of note are districts that have completely abandoned the practice, often after only a year:

- One high school issued "a directive to its teachers instructing them not to award zeros for assignments that were not completed" (Hanover Research, 2013, p. 14). A teacher who openly refused to implement the practice was fired, causing a great deal of public consternation. The minimum grading policy was removed several months after the controversial firing.
- In another failed attempt at no-zero grading, school officials cited low participation and confusion as reasons for ending the program.
- Finally, one district deserted the idea of minimum grading after an email that was sent to teachers defining the policy led to large-scale resentment and outrage from teachers.

We can draw some important inferences from the schools that have had failed attempts at minimum grading/no-zero policies. Studies like the ones in Carey and Carifio's study provide great evidence that a somewhat nontraditional grading change, like a minimum grading/no-zero policy, can lead to a positive impact on achievement. However, far too often the evidence is discounted or even refuted, based more on the delivery of the evidence than on the quality of the evidence itself.

Lack of Teacher Voice

In a 2003 *Harvard Business Review* report, W. Chan Kim and Renée Mauborgne share their research findings around how employees react to decisions that impact them. Kim and Mauborgne note that people most often feel satisfied and support decisions they disagree with when they understand the process for making them and feel their input was heard. The reverse is also true—people will feel very dissatisfied if they do not understand the process by which decisions are being made, and even worse if they feel they were wrongfully excluded from sharing valuable input. A specific example Kim and Mauborgne cite is a woman named Jane who had been issued a traffic citation for making an illegal turn. Jane was livid and felt the ticket was unfair, so she chose to appear in court to fight it personally. Jane went to court to speak on her own behalf. The judge threw the ticket out and ruled in her favor before she gave any commentary as to why she was fighting it. When she was asked about how she felt afterward, Jane stated she was even more frustrated and unhappy. The outcome was very positive for Jane, but the process for getting to that outcome left her feeling less than vindicated and desiring more than summary justice.

When people (teachers) are protecting something they don't want to lose (grading autonomy), they are going to be even more willing to fight to keep what they have but also for the opportunity to share feelings and reasons why. Middle and high school leaders can learn a great deal from Kim and Mauborgne's (2003) study when preparing to engage in any grading changes in their schools. Their example provides direction for what *not* to do. There have been far too many futile attempts at reforming grading practices and policy at the secondary level to keep track of. Many have failed specifically because the reform process consisted of little more than administrative mandates and noncollaborative edicts for teachers to implement grading practices they either did not understand, disagreed with, or both. When grading change decisions are made in this manner, it leads to increased teacher frustration, apathy, and at times even vengeance.

This is not to say teachers do not share their feedback. When it comes to mandates, though, the feedback teachers provide is often either not helpful because it is done in a vacuum—such as in staff rooms or in the parking lot, because there isn't an avenue provided for them—or it comes too late, after changes have been approved for implementation. When the latter happens, often schools and systems respond by doubling their efforts in a futile attempt to get some level of cooperation. Secondary teachers *will* voice their opinions related to grading. It does not take very long to hear a great deal of teacher frustration or indifference to changes in grading policies after they have been mandated without dialogue, input, or questions about how to implement new grading practices. Sit in any staff lounge shortly after an announcement that grading changes are coming, or even being considered, and you will hear a plethora of concerns, frustrations, and challenges about the idea. And based on the gap in the research, we can understand why.

The more school and district leaders can make every effort to ensure that all teachers, perhaps especially those at the secondary level, are part of the early and ongoing discussion around possible grading practice changes, the better chance these types of comments will not occur in print or in voice. Then when grading policy and practice changes begin to be implemented, it may be easier to assist and encourage teachers to attempt the practices with students and monitor their impacts on student achievement, leading to a more successful system overall.

We Must Fill the Research Gap

Secondary teachers are often encouraged to experiment with new instruction and assessment practices in their classroom. This helps teachers determine, based on student evidence, the impact these new strategies do or could have on student learning and notice necessary adaptions they may need to make for their specific classroom setting. They haven't been encouraged, or in some cases even allowed, to do the same with grading practices.

Karon Lee Webster (2011), principal in North Clackamas School District in Oregon, did a doctoral study that focused on high school teachers' perspectives on and implementation of effective grading practice in their classrooms. She notes that perspective and voice from high school classroom teachers is relatively absent in the research on grading practices. Webster found a gap in the research (p. 55). She argues that quite often grading policy and practice changes for secondary teachers have been mandated without teacher input and without giving teachers an opportunity to create their own findings through classroom action research. One of Webster's interviewees said, "They just up and changed their whole entire grading policy, and they did not ask a single teacher if they wanted that or not, and teachers are up in arms" (p. 192). Teachers were simply told to implement new practices. This has repeatedly led to teacher apathy and indifference related to attempted changes in grading.

Are Webster's Findings Surprising?

Webster (2011) cites the following studies that show a strong case to support her argument of an existing gap in the literature:

- Duncan et al. (2009) determined that there was a "lack of understanding in grading practices from the point of view of the teacher" who would ultimately be the individual to implement and improve existing practices.
- Truog and Friedman (1996) propose that a possible, logical, and most likely plausible reason for the gap between recommendations provided in grading literature and teachers' willingness to implement them relates to teachers not being at the table for discussion.
- Goodson and Hargreaves (1996) demonstrate the importance of teacher perspective associated with changes in grading practices due to the complexities of their job.
- Griswold (1993) suggests that adjustments and changes in any practice originate at the classroom level.

Webster's research indicates that our secondary schools have neglected to gather evidence from some of their most valuable resources: the teachers. It's no wonder, then, that teachers feel undervalued and resentful when mandated to change their grading practices.

CLOSING POINT: TEACHER ACTION RESEARCH

Middle and high school leaders must provide the opportunity and expectation that teachers conduct their own action research and make some of their own discoveries about changing practices related to grading. The same tactics teachers and teams use to monitor effectiveness of instructional strategies need to be used with grading practices. Once teachers attempt this, they need to note the impact these practices have on student achievement, both academically and behaviorally, to determine adjustments in the future. This will lead to evidence-based grading practice changes that originate from classroom practices rather than PowerPoint mandates that dissipate like smoke from a chimney on a cold winter evening. This will effect the best possible change—the kind that is owned and appreciated from having learned why we did something right alongside how we did it.

In the final chapter of this book, we will explore specific protocols for teachers to conduct action research in their classrooms, departments, PLCs, and so on related to grading practice changes. This is critical for middle and high school teachers to be able to monitor the effects on student learning by the most important factor that can impact achievement: the teachers. In the intervening chapters, we'll examine specific strategies, actions, and frameworks for improving the effectiveness and impact of grading practices that could be used in any middle or high school.

Activity 1.1: Probability of Implementation

The following are examples of grading practices we will explore in detail throughout the book. As a classroom teacher, imagine your school principal has strongly recommended, but not mandated, these grading practices to be implemented in classrooms. Rate each from 1 to 5, with 5 meaning it is very likely you will implement the practice with fidelity to determine effectiveness and 1 meaning you are not likely to even try.

Grading Practice	Quick Description	Implementation Probability (5 being highest)
Changing the no-late-work penalty to be nonacademic	Teachers can issue penalties for late work but cannot deduct points from students' academic grade	1 2 3 4 5

Grading Practice	Quick Description	Implementation Probability (5 being highest)
Amnesty days	Scheduled days in the curriculum calendar devoted specifically for students to make up work missed for any reason without penalty	1 2 3 4 5
Minimum grading system	A grading system in which any grade used in determining a student's final grade has parameters on how low it can be	1 2 3 4 5
Early final exam	Scheduling and administering final exams a week or two early to determine which students need specific help and which students have mastered essential content	1 2 3 4 5
Eliminating averaging grades	Using the most current and preponderance of evidence from student work and performance to determine vs. calculate grades (using current level of proficiency or demonstration at the end of the semester related to mastery of essential content vs. computing all of the attempts at reaching mastery)	1 2 3 4 5

(Continued)

(Continued)

Grading Practice	Quick Description	Implementation Probability (5 being highest)
Selection syllabus	Creating multiple tasks for students to select from to meet academic standards	1 2 3 4 5
Reporting behavioral elements separately from academic performance	Using only student academic work samples to determine any letter or reported grade, reporting elements such as effort, timeliness of work turned in, and so on separately (if the school does not have a separate reporting mechanism or standards-based report card, these elements are kept out of determining the letter grade)	1 2 3 4 5

This same activity will appear again in a later chapter. You may find that your perspective changes after you've read deeper about the specifics related to such grading practices, implementation steps, and case study examples. At the very least, you will likely be able to better understand your reasoning for your perspectives.

CONCLUSION

Secondary teachers have experienced a great deal of loss over the past 15 years in terms of what actions they have control over. Grading practice is still the one area where many perceive their freedom hasn't been taken away. Changes to grading practices issued through edicts and mandates will only cause teachers' grip to be even tighter. The more school and district leaders can make every effort to ensure that all teachers, perhaps especially those at the secondary level, are part of the early and ongoing discussion around possible grading practice changes, the better chance that teachers will not speak out against them. Then when grading policy and practice changes begin to be implemented, it may be easier to assist and encourage teachers to attempt them with students and monitor their impacts on student achievement, leading to a more successful system overall.

KEY IDEAS

1. The standards movement and loss of perceived academic freedom have caused teachers to fiercely protect their hold on grading practices.

2. Change is tough for all of us, and facts and fear rarely evoke the desire to significantly adjust behavior.

3. There is a significant gap in the evidence around secondary grading practices that includes teacher voice and action research.

4. We change belief by changing behavior, and support is needed.

REFLECTION QUESTIONS

1. How has the standards movement changed what is taught and how it is taught in your school?

2. What changes related to improving instructional practice and its impact on achievement have been successfully implemented in your school? Why do you feel they were successful? What can be replicated when looking at any changes related to grading practices or policies?

3. How have teachers in your school been supported or encouraged to conduct their own action research?

Determining Why 2
Grading Changes
Are Needed

Middle and high school parents have passionate opinions about grading. Secondary students also view grades much differently than they did in elementary school because grades begin to have many consequences (ability to take next course, honor roll, potential scholarships, etc.). This usually means that changing grading policies and practices involves working with a much larger group than just teachers. Many schools, not wanting to engage with a topic on which people have a reasonable amount of passion related to it, avoid addressing changing grading practices altogether and leave them to individual teachers. Or worse, they tinker.

Do you ever tinker with things? My wife will say often that I like to "tinker with rearranging the garage." She's right—I often spend long periods of time without ever having the result of a garage that doesn't look like a tornado just came through. Tinkering means to keep yourself busy on something without necessarily achieving useful results. When we *only* tinker with things, we never develop expertise. If a handyman you're considering hiring to do odd jobs around your house advertises on his webpage that that he likes to "tinker with fixing things," would you hire him? I would think not. Tinkering conveys a lack immersion and expertise. Handymen become experts—not tinkerers—by trial and error, experimenting with fixing things and learning the fine intricacies about their craft. Then they can better assess what they're trying to fix and know which tools give them the best chance to repair what they're charged with.

Secondary school teachers and leaders must develop expertise around fixing any issues with grading the same way. Far too often, though, schools only tinker with grading issues. When they focus on superficial issues like developing a new scale for letter grades and avoid the more deep-rooted issues, schools simply promote the status quo around traditional grading practices.

GETTING PAST TINKERING

How schools decide to address the topic of grading practice changes will ultimately impact their results. If building or district leaders simply mandate grading changes, teachers feel as though their voice is unimportant, which leads to indifference, and fidelity of new practices is unlikely. Worse, however, is when grading changes focus on superficial issues because of the fear of having to deal with a passionate topic. Grading change discussions that address only technical changes such as adjusting the grading scale or moving from letter grades to percentages on report cards never address deeper problems with grading.

International educational researcher Susan Brookhart (2011, p. 11) cautions schools that address only superficial grading changes and avoid dealing with deeper issues that they will miss out on progress toward more effective grading practices, and the results could even be harmful. Fiddling with a challenging issue will not lead to finding effective solutions.

Schools must consider three important concepts when moving grading change discussions past tinkering and into solution building:

1. Tradition musn't trump evidence.

2. Begin with why.

3. Build a clear plan.

TRADITION MUSN'T TRUMP EVIDENCE

Tradition is a word with many connotations. In the frenzy of change, people passionately attempt to hold onto things that are sacred. In families, traditions are passed on for generations as a way to honor the past and because often they work. Tradition can lead us to consider not changing existing practices. This happens often because we say to ourselves: "That's how we've always done it." Many grading practices in middle and high school fall under the *always been that way* category.

Instant Replay—Breaking Tradition

A sacred tradition in sports is that players and coaches should never argue with an official. In baseball, umpires are part of the game, and while they get most calls correct, they miss some and we must deal with it. If we grew up playing ball, we grew up with this ideology. Many of us likely also grew up with the belief that teachers' grading judgment was theirs and also not to be questioned.

All of the four major North American sports (football, basketball, hockey, and baseball) now use some form of instant replay. If an important call on the field was possibly made in error, coaches or even officials them-selves can check monitors and see whether the call was correct. If it wasn't, they stop and get it right.

This would have been *unheard* of a generation ago. Instant replay became commonplace over time because of developments in technology. Officials now have the ability to look again at the evidence of a play that just happened. Most people who play or watch sports enjoy knowing that winning and losing because of a blown call is much less likely to happen today than even 10 years ago. Officials do not want to make mistakes. They desire to be as good at what they do as the players playing the game. Similarly, Jim Collins (2001), author of *Good to Great*, notes that in great companies, technology is the accelerator that increases the quality of what was already really good (p. 144).

Major League Baseball was very slow and reluctant to move to any form of instant replay, however. Baseball has such a tradition in American history, many consider it a fiber of Americana. If you don't believe me, I'll bet anyone over the age of 35 reading this book can fill in the missing word to this jingle: "_ _ _ _ _ _ _, hot dogs, apple pie, and Chevrolet." Baseball also has many unwritten traditions that people close to the game are aware of. One of the traditions held dear by baseball enthusiasts is that an umpire's call is final—period. You argue with him, and you will be thrown out of the game. Countless players and coaches have been swiftly ejected for arguing with umpires. As the other major sports instituted replay over the past 15 years, baseball held its ground. But then as more and more calls that were missed were showing up on SportsCenter every night, sentiment was growing to break a century-old tradition and bring instant replay to baseball. The largest outcry came in 2010.

Egregious Error Opened the Door

In 2010, Armando Galarraga, a pitcher for the Detroit Tigers, was one out from a perfect game. A perfect game occurs when a pitcher gets all 27 batters out without any of them reaching even first base safely. The feat is extremely rare. As of April 2014, only 23 pitchers have ever thrown a per-fect game, and no one has ever thrown two. In a game against the Cleveland Indians, with two outs in the ninth inning, a routine ground ball was hit to the first baseman, who flipped the ball to Galarraga as he covered first base, beating the runner on a close—but obvious—play by at least a half step. Jim Joyce, a well-respected, 29-year umpire called the runner safe, incor-rectly eliminating Galarraga's attempt at baseball immortality!

Replay evidence showed that the play was not that close by Major League Baseball standards. It still was a blown call, and while it did not impact the result of the game (Detroit beat Cleveland 3–0), an immediate Internet, TV, and social media uproar ensued. Irate fans called into talk shows for days, vehemently demanding the call be changed. Major League Baseball even received calls from U.S. legislators suggesting Galarraga's name still be added to the record books of perfect game pitchers because of the obvious mistake.

Many people perceived that Galarraga's perfect game had been taken away from him by an umpire's blown call. If the play had been more complicated—one that could have gone either way and still have been incorrect—most people would have said, "That's baseball and the umpires are part of the game." People were angry because clear evidence showed just how incorrect the umpire was. Commissioner of Major League Baseball Bud Selig mentioned the next day that baseball was going to begin looking deeper at instant replay. The tradition not to ever question an umpire's judgment no longer seemed right if such an obvious mistake could have been immediately fixed.[1] (In 2014, baseball rules allowed for expansion of replay similar to other professional sports.)

Teacher Grading Traditions

Schools have long held onto a tradition that it is unacceptable to question a teacher's final grades. This belief is entrenched in many classrooms, schools, districts, and communities. Perhaps maybe because we've all had grades done to us. James Allen (2004), a professor in the Department of Educational and School Psychology at the College of Saint Rose, in Albany, New York, notes that teachers received hundreds of grades from teachers during their time as K–12 students and from college professors in their teacher preparation programs. Teachers then start their careers and take on the responsibility of assigning grades to their students. They were not allowed to challenge their teachers' final determinations, and now their students or their parents should not be allowed to question them either! Allen states, "Their perception regarding grades comes from their own long experience as students" (p. 222).

Examples of Uproar When Teachers' Final Grades Were Challenged

Luella High School, McDonough, Georgia: Teachers claimed they received an email from school administrators encouraging them not to fail students within two points of passing but rather, "at the very least be sure that those students receive a grade recovery contract." Allegations in a news story claimed that students who were well below passing

---

[1]In a confidential survey of 100 Major League players conducted by ESPN in 2010, Jim Joyce was voted the best umpire in the game (ESPN, 2010).

were simply moved to a passing level. "I think it is wrong, I think it is cheating the kids and it is cheating the parents," one teacher said. "Somebody needs to say something about this. Somebody needs to make this known" (quoted in Paluska, 2013, para. 4).

Woodbridge High School, Irvine, California: A news story addressed allegations that a teacher had refused to respond to requests from students and parents about a certain test grade that significantly impacted final grades (Martindale, 2012). The teacher in question had called in sick during the last 5 days of the school year (including final exam days) and did not respond to administrators' communiqués during that time. School officials deleted the test in question for all students since they were unable to address the concern with facts from the teacher. Students' final grades were not increased nor decreased. The article notes that even though the teacher had not communicated with parents, students, or school leaders to an acceptable level, and significant evidence existed to prove that the grades in question may likely have been inaccurate, some people still had deep concerns regarding the administrative action that took place.

Activity 2.1: What Separates Students in Terms of the Grades They Receive?

Students	Academic Characteristics and Traits	Behaviors and traits	Personal Characteristics and Traits (including parental involvement)
High-achieving students—A's and above			
Middle to average B–C students			
Underachieving, but not failing students			
Failing students			

Grading Instant Replay?

Joel McKinney, assistant superintendent of Frankfort Community Schools in central Indiana, and former high school principal, recently shared with me how he and one of his teachers dealt with having their final grading decisions questioned. A young man, Aiden, received an F for his final grade in Advanced Placement (AP) chemistry. Aiden's parents, who are very involved in his education, immediately requested a conference with the teacher and administration. The group convened and did a quick analysis of his teacher's grade book. It showed multiple—in fact, many—missing assignments. Aiden's parents, seeing this evidence, agreed the grade was deserved.

Two weeks later, Aiden got the results from his AP chemistry examination: He received a 5 (the highest possible score). Now this new evidence showing his obviously high level of mastery in chemistry content led to a second and more intense conference with his parents, Joel, and the teacher. This time, Aiden's parents asked a firm but fair request: "Help me understand how he could fail the course while demonstrating that level of subject mastery?" After some heated discussion, Joel asked Aiden's parents if the school could examine all the evidence and reconvene in a few days.

*Joel debriefed with the teacher afterward. She asked him if he would make her change Aiden's grade. Joel told her matter-of-factly that he would **never** ask any teacher to change a final grade. He did, however, request that she sleep on it and decide the next day if the grade made sense. Ultimately, Joel, the teacher, Aiden, and his parents came to a resolution. The teacher (and by extension, the school) would offer Aiden a stipulated second chance: He would need to create and conduct, on his own, several challenging lab experiments for a project akin to his interest and mastery level. Aiden needed to do so during a 2-week period over the summer. The teacher changed Aiden's final grade to a B after he successfully submitted detailed reports of these labs. (See Chapter 4 for more on stipulated second chances.)*

Most educators and parents would find this compromise reasonable. Aiden obviously had mastered deep levels of chemistry content. Did he need to learn some discipline and work ethic? Maybe. Was Aiden an F student, needing to repeat the entire chemistry course for high school credit when most colleges, based on his AP exam score of 5, would offer him college credit? Most assuredly not. Some might say Aiden didn't need to do lab work when he had already demonstrated mastery of content and he actually deserved an A instead of a B. Others may believe that if Aiden wanted an A, he should have done the work, and he deserves whatever grade he received based on the classwork. However, it would not be accurate to say Aiden is an F student academically in chemistry. Due to the disparity in the evidence, this situation called for a grading instant replay.

Practicality

While this example seems clear and came to a resolution, it is not indicative of all such situations, so it deserves to be considered with some practicality points in mind.

Practicality Point 1: This example is real. It is also an outlier. A student possessing mastery at an AP level but ending up with an F is rare. Schools and districts should not make and enforce new grading policies for outlier situations. Schools need to approach all grading decisions by looking at the evidence and applying common sense. This example also should not support the notion that demanding parents should always be allowed to challenge grading decisions. In this case, the extremity of the error called for a grading instant replay.

Practicality Point 2: Never should we think every grading decision should be scrutinized. The difference between an A– and a B+, or even between a B– and a C+ would have been quite different. Again, common sense needs to win. Also, students who turn in their work late or not at all are not immune from consequences. Granting students the opportunity to complete work, perhaps only on their time (after school, on weekends, or during the summer) can allow them to learn responsibility without distorting the accuracy of their grades.

Practicality Point 3: Finally, the chemistry teacher in this example is an excellent teacher. She is well respected by her colleagues and admired by her students. She consistently engages students at deep levels and challenges them to high levels of learning. All good teachers make mistakes—great ones fix them.

Middle and high school educators must ensure student grades are never far from an expected level of accuracy. They must expect accuracy from teachers in important grading situations, just like umpires are expected to not miss obvious calls in key games.

Setting a high standard for accuracy will not be accomplished by allowing tinkering, though. Tinkering with grading changes will not get schools to address deeper grading issues such as determining an acceptable level of accuracy. Truly fixing grading problems involves us moving past tinkering and examining *why* existing grading practices are not working.

BEGIN WITH WHY

Why virtually always needs to precede *how* before people will embrace any level of change; this is especially true if people hold strong opinions related to the proposed changes. Kim and Mauborgne (2003) demonstrated that explaining the rationale for decisions to people can double the amount of their buy-in. Helping people discover the whys versus just telling them will augment their buy-in to changes even more.

Reasons for possible grading practice changes must be shared and understood at some level before making them. The following four examples of why secondary schools should move to deeper discussions around changing existing grading structures might be great starting points for your school.

Why 1: Expectations Impact Grades

Grading practices that are heavily influenced by teachers' expectations of students lead to grades not accurately reflecting abilities (Hanover Research, 2011). In researcher Robert Rosenthal's landmark 1968 study, a group of teachers were incorrectly informed that certain students had been placed in their classrooms because they had demonstrated high levels of intellectual growth. This was not true. They had actually been selected at random. These students who were expected to be more intellectually capable demonstrated significantly greater intellectual ability and greater achievement than other students by the end of the school year (Rosenthal & Jacobson, 2003).

In a more recent study, Tomas Guskey (2011) found a strong correlation between high school students' initial semester grade and their final grade at the end of the academic school year. His findings pose challenging questions to high school teachers and administrators: If teachers can make accurate predictions of their high school students' final course grades based on evidence gathered during the second week of the academic term or school year, are we making adequate and effective use of the 34 weeks of instruction that fall between? Does the first achievement grade affect teachers' expectations of what their students can do? (p. 95).

Effort

Effort is a completely subjective term. Teachers cannot objectively gauge how much effort a student exerts for a given task. When teachers believe they should reward effort based on their belief about how hard something should be for students, they are allowing their own morals to come into play. Teachers, at all levels, let their ethical judgments influence the grades they assign (Zoeckler, 2005). Teachers' perception of effort impacts both high- and low-achieving students' grades.

Teachers often perceive that high-achieving students expend more effort, leading them to allocate higher grades than these students necessarily deserve. Christine Rubie-Davies (2008), associate professor and the Head of the School of Learning, Development and Professional Practice at the University of Auckland, notes that this bias is exacerbated if the student work is borderline: "If a teacher has high expectations for a student, a higher grade is likely to be allocated to that student's work, whereas if the teachers' expectations for a student are low, then there is greater probability a lower grade will be assigned" (p. 257). In another study, lower ability students who needed additional time to complete homework were perceived by their teacher as having tried harder, and they earned higher grades for the work (Jussim & Eccles, 1992). All these studies show that grades based on perceived effort cannot possibly be objective and therefore are inaccurate.

Why 2: Grades Are Feedback

Effective school practices (grading included) by definition should lead to increased student achievement—both academically and behaviorally. For schools to have effective grading, we must first acknowledge one critical point: Grades are feedback—always have been, always will be.

As of April 2014, feedback ranked 10th of over 200 influences on student achievement in Professor John Hattie's (2008) *Visible Learning* meta-analyses, and it doubles the rate of learning. Feedback is effective for learning when it is corrective in nature, specific to established criteria, is provided timely enough that students can apply it prior to the next assessment, and allows students to learn from it in the absence of the teacher.

But feedback in the form of a stand-alone grade misses the mark on all of these. Noted Duke University researcher Ellis B. Page's ground-breaking 1958 study demonstrated that achievement was highest for high school students receiving free comments to improve their work compared to letter grades alone or even letter grades with comments. Butler and Nisan (1986) affirmed that when student work is returned with comments and a grade, students focus on the grade and ignore the comments: "Descriptive comments have the best chance of being read as descriptive . . . [when] they are not accompanied by a grade" (p. 213). These two studies provide both a research base and a commonsense perspective on why secondary schools looking to make significant changes in grading practices need to address deeper grading issues like feedback as opposed to just adjusting grading scales.

Inheriting Standards-Based (Referenced) Graded Students

More elementary schools have moved to using standards-based (referenced) grading and having standards-based (Referenced) report cards than middle and high schools have. Many more students will then be entering middle school in the coming years having received more specific and criterion-based feedback during elementary school as opposed to just a single letter grade. If middle and high schools plan to continue to use single letter grades as their primary reporting method of student achievement, ensuring their grades have a high level of accuracy related to academic achievement will need to be a paramount priority.

Grades: Feedback for Adults

Parents and guidance counselors review and act on the feedback students receive in the form of letter grades. They make inferences based on what academic level of performance they perceive students have attained based on the grades they receive. If no other information is provided with their grades, which is often the case, decisions regarding subsequent course placement are based solely on assuming the grades are accurate. When a significant gap exists between the feedback students receive in the form of a grade and their level of academic ability, subsequent actions impacting their school careers are then based on false evidence.

During a course team meeting, Matt Smith, former principal at North High School in Des Moines, Iowa, challenged a group of his teachers who were discussing seven students who showed a high degree of proficiency and, at the same time, apathy in their classrooms. The teachers agreed that most if not all of these students' negative behaviors were attributed to boredom. They noted that all seven of the students either were repeating a class they had already taken or had been placed in a lower course level due to poor grades (D or D–) in the prerequisite. The school district had done away with guidance counselors several years prior in order to place instructional coaches in classrooms. That left school administrators to do more of the student scheduling, often based on teacher grades and recommendations. Matt challenged his teachers to consider how their grading decisions were leading to additional hurdles the following year.

Why 3: Avoid Inflation and Deflation

Initial grading change discussions very often tinker around issues like the elimination of zeros or allowing late work devoid of academic penalties. Schools attempt these changes to prevent students from failing courses by deflated grades. Meanwhile, they must also be cautious to ensure the grades students receive are not inflated. When grades overestimate students' current level of skills, students receive false impressions of their abilities and the support they will need in the next course, in college, and beyond. Both inflation and deflation occur when grades are unrelated to academic achievement. Above all else, grade accuracy is crucial.

Figure 2.1 Defining Grade Inflation and Deflation

Grade inflation: Increased grades without an accompanying increase in academic achievement

Lack of grade reliability: Increased grades over time despite the same level of achievement *or* different grades despite the same level of achievement during the same time period

Grade deflation: Decreased grades without an accompanying decrease in academic achievement

---

Grade Inflation Impact

A 2005 study by ACT found that over a 13-year period, high school grade point averages (GPAs) for ACT-tested public high school graduates increased by about 6.25%—without an accompanying increase in the average ACT Composite score. In its 2010 *College and Career Readiness Report,* ACT notes that just under one in four high school graduates met all four college readiness benchmarks for reading, English, science, and math (p. 8). The same report notes that only about 55% of incoming college freshman were prepared for college-level reading. The study goes on to say that the increase in GPA may actually be as much as twice the noted 6.25%, due to the fact that so few Ds and Fs are given out in high school, effectively reducing the grade range (from a range of A to F to a range of A to C). "Due to grade inflation and other subjective factors, post-secondary institutions cannot be certain that high school grades always accurately depict the abilities of their applicants and entering first-year students" (ACT, 2005, p. 4).

Similarly, a 2004 National Center for Education Statistics report estimates that 42% of community college freshman and 20% of 4-year college freshman need at least one remedial course (Colvin, 2005). Other studies have determined grade inflation is as much of an issue as grade deflation (Conley, 2000; Godfrey, 2011; Schmidt, 2007; Schneider, 2010).

Monitoring Inflation and Deflation

During my tenure as a high school administrator, teachers submitted names of all students in danger of failing on their D/F report every 4.5 weeks. The purpose was for the school to identify which students—and perhaps which teachers—needed specific and intentional support. I had as many concerns about the grading practices of teachers with zero potential failures as for teachers reporting a 60% failure rate. Our school external assessment results did not convey that every student was proficient or close enough to have zero Ds or Fs (inflation), nor that almost two thirds were lacking essential skills (deflation). This monitoring method proved effective in our school, and similar methods may be beneficial for other schools as well. (See Appendix A for more on this topic.)

BUILD A CLEAR PLAN

International researcher Daniel Pink (2012) in his best-selling book *To Sell Is Human: The Surprising Truth About Moving Others*, notes that every one of us sells every day—even if we aren't trying to sell products or services for a living. We attempt to sell others on our ideas for following directions, our children on brushing their teeth before bed, and students to complete their homework daily. In fact, Pink notes that individuals in the field of EdMed (education and medicine) are the largest-growing group that sells to other people every day. Pink stresses that to move others on the ideas we're pitching (like changing grading practices), we can be somewhat vague in guiding people in how to think, but we must be clear when we're directing them to act.

Middle and high schools can move past tinkering and into addressing deeper grading issues by having a certain level of clarity on *how* to begin. Three ways to help teachers have a clear grasp on the plan to get started are to examine the benefits and drawbacks of grading changes before implementing or dismissing them, to conduct grading experiments, and to communicate the grading replay rules for teachers.

How 1: Examine Benefits and Drawbacks

There are pluses and minuses to everything we do in life. When the benefits of taking an action outweigh the drawbacks, we can feel more confident in following that path. Not every instructional or assessment practice will be equally effective in each school or each classroom. Variables such as student makeup, subject matter, teacher pedagogy knowledge, and teacher effectiveness in implementing practices come into play. We would expect these same types of variables with grading practices.

Examining Benefits and Drawbacks of Grading Changes

When educators examine the benefits and drawbacks of grading practices, several positive things occur. First, they gain clarity on which changes to consider for implementation. Second, teacher voice is augmented as discussions identify practices with potential merit as well as places for caution. Third, grading practice hypotheses can be created for testing.

Several years ago, I was working with a team of high school teachers and their principal from St. Louis. They were considering several changes to traditional grading practices. One was to begin administering final exams 1 to 2 weeks prior to the end of the semester. The principal stated that he liked the idea but wanted to see how the teachers viewed it.

First we discussed drawbacks to the existing practice of administering finals at the very end of the semester. Teachers said they dreaded the mad dash of grading, scoring, and then calculating final grades within a short time period. One teacher added that she was always even more stressed if her grade determined whether a student would walk or not at the graduation ceremony. Another teacher mentioned that students never received feedback and exam results were never used formatively. A final drawback was that it was often too late to help students who missed key concepts and needed just a bit more focused instruction to develop mastery. One teacher summed up by saying finals were "simply a seal of approval for some students and an autopsy for others."

As downsides for keeping end-of-year finals were voiced, benefits for keeping the current format were shared as well. Some teachers felt their current end-of-year administering of final exams gave a way to hold students accountable (mostly for behavior) until the very end of the year. Another teacher stated that she felt she would need as much instructional time as possible before assessing students on a final.

Helping to facilitate their discussion, I asked them to list the benefits and drawbacks for comparison. Figure 2.2 highlights their summary points. (Early final exams are described in more detail in Chapter 5.)

Figure 2.2   Benefits and Drawbacks of Early Final Exams

Early final exam: Offering an option for students to take and complete a final exam 1–2 weeks early.	
Possible benefits	**Possible drawbacks**
Students demonstrating proficiency early are able to move on to more engaging enrichment work.

Teachers can identify students who need specific help in critical areas in enough time to provide more instruction. | Teachers might need to create a second version of the final exam.

Students might mentally shut down early after passing.

Students might become disruptive with no incentives for positive behavior. |
| **Likely questions or concerns:**

Who will be responsible for creating the second version of the final?

What is our plan for reteaching skills missed?

What is our plan/expectations for students who pass early?

What are other courses/departments doing? | |

Ultimately, changing or not came down to logistical issues. Several teachers shared a concern that if they made this change, there would likely be students who become proficient and pass the course well before the end of the semester. One teacher quipped, "Then what would we do with them?" The principal, having listened openly to both the benefits and drawbacks, asked one question: "What would be worse: having more students pass early or having some not pass at all?" His tone had both sympathy and sarcasm. He wanted to ensure they realized that certain benefits and drawbacks carried more weight than others. Students finishing the courses early would be a new challenge for his teachers to address. Time would need to be invested to determine how they would deal with students having passed the course, perhaps with a high grade, and still have 8 days of school left. Finally, the teachers determined that the benefits of an early final exam far outweighed the logistical challenges or drawbacks of keeping it at the very end as in past years. They planned to attempt the practice the following spring.

Examining the benefits and drawbacks of changing grading practices must be done with clear, not rose-colored, glasses. Leaders must respect and listen to the challenges predicted and shared by teachers. Likewise, teachers must play an active role in discussions around possible grading practice changes. Dismissing the drawbacks teachers mention related to changing grading practices only increases the gap in the research we explored in Chapter 1.

Activity 2.2: Benefits and Drawbacks of Changing Late Work Penalties

A change in grading practice that many schools wrestle with revolves around late work submission penalties. Please list some benefits and possible drawbacks for your classroom, team, professional learning community, department, or entire school related to changing such penalties. Do this either independently or with a team.

Proposed Change in Grading Practice: Separating academic and nonacademic penalties and consequences: Not penalizing students for late work with a deduction in academic points. (Other possible consequences: loss of privileges, having to cite additional sources before resubmission, adding additional element to the work, etc.)

Possible benefits	Possible drawbacks
Likely questions:	

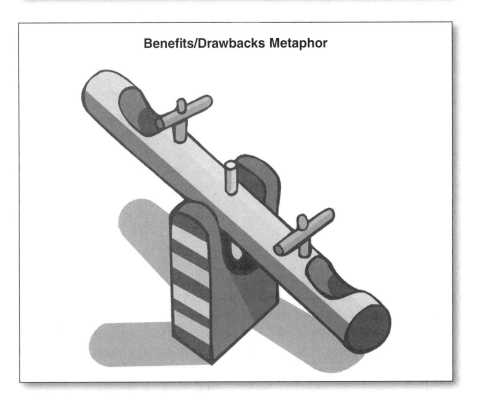

Benefits/Drawbacks Metaphor

What did you come up with? Do the drawbacks outweigh the potential benefits of using consequences for late work other than loss of academic points? In this exercise, if teachers or teams come up with more drawbacks than benefits for this possible change in grading practice, school leaders must respect their decisions. However, teachers should then be asked to similarly evaluate the benefits and drawbacks to existing grading practices, as in Figure 2.3.

Figure 2.3   Benefits and Drawback of Current Grading Practices

Benefits	Current grading practice	Drawbacks
	Use of zeros for missing work calculated into students' grades	
	Final exams administered on the final day of school with no chance for students to receive feedback and improve	
	Removal from course or drop in grade for unexcused absences alone (without considering academic performance)	
	Weighting final exams or single projects as 25% or more of total grade	
	Not accepting any late work	
	Averaging all attempts at proficiency to calculate final grade	

If we determine there are too many drawbacks for creating alternative consequences for late work other than point deductions, we also have to be able to look at current grading practices with the same filters.

How 2: Set Up Grading Experiments

Professional learning communities (PLCs) are commonly asked to review results and data from common assessments administered to their students. Discussion and dialogue then follows as teachers try to identify which instructional and classroom formative assessment practices yielded the best results. This is most powerful when they're analyzing results from pre- to post-assessments to see which teacher's students showed the most growth. Sometimes, there's disagreement between teachers as to the teaching practices they should use. If this happens, teachers often decide to use different strategies and then compare student results at the end of the unit. When the post-assessment results come in, PLCs look first to the teacher(s) who had the highest gains in student growth as a way for others on the PLC to replicate best practices. Every time they do this, they're conducting a scientific experiment around the impact of teaching strategies.

This same concept can be applied to determine how consistent or inconsistent teachers are at grading students with like scores over a semester.

Grading Experiments

The extensive body of grading literature has not determined any single grading practice accepted as the established standard of best practice. Instead, teachers hold a significant amount of agency in determining both how to calculate grades and what factors to incorporate when they do so. According to the *Encyclopedia of Education* (Guthrie, 2002), "grading is ultimately an exercise in professional judgment by teachers." The best way to test someone's judgment for accuracy is to conduct an experiment. The following example is a grading experiment you could conduct with all of the teachers on your PLC or even with the entire staff at your school.

Scenario: It's the end of a semester at your middle school, and grades are due tomorrow. The grades of one of your *typical* students, Jacob, are listed below. Calculate his final grade.

For the sake of simplicity, take into account the following points:

- There were 20 assessments or assignments included in your grade book. They are listed in chronological order (1 being at the start of the semester, 10 halfway through, and 20 at the end).
- Each one was of equal weight or importance.
- The course had a natural degree of scaffolding and building on concepts and skills from one topic to the next over the course of 18 weeks.
- Use any system you would like:

  - Scale 1: (Traditional) A:100–90, B: 89–80, C: 79–70, D: 69–60, F: 59 or below
  - Scale 2: (Numbering) 4-3-2-1-0
  - Scale 3: Any system that you wish or that your school currently uses

- If you are working with a team of five or fewer people, predetermine to all use the same scale. If you're working with a larger group of six or more, divide into Groups 1, 2, and 3 to calculate based on that corresponding grading scale.
- Determine Jacob's final grade as it would appear on his report card.
- If interested, please enter the grade at grading4impact.com/experiment. Please enter your final grade as well as which grading system you used. Results are tabulated and available on the site monthly.

Figure 2.4 Jacob's Scores in Your Grade Book

Assignment #	Grade	Assignment #	Grade
1	60	11	71
2	63	12	60
3	Not completed or turned in	13	70
4	89	14	82
5	61	15	Not completed or turned in
6	63	16	81
7	60	17	82
8	42	18	91
9	Not completed or turned in	19	96
10	Not completed or turned in	20	98

What is your final grade? _____

What grading system did you use? _____

Source: Adapted from Reeves (2011a, p. 33).

Challenge Reflection Question 1: If you did this work with a team or peers, how did your grades compare? Did everyone using the same scale come up with the same grade? If you completed it in a large group, what do the different scales' results tell you about the consistency you have in grading?

Challenge Reflection Question 2: Think back to the characteristics of A or B students versus D or F students that you listed in Activity 2.1 on page 35. Now compare those characteristics to the grade you gave Jacob. Do you know ***anything*** about Jacob related to the traits you see commonly in A or B students or D or F students?

I purposely used the name Jacob because a boy with that same name lives in my house. I'm fairly certain he'll portray characteristics on everyone's lists for both A and B students and D and F students when he arrives in middle school. He'll likely be driven to learn; he loves it. He tries hard at everything he does and asks questions *constantly*. He also is very disorganized, at times belligerent, and occasionally lazy. By the way, Jacob is 4 years old, but knowing he shares his father's DNA, he will likely continue to demonstrate all of those traits as a future adolescent. Do your results as a school or team match what the *Encyclopedia of Education* said? Is determining final grades currently the ultimate exercise in professional judgment by teachers?

As Much as Things Change, They Stay the Same

Reeves (2008) conducted experiments similar to the one with Jacob with over 10,000 teachers and administrators. He used just 10 mock grades instead of 16, and he used letter grades instead of percentages. His results show that teachers, even from the same school or same team, looking at the same student performance grades over a semester, might come up with grades ranging from A to F (p. 85).

Grading researchers Daniel Starch and Edward Elliot's (1913) results were eerily similar. They looked at 142 high school teachers grading two assigned papers written by freshman students in a Wisconsin high school English class. Grading on a 0-to-100 scale, 15% of teachers scored the first paper lower than 60, while 12% gave the same paper a 90 or higher. Similar results were found from their scoring of the second paper, with scores ranging from 50 to 97. Starch and Elliot note that teachers affirmed that neatness, spelling, and punctuation influenced their scoring. Others stated they "considered how well the paper communicated its message more than these elements" (p. 256). Based on this study, Starch and Elliot ultimately challenged the concept of percentage grades as a reliable measure of student achievement.

Oh, how little has changed in a century! While our society has walked on the moon, cured polio, eradicated smallpox, and invented gadgets to talk in real time to anyone on the planet, we struggle with the same problems of grading disparities.

How 3: Communicate Grading Rules

Let's go back to our baseball example. One hundred years of solid tradition was broken when instant replay allowed some calls that umpires make to be challenged. However, that doesn't mean that all umpire judgment was placed on the arguable (replay) table or that the importance of their skills and expertise was exacerbated. Some of their calls are still simply off limits to question.

The official rulebook for Major League Baseball has 117 pages. In the entire rulebook, only three words use all CAPITAL LETTERS. Rule 9 is specific to all aspects related to umpires:

Players leaving their position in the field or on base, or managers or coaches leaving the bench or coaches box, to argue on BALLS AND STRIKES will not be permitted. They should be warned if they start for the plate to protest the call. If they continue, they will be ejected from the game. (Major League Baseball, 2013)

In middle and high schools, teachers need to know what they can expect as schools dig deeper into grading change discussions. Teachers cannot fear infinite questioning of each and every grading practice they've been using. Schools must be clear as to what grading practices may be questioned and which ones will be considered off limits, for now. Perhaps final grades will not be argued with, unless there is an obvious disparity in accuracy between the evidence of student performance and their grade—then a replay may be in order. Schools that are up front about how grading calls will be determined at the school, team, and individual classroom levels have a better chance for teachers not to be defensive and look to "eject" someone questioning them.

CONCLUSION

Tinkering with superficial issues will not lead to effective changes around deep grading issues. First, traditions may need to be sacrificed in place of getting things right. Next, teachers must be led in understanding why grading practices need to be examined, and they must be provided with some clarity in how to get started. Schools must then allow teachers to have some structured freedom to, over time, test hypotheses related to grading practice effectiveness. Looking at relevant evidence for possible immediate replays and having clear starting actions will lead schools away from tinkering with minor grading issues and better prepare them to address deeper grading issues.

KEY IDEAS

1. Schools need to avoid tinkering with technical and superficial issues that detract from addressing more hidden issues in grading practices.

2. Questioning individual teachers' final grade determination has been a taboo topic because of tradition. We need to allow teachers the professional judgment they deserve, but we must also balance that with some level of ability to ask for replays.

3. It is critical to begin sharing and investigating why existing grading practice structures need to be examined.

4. Clarity of actions is needed to begin the process of changing grading practices.

5. Schools and teachers should examine both benefits and drawbacks of changes in grading practices.

6. Grading experiments can demonstrate how much variability and individual judgment and discretion are involved in grade determinations.

7. Teachers need clarity on what grading practices are going to be up for discussion and what, for now, may be theirs to determine the effectiveness of over time.

REFLECTION QUESTIONS

1. Are there any grading traditions in your school that need to be examined? In your classroom?

2. As a student or teacher, have you ever used or seen the need for a grading instant replay?

3. Does your perception of the effort students apply impact any of your grading decisions?

4. How do you look at the grades your current students received from their teachers last year as feedback to you? Do you feel their grades are truthful?

PART II

Practice Trumps Policy

Policy

3

A Starting Point, Not the Destination Finder

The word *policy* is defined as "a definite course or method of action selected from among alternatives and in light of given conditions to guide and determine present and future decisions" (Merriam-Webster, 2014b). Policies are formed to provide guidance for employees for what actions they should do in common or important situations. This guidance should help them make quicker and effective decisions when faced with multiple options. Organizations, including schools, also create policies to prevent stagnation in decision making as much as to increase fidelity of the actions themselves.

Companies can increase the fidelity with which employees adhere to their policies by having fewer of them to remember. Organizations can have fewer policies if the ones they develop are applicable across multiple situations and people. Multiple people with different perspectives and even job descriptions can apply a more general policy.

However, when companies create general policies in the hopes of guiding as many decisions as possible, they may not always consider the specific practices that employees will need to act upon for the policies to be effectively implemented. Companies, including schools, must ensure policy adherence doesn't lead to unpredictable results.

POTENTIAL FOR INCONSISTENCY

Policies themselves are rarely bad or good at their core. The practices people use to meet them will lead to either effective or ineffective results. The challenge middle and high schools face related to student grading is often discretionary application of grading practices stemming from their grading policies. Some school officials have an erroneous perception that if they simply establish a grading policy for their teachers, there will automatically be fidelity and consistency in its application across classrooms. As we saw in Tierney's (2011) study in Chapter 1, a large proportion of teachers (43%) somewhat followed grading principles, and one out of four simply ignored them.

Factors limiting grading policies from guiding effective grading practices include the following:

1. Vagueness, which leads to inconsistency;

2. Being overly constrictive, which leads to directing ineffective practice;

3. Focusing solely on the grading scale.

OVERLY VAGUE EQUALS INCONSISTENT

Secondary grading policies frequently allow for a tremendous amount of discretion in their application. With that discretion in hand, teachers implement practices that align to policies in their classrooms. This can lead to inconsistent actions across classrooms unless there is enough understood clarity. For example, most districts have some form of policy related to students turning in work late that often provides only recommendations or loose guidelines for how teachers individually will address the issue in their classrooms.

In February 2013, I analyzed the verbiage of 100 school district grading policies through a random Internet search of schools that placed their grading policies on their websites. I looked for how the school or district specifically addressed point reduction for late or missing work. As Figure 3.1 shows, almost 75% of the policies analyzed mentioned some recommendation of potential loss of points for late work submission. Of these, only eight had verbiage of any mandatory or consistent point deduction across classrooms for late work. The others were all individual teacher discretion.

Teacher Discretion Not Advised

When written grading policies allow large degrees of discretionary application, teachers in the same school can be completely adhering to the policy but still have inconsistent practices and results. The two teachers in the following example end up administering very different grades while both following the same grading policy.

Figure 3.1   Grading Policy Review: Point/Mark Reduction for Late Work

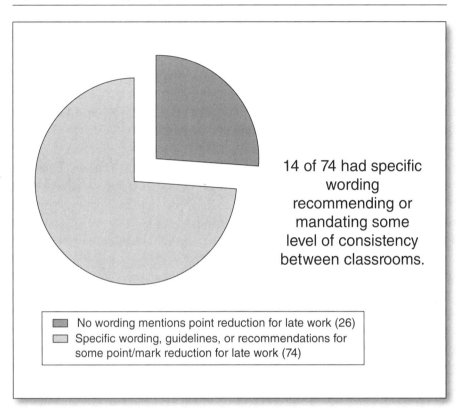

14 of 74 had specific wording recommending or mandating some level of consistency between classrooms.

☐ No wording mentions point reduction for late work (26)
☐ Specific wording, guidelines, or recommendations for some point/mark reduction for late work (74)

Mrs. Mitchell and Mandy, and Mrs. Smith and Sandy

Mrs. Mitchell and Mrs. Smith teach 10th-grade English across the hall from each other at West High School. Sophomores Mandy and Sandy are in their respective classes. Both students have demonstrated the same level of proficiency in writing over a 9-week grading cycle. Both girls often hand in their final drafts and submissions after predetermined deadlines, which are usually on Wednesdays to allow teachers to score and return assignments to students before the weekend.

The district grading policy states, "Work turned in past a deadline determined by the teacher may result in up to but not more than a 20% reduction in final grade." The policy offers no additional guidelines or recommendations. The two students produce work at very similar standards-based proficiency levels. The teachers, using state issued

(Continued)

(Continued)

rubrics, collaboratively score the assignments, and, based on the quality of the written work alone, both students would be awarded a B+.

Mrs. Mitchell, Mandy's teacher, is forgiving of the student's lateness, although she does still hold her accountable for the deadlines missed. She does not deduct points for Mandy missing the assigned deadlines. Instead, Mrs. Mitchell's consequence is to *allow* Mandy some additional *mandated* afterschool time on Thursdays and Fridays following the missed deadlines to complete her assignments. She calls these stipulated second chances (see Chapter 4 for more on stipulated second chances). These are opportunities for her students, like Mandy, to complete their late work with some form of penalty, usually additional time after school, before deducting any academic points from their grade. Since Mandy's work does demonstrate mastery of the course's essential standards and she utilizes the stipulated second chance provided to her, she receives a B+ on her report card.

Sandy's teacher is less forgiving of her lateness. Mrs. Smith deducts at least 10%, and usually the 20% maximum, for each of her missed deadlines. She does not offer Sandy any stipulated second chances, such as afterschool time. The consequence for Sandy is deducted points from her final grade. Sandy's academic work also constitutes that of a B+, related to level of proficiency of the content writing standards of the class. However, because Sandy's teacher includes process elements (deducting points for lateness) in her grading, Sandy receives a D+ on her report card.

Many middle and high school teachers and leaders would agree that this example is all too common. Two teachers in the same school, both adhering to the same grading policy, have students with very similar levels of mastery of content where one is deemed highly proficient and the other in possible need of academic intervention. Discretion is the real culprit. Both students for sure may need some work on time management and organization. However, both students have demonstrated proficiency requirements of the class related to the writing standards. The school's policy for addressing late work is credible in its intent. The policy was likely created to allow for multiple teachers to adhere to the same policy and have some level of difference in grading late work. This allowed for one policy to be written instead of multiple. The actual verbiage of the policy, however, allows for a large degree of difference in implementation of practice across classrooms in the same school. Schools must be acutely aware that grading policies alone, mandated or not, will not necessarily result in consistent grading across classrooms.

Activity 3.1: Policies Regarding Late Work

What are the school and district grading policies for late work submission?	Is any degree of discretion known or accepted related to these?	How do teachers on your course team or PLC address late work submissions?	How do teachers on your PLC monitor consistency across classrooms?

Hodgepodge Grading

When grading policies have a large degree of vagueness in their wording, teachers of the same course can adhere to them while implementing very different practices. This then leads to very different levels of accuracy between students' grades. Guskey and Bailey (2000, p. 41) recommend reporting grades based on three separate criteria: product, process, and progress. *Product* refers to student work and demonstration of proficiency related to concepts or skills from academic standards. *Process* relates to work ethic, timeliness of meeting deadlines, and even perceived effort. *Progress* considers the level or amount of improvement that students have made from the starting point of a grading cycle to the end. Many middle and high schools report academic achievement to all stakeholders (students, parents, counselors, and higher learning institutions) in the form of a single letter grade combining all three criteria. Guskey and Bailey call this "hodgepodge grading."

In the case of Mrs. Mitchell and Mrs. Smith, the school policy stated that "work turned in past a deadline determined by the teacher may result in up to but not more than a 20% reduction in final grade." (This is the exact wording of a grading policy from a high school in the United States.) This policy is imprecise and leaves a great deal of gray area to be determined by individual teachers. Using Guskey and Bailey's three criteria, most of us would agree that both Mandy and Sandy should have had the same product grade related to writing standards for their proficient work. Neither student was necessarily proficient in the process expectations of submitting work within a defined period of deadlines. We are unaware of any progress criteria considered in that example.

Helping Verbs Don't Help

Students (like adults) need deadlines to be reminded of responsibilities. A school or workplace where there are never any deadlines would be in chaos. Students (like adults) will miss deadlines. There must be some degree of expectation, perhaps in the form of grading policy, to address this. The policy Mrs. Mitchell and Mrs. Smith were using had an Achilles heel: the word *may*. Words like it (*could, might, possibly, well*) open the door wide for well-intentioned teachers across the hallway from each other to have large difference in their grade reporting. Mrs. Mitchell didn't ignore Mandy's lateness; she offered her a stipulated second chance to make up her work. Mrs. Smith did not offer one to Sandy. Both teachers adhered to the policy guidelines and were allowed to be very different in their grading practices because of the inclusion of the vague word *may* in their school's grading policy. Therefore, students demonstrating the same level of mastery for both product and process criteria received very different final grades (B+ and D+) at West High School from teachers teaching the same subject across the hall from each other.

Grading policies can far too often mask hodgepodge grading. Furthermore, in scenarios like this, students like Sandy are left with little to no leg to stand on for questioning or challenging their final grades. After all, the teacher followed the grading policy.

Always Consider Student Perspective

Schools analyzing their existing policies or considering forming new ones need to balance considerations for teacher freedom to implement changes in grading practices along with the perspective of the students themselves who are being graded.

Stephen J. Friedman (1998), professor at the University of Wisconsin–White Water, says that principals could more effectively monitor the implementation of grading practices in their schools by considering student perspectives. In his research interviews, he notes that teachers conveyed they often left off specific details in their written grading policies due to the belief that some students might not understand them. He notes that teachers admitted to him that a vaguely stated grading policy made it easier for them to adjust it for individual students and situations (p. 78). When this happens, students like Sandy are left with little recourse if a problem arises. What if Sandy and Mandy, and their parents, compared their work only to find little difference everywhere except their report cards? Would you want to be Mrs. Smith then?

Community Angst

Flower Mound, Texas, Lewisville Independent School District: Proposed grading changes have caused concern for some teachers, parents, and others in this community. One of the main issues relates to when students will be allowed to retake assessments to improve their grade. The policy states that if conceptual mastery was not reached by earning at least an 85% on the final exam, then the student could retake the exam.

The controversy relates to the vagueness of when a retake is permitted. The policy seems to imply that if conceptual mastery was reached, then a retake isn't permitted, and if conceptual mastery was not reached, students would be allowed as many retakes as they needed.

One community member commented to the local paper, "It is my opinion that the proposed grading policy is too vague and subjective. The proposed guidelines could be widely interpreted by different teachers and administrators" (quoted in Southwell, 2013, "Original Story," para. 18). Several parents shared concerns similar to this at a school board meeting to challenge the proposed changes to grading practices. (At the time of the article's publication, the policy hadn't been approved or even recommended to the school board yet; it was only in early draft form.)

Frustrated superintendent Dr. Stephen Waddell said that "changing grading practices is one of the hardest things to do" (Southwell, 2013, "Original Story," para. 13). In response to the emotional pushback from some of the perceived nebulousness related to students getting additional chances to retake an assessment, he said, "For those kids who do their work, and do it really well, and care about their grades, it doesn't hurt their education one bit whether another kid does or does not receive another chance" (Southwell, 2013, "Original Story," para. 19).

OVERLY CONSTRICTIVE POLICIES

The opposite of vague is explicit. Using overly explicit or rigid verbiage in grading policy can lead to just as many challenges as being overly vague. Schools and districts have challenges with effective implementation of grading policies when the wording is too direct.

Guiding Ineffective Practices

The desire for consistency and reliability often leads teachers to implement practices that are incongruent with research-based evidence. Teachers and school leaders can inadvertently impede learning and achievement simply by making sure everyone adheres to strict grading policies.

Assessment Practices

Grading policy verbiage very often flies in the face of the large body of research related to effective use of formative assessment. A critical attribute of any quality assessment is that it allows teachers to make reliable inferences from the student evidence of learning (Ainsworth, 2003, 2011; Popham, 2008; Stiggins, Arter, Chappuis, & Chappuis, 2004). Teacher inferences from student products and skill demonstration should be the primary evidence they use to guide their instruction and to give students feedback so they know what their next steps are.

When school and district policies mention or even direct teachers to take off a specific amount of points for work turned in late, teachers lose the ability to make reliable inferences from student work. Why is this so? Teachers must use the work students turn in for their grades but also to know what the students need next in the learning. Complete student effort and commitment are virtually diminished when they know a makeup assignment will receive only 50% of the points possible, no matter how stellar it is. Why put 100% effort in when 50% is the maximum reward? Can teachers then make quality inferences if they know student work is far from their best attempt? The grading policy itself leads to less reliable inferences that teachers can make from student work.

Homework Policies

Homework—its use, amount, purpose, and inclusion in a student's final grade—is often a point of contention in many secondary schools. Many parents judge the effectiveness of schools by the presence and amount of homework students bring home. What parents rarely, if ever, question is whether the child's homework is targeted to her or his current level of need for practicing particular skills. Homework and its impact on middle and high school grading is an important issue for schools to consider as they examine or plan to adjust their grading policies.

Hattie (2008) found high school teachers were most likely to assign homework for students to actually learn the subject matter themselves rather than from the teacher delivering instruction. The highest effect sizes or gains in achievement for homework were when students worked on rote practice, or rehearsal of the content. This was after having learned the material to some degree. When students are working on something for a grade while they are learning it, it's safe to say they are not practicing—not deliberate practice that refines skills and helps develop mastery. This is not just ineffective, it is detrimental to their learning. None of us can practice something and know if it's working if we haven't learned what *working* would need to look like. Based on the accuracy of answers students provide early in the learning process, grades are likely to encourage them to focus on the immediate goal of acquiring a certain number of those points. Students then concentrate much less on actually learning the strategies they are using and making connections for a bigger task they are working toward (Kluger & DeNisi, 1996).

Teachers need to use homework like any other strategy in the classroom. Some students need more practice than others, and some need different practice. Policies that direct teachers to count as a grade a certain amount of the homework they assign toward student final evaluations can truly be detrimental to learning and achievement, if done early in the learning cycle.

Example Homework Policy

Grading policies that have direct guidelines help teachers know what the level of consistency should be in their classrooms and across classrooms in the same school. The more direct the guidelines, the more the directions must lead teachers to effective actions. Here we will examine an actual high school homework policy that specifies how teachers should assign homework and then apply it toward final grades:

> Homework is for practicing and reinforcing fundamental skills to meet course objectives. . . . Homework should be graded and will be part of up to at least 20% and as much as 30% of students' overall grade along with other formative measures.

This first part of this policy fully supports studies and research related to the effective use of homework (Cooper, 1989, 2006; Darling-Hammond, 2006; Guskey & Bailey, 2000, 2010; Hattie, 2008, 2012; Marzano, Pickering, & Pollock, 2001) as a way for students to practice and reinforce skills. However, the same policy then mandates that one third of students' final evaluation of academic performance will be derived from practicing skills. Here, two aspects within the same grading policy are opposing forces. One fully supports the evidence of effective use of homework for practice, and the other is archaic and potentially minimizes the effectiveness of the same research. In addition, this policy has a large degree of vagueness in allowing as much as a 10% difference between classrooms.

Retention

Holding students back to repeat a year of school is one of the most deleterious actions on student achievement. Retention ($d = -.34$) is one of the few areas where it is difficult to "find any studies with a positive effect, and the few that do are hovering close to zero" (Hattie, 2008, p. 97). High-level grading policies have directed schools to implement one of the most detrimental practices on student achievement: mandated retention. Promotion gate policies have been implemented in Florida and New York City (Rose & Schimke, 2012). Schools where students are not meeting certain benchmarks, often in reading, at the end of specific grade levels are directed to intervene early in the students' educational career before they get too far off track. The intent is to be well commended.

Hattie's (2008) synthesis of numerous reviews in the literature demonstrate the overwhelming negative evidence around retaining students as well as how the detrimental effects increase over time. Hattie notes, "After one year, the retained groups were scoring 0.45 standard deviations units lower than the comparison groups who had gone on to the next grade level and were being tested on a *more advanced material*" (p. 98, emphases added). He goes on to conclude that retaining students doubles the chances of dropping out, and retaining them twice effectively ensures it.

Some studies have reported student achievement at lower grade levels was higher the following year for students who were retained, compared with those who were possibly socially promoted to the next grade (Greene & Winters, 2007). Nonetheless, the evidence is clearer regarding the negative impact on students in middle school and above. A study of Chicago Public Schools found eighth-grade retained students had a much larger probability of dropping out than their promoted peers, which wasn't the case with sixth graders. The researchers felt additional time in their educational career was on the side of the younger students (Jacob & Lefgren, 2007). London researcher C. T. Holmes (1989) concludes we would be hard pressed to find another educational practice so obviously negative.

Grading Policies Mandating Retention

Schools and districts at times are not always the inventors of the grading policies that mandate or highly recommend student retention. Sixteen states have mandatory retention laws in place (Rose, 2012). For example, for the 2012–2013 school year, Missouri law P5123 had specific guidelines for promoting junior high students based on their grades. For students to be promoted to Grade 8 or 9, they must meet the following requirements: receive a passing grade in communication arts (reading and writing), mathematics, science, and social studies. For students to be promoted to Grade 7, the same four classes are required and reading ability should be "strongly considered" (St. Louis Board of Education, 2012).

Sarasota County Schools has adapted policies to adhere to the Florida laws guiding retention for middle school students. It has attempted to ensure steps are taken to avoid retention if at all possible. Its policy directs schools to retain middle school students who fail more than two of the four core academic classes. Students who fail one core academic course may be conditionally promoted to the next grade. These students are expected to attend summer school to recover the course. Conditionally promoted students in Grade 7 or 8 who have not passed all courses of the previous grade must be passing all courses at the end of the first quarter to remain at that grade level. Students failing one or more courses will be returned to previous grade (Sarasota County School Board, 2015).

Neither of these examples was included to critique any district or state policy makers enacting policies they believe are in the best long-term interest of students. Retention laws are enacted predominantly to prevent social promotion. Students who demonstrate clear learning needs and challenges should not simply be passed on (literally or figuratively) to the next grade level or next school.

Verbiage in grading policy is needed to guide actions in schools to make sure non-proficient students get the support they need to get back on track. At times, retention laws are held in place and used only when schools need to have some leverage with students and parents when intentional non-learning is taking place. Schools might not create the retention policy, but they ultimately are the ones to implement it.

GRADING SCALE: THE GO-TO POLICY

Grading scales are not grading policies. They do not provide **any** guidance to schools, teams, or teachers as to what specific classroom grading practices should be implemented. In some school districts, their entire grading policies amount to little more than how they established a scale for grades (O'Connor, 2010, p. 216). Most systems for calculating or determining grades are on a 100-point scale. Grading scales have maintained their place in middle and high school grading polices because of several flawed beliefs. One, some believe that if schools increase the numerical average scale students must reach to earn a certain grade, then they have increased expectations and quality of instruction. This is far from being truthful. In almost every case, everything teachers use to determine the percentage is subjective: the assignments, tasks, point allotment for each, value of points reduced for lateness, etc. Two, if schools adjust the descriptions that accompany a grade or numerical average, teachers will change their grading practices to match that descriptor. This is the epitome of grading policy tinkering.

In my analysis of 100 grading policies, 94 specifically mentioned equating a percentage scale of points to a grade (see Figure 3.2).

Parents can influence schools to change or adjust their grading scales. I have personally heard many parents say they wanted their son or daughter to at least get a B because they know what that means. Middle school grading expert and author Rick Wormelli (2006) points out that many grading systems that schools advertise provide a descriptor next to the letter grade in school information literature (A= excellent, B = above average, C = average, D = below average, etc.). These descriptions provide fodder for parents and students to seek that connotation of being above average or exceptional without really considering what that term would convey about what they should know and do related to that class.

If parents and students believe every classroom applies the same grading practices to arrive at these terms accurately and consistently, they expect the same the following term or school year. But unfortunately, this isn't always the case. Sandy's (D+) grade in 10th-grade English may move to a B+ the next year if her teacher doesn't take off 20% for late work (or Sandy just gets stuff in on time!). She and her parents would then incorrectly perceive she has made great gains in her English skills, when there may not have been any improvement in her academic mastery. Worse,

Figure 3.2   Analysis of Grading Policies

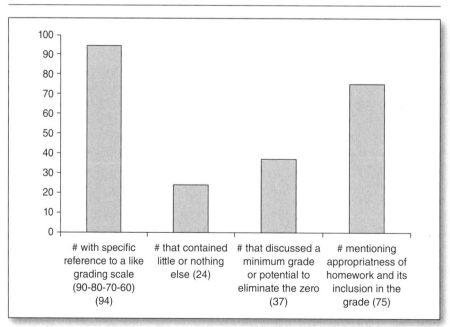

Mandy (B+) could have a teacher that never allows for late work to be submitted at all. Her skills in writing might even improve, but if her grade goes down significantly, many issues could then arise.

Statewide Grading Scale—South Carolina

Schools' grading scales policies are sometimes determined for them. South Carolina, for example, has a statewide uniform grading policy (see Figure 3.3).

Figure 3.3   South Carolina Uniform Grading Scale Conversions

Numerical Average	Letter Grade	College Prep	Honors	Dual Credit AP/IB
100	A	4.875	5.375	5.875
99	A	4.750	5.250	5.750
98	A	4.625	5.125	5.625
97	A	4.500	5.000	5.500
96	A	4.375	4.875	5.375
95	A	4.250	4.750	5.250
94	A	4.125	4.625	5.125
93	A	4.000	4.500	5.000
92	B	3.875	4.375	4.875
91	B	3.750	4.250	4.750
90	B	3.625	4.125	4.625
89	B	3.500	4.000	4.500
88	B	3.375	3.875	4.375
87	B	3.250	3.750	4.250
86	B	3.125	3.625	4.125
85	B	3.000	3.500	4.000
84	C	2.875	3.375	3.875
83	C	2.750	3.250	3.750
82	C	2.625	3.125	3.625
81	C	2.500	3.000	3.500
80	C	2.375	2.875	3.375

(Continued)

Figure 3. 3 (Continued)

Numerical Average	Letter Grade	College Prep	Honors	Dual Credit AP/IB
79	C	2.250	2.750	3.250
78	C	2.125	2.625	3.125
77	C	2.000	2.500	3.000
76	D	1.875	2.375	2.875
75	D	1.750	2.250	2.750
74	D	1.625	2.125	2.625
73	D	1.500	2.000	2.500
72	D	1.375	1.875	2.375
71	D	1.250	1.750	2.250
70	D	1.125	1.625	2.125
69	F	1.000	1.500	2.000
68	F	0.875	1.375	1.875
67	F	0.750	1.250	1.750
66	F	0.625	1.125	1.625
65	F	0.500	1.000	1.500
64	F	0.375	0.875	1.375
63	F	0.250	0.750	1.250
62	F	0.125	0.625	1.125
0–61	F	0.000	0.000	0.000
61	FA	0.000	0.000	0.000
61	WF	0.000	0.000	0.000
—	WP	0.000	0.000	0.000

Source: Retrieved from http://www.lexrich5.org/files/34690/South%20Carolina%20Uni form%20Grading%20Scale%20Conversions.pdf.

Grading Scale Descriptions

Sometimes we don't know what we don't know. Parents who state that they want their child to receive a B may believe that they know what the grade means related to a brief description that accompanies their child's report cards. Is this enough to ensure understandability, though?

In my analysis of 100 grading policies for middle and high schools, 88 used traditional letter grades. Of those schools, only 9 had descriptions of more than one sentence about the meaning of an A, B, C, D, or F. More than 70 used five words or fewer to describe any grade, and 81 used fewer than three words.

In Figure 3.4, schools 1 and 2 are very typical. Their descriptions are basically synonyms of each other, with school 2 leaving out its percentage grade, and both reference standards or the performance level of the student in their description. Let's examine school 3. It obviously intends to make a distinction between the grades administered to students by intentionally listing + and − next to the grades. However, different than schools 1 and 2, school 3 provides descriptions much more closely to being adjectives related to the students themselves. A student who receives a B (88%) in World History at school 1 would be told by the report card comment that he is (performing) *above standards*. At school 3, a student with the same percentage grade would be told by his report card that he is *excellent*. The feedback from the comments is now directed more

Figure 3.4   Three Examples of Secondary Grading Scale Grade Descriptions

School 1		School 2 (Did not provide percentages)		School 3	
Grade	Description	Grade	Description	Grade	Description
A	Above standards with exceptional performance (100%–90%)	A	Outstanding level of performance	A+ (98%–100%)	Superior
B	Above standards (89%–80%)	B	High level of performance	A, A–, B+ (97%–87%)	Excellent
C	Meets standards (79%–70%)	C	Acceptable level of performance	B, B–, C+ (86%–77%)	Good
D	Marginally meets standards (69%–65%)	D	Minimal level of performance	C, C–, D+ (76%–67%)	Average
F	Below standards (65%–0%)	F	Unacceptable level of performance	D, D– (66%–60%)	Below average
				F (59%–0%)	Failing

toward the student and not the quality of his work. This is a form of self-feedback which is least effective and at times detrimental to achievement (Hattie, 2008, 2012).

Also, at school 3 the difference between a good student and an excellent student could be the difference between 86% and 87%. At the same time, an average student who has a teacher bump her up from a 76% to a 77% went from almost being told she was below average to now being good. These kinds of descriptions are not enough to make the justification for these lines between average, good, and excellent—which are subjective terms that have different meanings to different students and parents.

The desire for statewide consistency in grading for all students in South Carolina is commendable. Policy makers and educational leaders have attempted to create a statewide policy to provide more reliability in the grades that students in South Carolina high schools receive. The hope is that grades across the state from school to school and classroom to classroom are consistent from this scale and that. The problem with this notion is that it assumes a great deal.

The policy (scale) as written would lead us to believe that if student A in a Columbia-area high school and student B in a high school in the Hilton Head area both obtain 84% mastery in a college prep biology course, they would both receive a C grade and earn 2.875 GPA points. For the grades of two students to be reliable to this degree in two different classrooms, let alone two different schools, both different teachers would need to have the following:

1. Similar practices for accepting late work with or without penalty and how that is factored or calculated into the final grade (All would have to have grading practices for accepting late work like Mrs. Mitchel *or* Mrs. Smith—no combinations or substitutions allowed.)

2. Similar levels of rigor for their assignments linked to the same standards for most if not all tasks

3. Relatively the same final exam or assessment addressing the same standards and expecting very similar success criteria to earn a certain or specific grade or points allotment

A statewide grading scale could provide some levels of grading consistency, but it is far from a silver bullet in terms of increasing reliability of grading in classrooms across the state, let alone within the same school. It is not just possible, but probable, that two South Carolina high school teachers using this same grading scale, adhering to the state policy, could easily still have grades that are inconsistent for two students demonstrating the same level of academic mastery. The opposite is also possible, and probable: Two students could receive the same grade but demonstrate very different degrees of content mastery.

CONCLUSION

Grading policies that are vague in their verbiage or that focus solely on the grading scale and lack specific guidelines often lead to inconsistent grades from classroom to classroom. This effectively creates a lottery system in which differences in grades are unrelated to differences in demonstration of proficiency. Differences in grades originate from the school's computer scheduling system that determines which teacher a student receives, who then determines which practices will be implemented. No wonder we have students like Mandy (B+) and Sandy (D+).

When schools create policies that have explicit language directing teacher practice, they must ensure this language is not incongruent with effective research to support it. Valuable grading policies need to be established, but to be effective they must be the guidelines that will drive *practices*. The same reasons that limit the reliability and consistency of grades for students across South Carolina (which has a statewide grading policy) would also render grades in one school just as unreliable without consistency of grading practices. The next chapter will move us from looking at policies to examining the specific grading practices they lead to.

KEY IDEAS

1. Schools and districts will not see meaningful short- and-long term changes in grading practices if they only scratch the surface in addressing current grading issues.

2. Schools and districts create (grading) policies to provide guidance for action. Inconsistency can and will arise from a variety of factors related to policy implementation.

3. Grading policies that are vague, discretionary, or too constrictive can lead to inconsistency of grades and hodgepodge grading.

4. Grading policies sometimes even mandate practices that are incongruent with effective research.

5. The grading scale, with its percentages equating to grades and anecdotes for student achievement, is the most common element in many grading policies. It alone will have little effect on accuracy of grades.

6. Relying on grading policy alone will not ensure consistency of grading practices across a state, district, or even school.

REFLECTION QUESTIONS

1. What are current grading policies that you or your teachers know are in place, and how are they adhering to them?

2. Are any policy guidelines constricting effective practice?

3. Are any policy guidelines allowing drastic inconsistency across classrooms even when they are being met?

4. Would a consequence other than point deduction for late work help students provide accurate evidence of learning so teachers can make accurate inferences related to their academic skill level?

Policy Into Practices

4

The Path to Effective Grading

How schools set effective grading policies is very similar to how stadiums create signage for patrons attending sporting events. The more specific and clear the directions on the signs, the faster and more efficiently they drive the flow of people to move in the proper direction. At the basketball game my son and I recently attended, there were two signs (Figure 4.1) to direct us to our seats, which were in section 15. They were simple to understand and *one* guided us in the *best* direction possible.

Had the signs provided only a vague description, such as in Figure 4.2, we still would have eventually found our seating assignment, but it would have likely taken much longer. Patrons likely would have been going in many different directions, and the traffic flow of people would have likely caused more bottlenecks. Specificity in the signage with enough detail, like in Figure 4.1, allows event workers to guide and direct patrons in the proper direction and leads to less confusion, less congestion, and fewer issues for game management.

Most patrons needed little help or guidance. They knew where they were going. However, there were a few sections that were obviously off limits to patrons. They were marked with a sign that said *Do Not Enter*.

Figure 4.1   Empowering Stadium Direction Sign

Figure 4.2   Vague Stadium Direction Sign

Event workers were posted close by to make sure no one went beyond the parameters they had established for patrons.

Effective grading policies in schools are established in a similar way. Grading policies should be clear and concise, guide teachers' actions where most are headed anyway, and provide a practical level of consistency between schools, within schools, and between classrooms (O'Connor, 2009, p. 216). Teachers inherently do not want their grades to be inconsistent, inaccurate, and incongruent with effective research, so they just need some guidance to help them to that end.

We learned in Chapters 1 and 2 that mandates are recipes for disaster when looking to implement grading changes in middle and high schools. Effective grading policies that will eventually lead to effective classroom practice must combine a certain amount of flexibility that allows teachers to adapt grading practices for their specific classroom setting and still be consistent with peers. Grading policies must also then provide teachers and leaders with concreteness to know what is off limits in terms of grading practices—just like the Do Not Enter signs at the game. Schools can accomplish both of these by establishing grading parameters.

Figure 4.3   Do Not Enter Sign

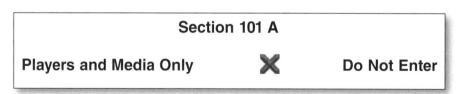

PARAMETERS, NOT MANDATES

Teenagers are extremely susceptible to the influences of their peers (Evans, Oates, & Schaub, 1992; Lavy & Schlosser, 2007). Parents often create parameters for whom their own children can interact with at deep levels or become friends with. My wife and I hope our boys become friends with youth who participate in activities, have involved parents, and plan to go to college after high school. We understand, though, that to mandate that would be constrictive and could lead them to rebel and intentionally ignore our guidance. We hope they select active youth who have solid plans for their future, but we don't mandate that. Hanging out with youth who commit crimes or use illegal substances of any kind, however, will be out of bounds. These are reasonable parameters.

Schools need to consider the same concept when creating grading policy. We have demonstrated how mandates were the significant factor in the failure of minimum grading policies in multiple districts. Schools and districts can provide clarity for teacher actions regarding grading practice by establishing parameters when forming or adjusting their current grading policies. Chapter 3 demonstrated that vague policies often lead to inconsistences, and constrictive ones can direct ineffective practices. When teachers have a clear understanding of how parameters were used for forming grading policy, they can be more effective in determining practices for their classrooms in how to adhere to them with consistency. Many other researches have called for some form of parameters of filters related to grading as well (Figure 4.4).

Parameters Define Boundaries

Parameters, when presented as guidelines and not as mandates, can provide and even encourage more teacher voice related to grading practices in the classroom and limit some of the resistance to implementing effective grading practice. These boundaries become the playing field for teachers as they experiment with converting grading policy into practices. Football teams have many, maybe hundreds of, plays they can execute in an attempt to score a touchdown. However, it is never acceptable for the players to go into the stands to catch a pass. That would be out of bounds. The area and perimeter of the football field are pre-established, large but not limitless. Anything that stays within the confines of the field has the chance to be an acceptable play.

Parameters Promote Safety

In life, parameters promote safety. Roads have lines and barriers indicating where cars may drive. Pedestrians may walk on roads where cars drive, but only in specific places designated for them in order to promote their safety. Drivers and pedestrians are aware of specific paths that walkers should take when crossing busy roads. These are clearly marked so

Figure 4.4   Researchers Seeking Parameters Related to Grading

Researchers	Source	Parameters
Tom Guskey and Jane Bailey	*Developing Grading and Reporting Systems for Student Learning* (2000)	Provide grading information around three key elements: • Product: Actual student work gauged against performance standards. • Progress: Improvement over time. • Process: Effort, work habits, attendance, class participation, and some forms of formative assessment.
Rick Stiggins	*Student-Involved Assessment for Learning* (2005)	Implement "bottom lines" for developing sound grading principles, such as the following: • Grade on achievement of pre-specified learning targets only. Do not factor in intelligence, effort, attitude, or personality. • Rely on the most current information available about student achievement. • Keep grading procedures separate from punishment. • Change all policies that lead to miscommunication about achievement. • Advise students of grading practices in advance.
Ken O'Connor	*How to Grade for Learning, K–12* (2009)	Use guidelines for grading, such as the following: • Relate grading procedures to learning goals. • Use criterion-referenced performance standards to determine grades. • Limit grades to individual achievement. • Sample student performance; do not use all scores in grades. • Grade in pencil and change if needed. • Crunch numbers carefully, if at all. • Use accurate assessments and evidence. • Involve students in the learning and grading process.
Doug Reeves	*Elements of Grading* (2011)	Schools should consider four primary boundaries related to grading policies: • Accuracy: Grade reflects performance of student. • Fairness: Grade is not influenced by gender, socioeconomic status, or factors unrelated to academic performance. • Timeliness: Students receive a "steady stream of feedback" not just for evaluating performance but also for improving it. • Specificity: Grade is not an evaluation but is feedback.

drivers can keep their eyes out for where pedestrians may be to maximize safety for both drivers and pedestrians. Setting parameters for grading decisions can guide how grading policy will be formed and can provide more safety in grading—safety from drastically inconsistent practices, safety from policies that lead to practices incongruent with research-based best practices, and safety from drastic inaccuracies of grades between students demonstrating the same level of proficiency.

Parameters Reduce Voice Gap

Establishing parameters also assists secondary schools in reducing the gap in teacher voice related to grading practices. In *Nine Characteristics of High-Performing Schools*, researchers Sue Shannon and Pete Bylsma (2007), directors of research, assessment, and accountability for Washington State's Office of Public Instruction, note, "Not one method of grading and reporting serves all purposes well. Since one method cannot serve all purposes, schools must identify their primary purpose for grading and reporting" (p. 80). We will likely never discover *the* one way to grade. Providing teachers with an appropriate level of structured freedom in their grading decision making allows teacher voice to be promoted while decreasing potential grading inconsistencies.

Parameter Promoting Consistency

Mandy and Sandy

Mrs. Smith and Mrs. Mitchell's school's grading policy had been established the year before, with the parameters that teacher grading practices must lead to increased reliability of grades across classrooms of like subjects. If Mrs. Mitchell shares that she gives Mandy stipulated second chances on Thursday afternoons to make up missed work with the penalty being time, not point deduction, and Mrs. Smith refuses to use that or any similar practice for Sandy, and her only option for penalty is reduction in points, that would be out of bounds. The conversation would need to continue between the teachers to determine methods and practices to ensure accuracy in grading between classrooms. If they cannot agree, then administration would need to facilitate the discussion to come to consensus.

Guiding Questions for Establishing Grading Parameters

Schools can use guiding questions to establish their parameters related to grading policy. These will help guide classroom grading practices based on established policy as well as evaluate existing grading policies for possible revisions:

1. What is the *mission* of our grades? What do we want them to do for students and parents? What do we want our grades to convey?

2. Are our grades *truthful?* Do our grades convey to students, parents, guidance counselors, and subsequent teachers an honest assessment of agreed-upon curricular learning goals and intentions for each course?

3. Do our grades have an acceptable level of *reliability?* Would the grade a student receives from one teacher be similar to another teacher for the same demonstration of mastery?

4. Are the grades we give students *impartial?* Are we providing an expected level of consistency in grading experiences and practices across classrooms (which may impact reliability)?

5. Do students and parents *understand* what the grades mean? Can they determine what aspects of curriculum students have mastered and what their next learning steps are from their grades?

Figure 4.5   Grading Parameters

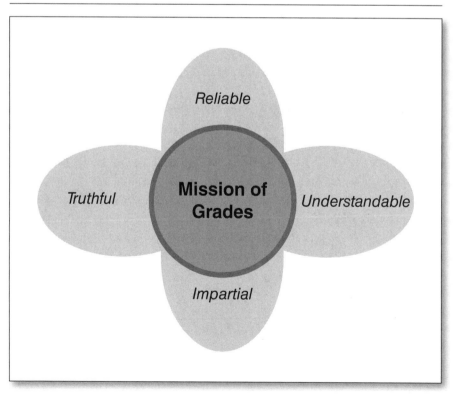

Mission for Grades

Before schools establish their parameters, they must determine their core mission for grades. Establishing a mission for grades helps schools form policies and guide all grading decisions. This promotes consistency and effectiveness of grading practices at the school and classroom levels. A mission for grades may be short and concise, like Guskey's (1996) recommendation that schools "use grading and reporting methods to enhance, not hinder, teaching and learning" (pp. 20–21). Similarly, O'Connor (2009) provides that "grading is fair, consistent, and meaningful" (p. 252). Once the core mission is established, then parameters are formed.

Truthfulness

Truthfulness is an essential parameter for middle and high school grading policy and practice. The grades students receive must reflect a high level of accuracy regarding their current performance, at appropriate levels of rigor for the learning expectations of that class. Leaders in middle and high schools must ensure that teacher practices for determining grades evaluate student performance related to content and academic objectives outlined for the class. Teachers of like courses must determine what levels of academic performance are expected from students in order to receive specific a grade. Teachers within a vertically aligned set of courses where one is a prerequisite for another also must ensure their grades represent accurately the academic level that students progressing into the next subsequent course would be likely to demonstrate. If a grade is determined by evidence that is significantly unrelated to curricular learning goals, it becomes a misrepresentation—and is dishonest and perhaps even deceitful.

Example of Diminished Truthfulness

The truthfulness of student grades is radically diminished by

- disproportionately including nonacademic factors (effort, timeliness of assignments, attendance),
- providing points for work that is unrelated to the content standards of the class,
- providing points for work submitted at the rigor levels well below what would be expected for the course.

(Continued)

(Continued)

Bert, Jim, and Steve all end up with a C+ in their 11th-grade U.S. history course. Their U.S. history teacher, Mr. Whipkey, runs his class as a project-based course. The last major assignment for the semester is heavily weighted, as it covers a large amount of course content. Students are required to conduct research and argue some of the main causes and long-term impacts of the Korean Conflict. Students are expected to work independently and present their findings to the class via a PowerPoint presentation.

Bert is a hard-working, likable student who has struggled to get by for most of his school career. He likes creating PowerPoints. His dad is a graphic designer and offers help, tips, graphics, and images that wow Bert's classmates and teachers whenever he gives a presentation. For his project, as always, his slides are professionally sharp, images are crisp, and transitions and effects are eye-catching. However, his ability to clearly articulate a true understanding of the causes, impacts, and effects of the Korean Conflict is far from accurate or proficient. Bert, like on many other projects he has submitted, receives 95 out of 120 points, mostly for the quality of his slides and graphics. Mr. Whipkey often assesses students as much on their slide quality as on the content knowledge they demonstrate. Bert's final grade is a C+.

Jim is very interested in and passionate about the history of wars and conflicts. His dad is a former marine, and Jim has lived for several years on military bases and attended schools with other military children. Jim's grandfather served in Korea. For this project, Jim researches in depth and examines the causes of the Korean Conflict and includes some firsthand accounts of the happenings there, even challenging some of the textbook's depictions of events. He develops and shares a solid argument about what were the main causes and impacts of the event in Korea, even more detailed and thorough than Mr. Whipkey could have. Jim is able to handle questions on his feet, and his answers convey the type of understanding of the conflict that Mr. Whipkey has never seen in any previous student. While Mr. Whipkey commends Jim for his arguments in front of the class, he deducts a great deal of points for Jim's overall project grade. Jim's PowerPoint falls low on several categories on the rubric. His images are poor, he uses large amounts of text on slides with some spelling errors, and it is 2 days late. Similar to his other project grades, Jim's final grade on this and for the course is a C+.

Steve struggles a great deal. He has never been identified as having any learning or other disability that would qualify him specifically for education support or accommodations. His parents are hardworking people who have seven other children. Steve is the oldest, and compared to his siblings, it seems he often receives less support from his parents related to keeping up with his academic progress. They are just trying to get him out the door and into college to free up a room in their overly crowded home. (Mr. Whipkey heard them say this during open house in the fall.) Mr. Whipkey often gives Steve the benefit of the doubt and grades much higher than Steve deserves. He knows Steve needs a C+ or better in his class this spring to keep his GPA above 2.5, which is the threshold for the community college Steve is planning to attend after graduating from high school. This assignment is no different than others. Steve's research and argument are subpar and well below the standards on the rubric. In addition to providing additional points for slide effects like he did for Bert's, Mr. Whipkey gives Steve a much lower level task that simply requires him to share basic facts about the war: dates, casualty numbers, costs, places of battles, and number of episodes of the TV show *M*A*S*H* that highlighted actual combat. Steve's work is not at all aligned to the rigor of the content standards. He is awarded a C+ as well, however.

Mr. Whipkey's grading practices exhibit diminished truthfulness, a problem that appropriate grading parameters could prevent.

Reliability

Grades have reliability when similar performances between two students receive the same grade from one classroom teacher as they would from another teaching a similar course. Schools need to consider this parameter as a form of quality control. Students, parents, and other teachers in the same school should expect a minimum level of grading consistency for similar demonstration of skill, from one classroom to another. Guidance counselors make many decisions about the placement of students based on grades they have received. Their ability to make proper placements of students is seriously impacted when grades from one classroom to another are unreliable. Schools that have high levels of reliability of grades between classrooms never have student or parents requesting a specific teacher because they perceive them as offering easy As.

Impartiality

Grading is impartial when determining that the quality (or lack thereof) in student work is not impacted by who students or their parents are. Friedman (1998) strongly encourages principals to demand that teachers are fair and impartial when determining student grades. He describes a situation in which a teacher raised the final grade of one student because the student's parents had determinedly complained. Friedman wonders about other students in the class who might be less vocal or fearful of challenging. Why should students whose parents advocate more or just more audibly be rewarded? (p. 81).

Impartiality of grades as a parameter also guides teachers to not overly punish students in point or mark deduction for a perceived lack of effort nor inflate grades with additional points because they struggle more than others. Thus, the impartiality parameter fully supports having more truthfulness.

Understandability

Finally, parameters for establishing and implementing grading policy should ensure that student grades convey clarity as to what the students' next steps in learning are. Parents, counselors, and subsequent teachers must be able to comprehend these from the grades students receive. These parameters will guide grading practices and actions to ensure the meaning of grades has a level of clarity and accuracy as to what any grade tells someone about a student's performance.

Figure 4.6   Examples of Grading Policies and Practices Matched With Practices Parameter Questions

Parameter	Example of middle and high school grading policies	Example of grading practices that would adhere to them	Example of out-of-bounds practices
Truthfulness	For a grade of B: Students must exhibit mastery with evidence at or above the 80% level on appropriate standards-based assessments.	Common summative assessments included in grade determination will assess only district priority standards.	Teachers deduct points or offer critical feedback unrelated to the standards, objectives, or learning intentions of a lesson, unit, or course.
	In addition to an academic grade, students will receive a work ethic grade. This supplementary grade will include how students were assessed on their ability to act responsibly, behave appropriately, and work diligently while at school. Additional comments will be included on the report card.	The professional learning community (PLC) will collaboratively create a course syllabus of learning intentions from specific academic standards for the course as well as acceptable success criteria for student work to be considered exemplary, proficient, or progressing.	Teachers offer extra credit points that are unrelated to standards or objectives of the course. (Points come from more work or more time spent on a project, bringing supplies to class, etc.)

Parameter	Example of middle and high school grading policies	Example of grading practices that would adhere to them	Example of out-of-bounds practices
Reliability	To increase the consistency and quality of grading, isolation in grading will not be an option in our school district. All middle and high school teachers are required to meet in monthly PLC meetings after school hours to discuss grading practices and reactions to student assessment evidence.	PLC and course-level teams will meet regularly (at least twice per month) to collaboratively score anonymous student work.	When grading, teachers include factors at any disproportionate level or differently than teachers of like classes. (Teachers of like courses never collaboratively score any work or rarely if ever have structured dialogue and discussion for determining appropriate assignments, assessments, etc.)
Impartiality	On informal assignments, students who have made a reasonable attempt, as determined by the PLC, will receive a minimum score and will be given specific feedback to improve prior to resubmission. All students in like courses must receive the same opportunities regardless of their assigned teacher.	All students will be offered the same amount of multiple attempts at revision of assignments as well as stipulated second chances for assignments missed.	Teachers refuse to use agreed-upon stipulated second chances for students to attempt making up work before deducting points from their grade.
Understandability	Learning objectives and grading criteria will be explicitly communicated to students and parents at the beginning of the course. Course-alike teachers at each site will have similar syllabus expectations.	Teachers will create a common syllabus with assignments and tasks linked to specific course objectives and will share it with students at the beginning of semester. (See Chapter 7 for examples.)	Teachers in a PLC do not share with students and parents specific criteria that students should have mastered that correspond to specific grades.

EFFECTIVE POLICY = EFFECTIVE PRACTICES

Middle and high school leaders must acknowledge that it is erroneous to believe that a new grading policy, regardless of how firmly mandated, will automatically be implemented with fidelity. Policy alone is not sufficient. The actual classroom grading practices that teachers implement will have the most impact on students. Subject matter will at times determine differences in how classroom grading practices are implemented. A few core grading practices applicable at the school level should be considered essential: teacher collaboration, collaborative scoring of student work, and multiple opportunities for success.

Core Practice 1: Teacher Collaboration

Middle and high schools can increase the fidelity and effectiveness of implementation of grading practices through effective collaborative structures. Too often, grading decisions take place in a large-group setting without having protocols for the discussion. Without structure, dialogue about grading changes can be very counterproductive. Friedman (1998) notes:

> Teachers tend to find a way to have their grading policy reflect their own deeply held beliefs (not necessarily knowledge) about how students should be graded, even if building or district-level grading policies exist. Often, this is a reflection of how their own teachers graded them and is characterized by a strong sense of ownership. (p. 77)

That is far from the type of collaboration needed in order to create and implement effective grading practices.

Effective PLC-Challenging Beliefs

Many middle and high schools have some form of professional learning community (PLC) models in place for collaboration. Effective PLCs have the capacity to promote and sustain the learning of all professionals in the school community and thus impact student learning from the adjustments in practice that teachers make. It is, however, critical that the collective purpose of "enhancing pupil learning is the foremost concern" (Bolam, McMahon, Stoll, Thomas, & Wallace, 2005, p. 145). Grading practices have to be an expected aspect of their discussions. PLCs must dedicate specific time for collaborative concentration on monitoring how their grading practices are impacting student achievement. Effective PLC dialogue focuses on improving student performance. The goal of their PLC cannot simply be to be a PLC, in which teachers talk only about their actions and collaborate around how their actions are impacting students. Status-reporting PLC meetings will not lead to achievement, nor will they help teachers increase truthfulness, reliability, impartiality, or under-standability in their grading practices. These collaborative discussions are where secondary schools must look first as a place to minimize the gap in teacher voice regarding grading.

Effective collaboration around grading as a core practice can begin to challenge certain existing beliefs teachers have about grading practices. Hattie (2012) notes, "Powerful impacts in our schools relate to how we think . . . and underpin our every action and decision" (p. 159). Hattie goes on to mention that teachers have "theories of practice" for how to accomplish all they have to do within an established set of resources, such as the available time they have. He also points out that, over time, as experience in teaching increases, teachers' theories of practice (e.g., grading practices) become more pervasive in teachers' minds as the best way to do things.

Using Collaboration: Mrs. Mitchell and Mrs. Smith (Mandy and Sandy) Improved

Mrs. Mitchell and Mrs. Smith engaged in a dialogue during a recent PLC meeting. Mrs. Mitchell shared how she gave her students time to complete work after school as a stipulated second chance of additional time on Thursdays and Fridays. She asked Mrs. Smith if she used any practices similar to this. Mrs. Smith was at first resistant to the idea, but agreed to try it. Together, the two teachers came up with other possible strategies to provide additional time but still hold students accountable for doing their required work. They also deter-mined a few indicators to look for over time if the second-chance strategy was proving to be effective. Mrs. Mitchell and Mrs. Smith decided that if more students were increasing the quality of their writing from revisions during these second chances and if fewer students were missing deadlines, they would be more inclined to continue the practice. The two teachers intentionally focused their col-laboration and increased their chances for reliability and truthfulness of the grades they were administering.

Example: Expected Grading Collaboration

Fontana Unified School District in California has written into its board-approved secondary grading policy recommendations for teacher collaboration as an expectation. Using the district's existing PLC model, several parameters are explicit in the policy as recommended practices:

- PLCs will have agreed-upon like-weighting and like-categories for determining student grades.
- If a student has made a reasonable attempt to complete an assignment, as determined by the PLC, the student will receive a grade no lower than 50% on informal assignments.
- Teachers shall allow students to retake assessments within the guidelines established by the PLC. Final exams are not included in this, since they coincide with the end of the grading period. Assessments should be retaken within a reasonable amount of time to be determined by the PLC.
- Extra credit may be offered only under the guidelines established by the PLC and may be given only for the completion of standards-based work.
- PLC members should work together to create a common syllabus that includes assignments that are both formative and summative (Fontana Unified School Board, 2011).

Fontana Unified has included in its secondary schools grading policy strong recommendations that the practice of teacher and team collaboration related to grading practices and grade determination should be the norm and parameter for grading decisions. The policy guides teachers into the parameters of reliability and impartiality by encouraging them to collaborate around decisions such as determining weight limits for assignments to prohibit any one assignment from distorting the accuracy of the grade. It also ensures that assessment make-up time should be reasonable, not infinite, and must be the same for all teachers. Kimberly Mac Kinney, former director of secondary instruction for Fontana Unified and now chief academic officer for Oro Grande School District, said, "The increased collaboration in grading has led schools to better determine which grading practices across classrooms are having the greatest impact. Those are now being replicated by our teachers." This approach has proven effective for this school district.[1]

Core Practice 2: Collaborative Scoring of Student Work

Collaborative scoring of student work is a core practice to increase the reliability of middle and high school grades. In *Classroom Grading and*

---

[1]Used with permission from Kimberly McKinney of Oro Grande School District.

Assessment That Work, Marzano (2006, p. 61) notes that when two teachers used a common scoring system for the same work, the reliability of the combined score was found to be as high as .82. In her dissertation, high school principal Mary C. Pauly (2009) defines *collaborative scoring* as "teachers gather together to use a standards based rubric to score student work" (p. 14).

The more teachers score work together, the more the reliability and impartiality of their grading practices grow exponentially. Reliability in grading increases when teachers grade sets of student work samples anonymously. This removes any preconceived personal beliefs or perceptions about individual students' ability during the scoring and grading process. This addresses Zoeckler's (2005) caution that all teachers have the ability to let their moral judgments influence the grades they assign.

Core Practice 3: Multiple Opportunities for Success

Providing students with multiple opportunities to demonstrate proficiency is a core grading practice that all middle and high schools can implement immediately across classrooms to increase effectiveness of grading on student achievement. When students have several chances to revise and improve work, they view trial and error as a way to learn from mistakes. Teachers must provide students with multiple opportunities to practice skills when their errors aren't counted against them. Students who have a chance to prove proficiency over time develop perseverance, resilience, and grit. This increases how they value and more effectively utilize teacher feedback.

One Measure Is Rarely Accurate

Assessment expert Rick Stiggins (2005) quips that "grades must convey as accurate a picture of a student's real achievement as possible. Any practice that has the effect of misrepresenting actual achievement of agreed standards is unacceptable." The notion that a single evaluation of student performance would be representative of a student's true achievement level is ludicrous. Friedman (1998) mentions that many teachers "like to point out to students that they can learn from their mistakes" (p. 79). However, if teachers don't offer multiple opportunities for students to display proficiency, they are *not* allowing students to learn from their mistakes.

The systemic practice in a school of providing multiple opportunities for students to revise their work increases consistency between teacher grades while also increasing reliability, truthfulness, and impartiality. When student grades are determined based on students' true demonstration of proficiency, rather than by the averaging of each student's individual attempts, consistency of grades between teachers increases dramatically.

Make-Up Testing

Teachers and administrators sometimes misconstrue multiple opportunities as meaning students have infinite chances to retake the same test. Any true quality assessment has three main attributes: purpose, evidence, and inference. First, teachers must decide on the *purpose* of their assessment (what standard concept or skill is it assessing?). Then they must determine how they'll be able to make accurate inferences from the *evidence* students provide. If a student was to take the exact same test over and over, and on the fifth try finally score a passing or proficient grade, the teacher would not be sure the student hadn't simply memorized the answers. The teacher would not be able to make an accurate inference that the student mastered essential material. Teachers can create several versions of tests to prevent students from memorizing answers on their first try (Fisher, Frey, & Pumpian, 2011, p. 47) or have alternative assessment methods to provide them with multiple avenues for accurately assessing and grading students.

Common Core State Standards

The Common Core State Standards were designed to help teachers guide students to develop the critical learning skills needed to be ready for college and careers. The standards convey both implicit and explicit expectations for multiple opportunities for students.

Language Arts: Writing

Offering students multiple attempts aligns directly with the Common Core writing standards for language arts. The standards for writing use a key word multiple times: *develop*. *Develop* is defined as "to bring out the capabilities or possibilities of, to bring to a more advanced or effective state, and to cause to grow or expand" (Merriam-Webster, 2014a). Bringing out a student's capabilities to develop writing takes time, feedback, and trial and error.

Ninth- and Tenth-Grade Writing Common Core Standards that use *develop* as the skill:

- CCSS.ELA-Literacy.W.9-10.1b: *Develop* claim(s) and counterclaims fairly, supplying evidence for each while pointing out the strengths and limitations of both in a manner that anticipates the audience's knowledge level and concerns.
- CCSS.ELA-Literacy.W.9-10.2b: *Develop* the topic with well-chosen, relevant, and sufficient facts, extended definitions, concrete details, quotations, or other information and examples appropriate to the audience's knowledge of the topic.

- CCSS.ELA-Literacy.W.9-10.4: Produce clear and coherent writing in which the *development,* organization, and style are appropriate to task, purpose, and audience.
- CCSS.ELA-Literacy.W.9-10.5: ***Develop*** and strengthen writing as needed by planning, revising, editing, rewriting, or trying a new approach, focusing on addressing what is most significant for a specific purpose and audience.

The core practice of multiple opportunities will be essential for students to develop their skills in writing. "To build a foundation for college and career readiness, students … *develop* the capacity to build knowledge on a subject through research projects and to respond analytically to literary and informational sources" (Common Core State Standards Initiative, 2014a; emphasis added).

Math

The concept of multiple opportunities to demonstrate proficiency is also firmly emphasized in the Common Core math standards. *The Standards for Mathematical Practice* guide teachers to *develop* skills or math expertise in all of their students. Two examples are shared below.

Persevere and Persist in Solving Problems

The first standard of mathematical practice states that students should "make sense of problems and persevere in solving them." When students persevere, is it safe to say we should expect some mistakes? Students would then continue to work on whatever it is until they get it. Teachers assisting students in persevering at anything would never stop every time they made a mistake, write it down, and remind them that that mistake will count against them in the end.

Model With Mathematics

Another standard of mathematical practice to develop in students that calls for multiple opportunities is for students to *model* with mathematics. The description of the full standard states: "[Students] routinely interpret their mathematical results in the context of the situation and reflect on whether the results make sense, possibly improving the model if it has not served its purpose" (Common Core State Standards Initiative, 2014c, "Model With Mathematics"). Students improving their model would imply that they are on at least their second revision of work, formulas, and so on. A traditional grading practice of counting each error into the average of a student's grade at the end of a unit or course would simply be incongruent in helping students meet this practice.

In both the English language arts and mathematics Common Core standards, there is a clear emphasis on schools ensuring that students have multiple opportunities to demonstrate proficiency.

Stipulated Second Chances

We all have to acknowledge that life is full of do-overs. Often, however, they come with stipulations. For example, teachers who do not pass their exam for certification always have the chance to retake it—with the penalty of the cost of the test and additional time dedicated to studying and retaking the test. Other examples include income tax extensions that can be filed for a fee and people who pass the bar exam on the fifth try are still called attorneys.

One other common example is acquiring a driver's license. People who pass their driving test on their third or fourth try don't have to pull over when it rains. A related example has to do with traffic violations such as speeding or ignoring traffic laws, which devalue the license by adding points against your driving record. These points carry the cost of increased insurance rates, and after a certain number, the privilege of driving legally can be taken away. These points can be deducted and removed from driving records through a stipulated second chance. In Indiana, the stipulation to remove four points for two speeding tickets is $70 and successful completion of a 4-hour online defensive driving course. (Trust me on that one—I know all about it.) Real-life second chances happen every day and they all come with stipulations. The cost is usually money, time, or both.

Stipulated second chances are a way to provide middle and high school students with multiple opportunities to show proficiency. They have helped many teachers be able to feel less concerned about allowing additional attempts for students who may have, let's say, thumbed their nose at them. Many teachers have a strong desire, and rightly so, to make sure their academic teaching does not ever completely eliminate their ability and calling to teach students some degree of responsibility and accountability.

I mentioned that in real life, stipulated second chances often cost money. Students have currency that their teachers can barter for in exchange for giving second chance stipulations to be able to make up work, retake tests, or show proficiency on the second or third or fourth attempt—it's their precious time. When students lose the privilege of time that may have been expected to be free, teachers can increase their achievement and still provide them with a dose of real-world experience for missing deadlines or failing to follow through on responsibilities. Multiple opportunities can actually increase students' responsibility to learn without distorting the accuracy of the academic grade.

Teachers have many options for stipulated second chance scenarios that they can use to offer students multiple opportunities without reducing grades. Figure 4.7 lists a few examples.

Stipulated second chances are of course not foolproof. The examples in Figure 4.7 are from teachers I have personally worked with who have implemented these in their classrooms. None have been perfect in getting every student to consider not missing deadlines, but they have in each case reduced the number of students dismissing the idea or just blowing off the work and taking the academic loss in points. Teachers have used these and countless other ways to stipulate multiple opportunities for students without threatening to reduce points, thus minimizing the loss of reliability and truthfulness in student grades. Offering stipulated second chances also teaches an accurate life lesson to students: The world is filled with second chances, but they are rarely free. Middle and high schools can teach students this important lesson without it having any immediate cost to their academic grade.

Stipulated second chances add fairness in grading as well. Students are now more in charge of their grades based on whether they accept the stipulations. If they do, then their academic grade will not suffer. If they do not, they have made the choice to turn down a very good offer. Most schools will find that many, if not most, students will be willing to take them up on it.

Figure 4.7   Examples of Stipulated Second Chances

- Teachers allow students to make up missing work before or after school (or during any designated free time).
- Students' late work submissions must be accompanied by a parent note, conference, or phone call.
- Written work must include additional sources and be cited properly.
- Students have to miss an activity or extracurricular event for missing work until work is submitted close to or at standard.
- Work must be polished and made ready for submission to a journal, school or local newspaper, or school board (stipulated second chance is met whether or not the external publication accepts the submission).
- Students must share work with the class via presentation or some mode of technology (adds rigor and meets Common Core speaking and listening standard CCSS.ELA-Literacy.SL.9-10.5: "Make strategic use of digital media [e.g., textual, graphical, audio, visual, and interactive elements] in presentations to enhance understanding of findings, reasoning, and evidence and to add interest" [Common Core State Standards Initiative, 2014b]).

Stipulated Second Chances Built Into Grading Policies

Iowa

Des Moines Public Schools recently commissioned a districtwide task force to revamp and recreate its grading policy. I was fortunate to facilitate several of the early meetings and discussions related to this process. One of the early decisions the committee agreed on was to have stipulated second chances be a common practice in Des Moines classrooms. There was consensus that students should be held accountable for completing work and demonstrating proficiency of standards. However, the adults in the system were also expected to be held accountable for providing those opportunities. The policy specifically says:

> Retaking a particular assessment will be allowed. Schools may implement some provisions that require students to earn a second chance (this is a site-based decision). If a student has scored poorly on a standard and wants to try again, the student may engage in learning opportunities prior to the attempts. The student needs to practice the skills being measured before retesting on a specific standard.[2]

Indiana

The Metropolitan School District of Wayne Township in Indiana states that evidence from standards-based assessments should be included in grades and that multiple but not infinite opportunities should be offered:

> [If] the student does not exhibit mastery at the 70% level on the appropriate state standards as evidenced on standards-based assessments. Student receives an "I" until mastery at 70% is obtained or opportunities to improve grade have been exhausted.

How many multiple opportunities should students receive, and when are opportunities exhausted? The answers to these questions are left to the discretion of teachers or teams. Obviously, logistical factors are considered. The policy provides parameters for teachers and PLCs to impartially use their professional judgment related to multiple opportunities and number of attempts at proficiency. *Exhausted* is a relative term. If students are attending additional tutoring, meeting extended deadlines, and showing progress and effort, it would be safe to say they are using their opportunities. If students do not attend tutoring, continue to miss deadlines, and refuse to submit work, this might constitute an exhausted opportunity. What is clear is that not offering students these additional chances for learning would mean not adhering to the parameter of impartiality and thus would be out of bounds.[3]

---

[2]Used with permission from Des Moines Public Schools.

[3]Used with permission from Metropolitan School District of Wayne Township.

CONCLUSION

My son is grateful for the signage at our favorite stadium, which helps him guide us toward our seating section for each sporting event. The signs lead us in the right direction to get close to our seats faster, but they aren't enough. The information printed on our tickets and the guidance of ushers are what ultimately get us to our exact seats.

Grading policy and practice work hand in hand the same way. Policy will guide and, if aligned with parameters, direct teachers to effective practices. Core practices such as collaboration, collaborative scoring, and providing multiple opportunities align with parameters such as truthfulness and reliability of grades and must be able to be adapted by teachers in individual classroom settings.

The next set of chapters will begin to address specific practices related to failure prevention, credit recovery, and standards-based grading. All will focus on more specific grading practices teachers can implement in their classrooms. As you read them, keep in mind that grading policy is simply the signage that gets us going in the right direction in the stadium—the implementation of effective grading practices is what gets us to our exact seats.

KEY IDEAS

1. Grading policy without additional guidelines can lead to inconsistency in grading.

2. Effective grading practices have more impact in classrooms than any set district or school policy.

3. Policies can and should provide guidance, but they need additional guidelines and recommendations.

4. The overall mission of grades, their truthfulness, reliability, impartiality, and understandability are parameters schools should use when creating grading policies. These will then guide fidelity of grading policy implementation by determining specific grading practices to be implemented with students.

5. Core grading practices of teacher collaboration, collaborative scoring, and multiple opportunities for success can help middle and high schools increase the consistency and reliability of their students' grades.

6. Multiple opportunities can mean stipulated second chances (mirroring real life), where consequences are in place for late or missing work, but they do not immediately lead to a reduction in points.

REFLECTION QUESTIONS

1. Are your grading practices, explicit or implicit, within the confines of your grading policies? Are further recommendations and guidance needed?

2. What parameters would your school need to establish before adjusting current grading policies or practices in your school or district?

3. How do you view multiple opportunities for students to demonstrate proficiency as stipulated second chances?

PART III

Grading Practices to Prevent Failure, Recover Credits, and Increase Grading on Standards

Preventing Unnecessary Failure

5

In Chip Heath and Dan Heath's (2010) *New York Times* best-seller *Switch: How to Change Things When Change Is Hard*, they talk of "shaping the path" to make it easier to navigate changes in our lives. They recommend as an example, for people who have a tendency to hit the snooze button over and over in the morning, placing the alarm clock on the other side of the room. Then when it goes off, instead of being able to just reach over and hit snooze, people actually have to get out of bed to shut it off and are and less likely to stay in bed.

A friend mentioned to me recently how he shaped his 10-year-old son Jack's path, after a cavity was found during a visit to the dentist. Daily tooth brushing had been a bit problematic for Jack, especially in the morning. Jack would come downstairs for breakfast before school and, like a normal 10-year-old, he would procrastinate getting his backpack and other materials ready. When the bus was about to arrive, running upstairs again for tooth brushing was the last priority. Jack would be out of time and out the door before having a chance to brush his teeth. After the dentist report, Jack's dad decided to follow the Heath brothers' advice. He placed a toothbrush in the bathroom downstairs to make it less easy for Jack to have an excuse not to brush his teeth. Jack no longer has to go back upstairs after breakfast during the franticness of the morning. Jack's path is now shaped. He still has to do the brushing, but it is easier for him *not to fail.* (I know this story resonates with many parents who have children in his age bracket.) Jack's dad provided support for him to be successful. He doesn't brush his teeth for him.

IMPACTS OF STUDENT FAILURE

When a student drops out of school, it's far from a one-time event. Over time, young adults see the number of failures mount, eventually fail to see the relevance of continuing to try, and completely disengage over time. The number of high school dropouts in the United States is staggering: 1.2 million students, or 1 every 26 seconds (Amos, 2011). High numbers of student dropouts is one of the most negative data points for any school or district.

The impact lingers well past dropout day. In Cox's (2009) study, adults who dropped out stated that past failures seriously affected their confidence 9 years after high school. As these students move into adulthood, lingering fear of failure prohibits many from acquiring skills needed to better their lives and society as a whole. "The average high school dropout will cost taxpayers over $292,000 in lower tax revenues, higher cash and in-kind transfer costs, and imposed incarceration costs relative to an average high school graduate" (Sum, Khatiwada, & McLaughlin, 2009).

Activity 5.1: Local Effect of Student Failure

For your school, brainstorm some specific causes for student failure, those caused by student actions as well as actions of adults. How do these failures affect both students and adults?

	Factors contributing to students failing courses	Impact of students failing courses
Originating with student		
Originating with adults		

Prevent vs. Endure

A professor of mine at Butler University, Dr. Steve Heck, often said, "Amateurs react and repair; professionals prepare and prevent." Secondary schools must look at preventing failures as a primary basis for preventing potential dropouts. A longitudinal study of Chicago Public Schools found clear evidence that students receiving one F in their ninth-grade fall semester were 15% more likely to not graduate, and multiple Fs added another 15% to this rate (Allensworth & Easton, p. 6).

There is clear and abundant evidence that success in ninth and tenth grades is a strong predictor of graduation and success beyond high school (Allensworth & Easton, 2005; Balfanz, Legters, & Jordan, 2004; Cahill, Lynch, & Hamilton, 2006; Orfield, 2004; Roderick & Camburn, 1999). Ninth grade has been identified as the most critical point to intervene and prevent students from losing motivation, failing, and dropping out of school (Gainey & Webb, 1998, p. 2). In a 5-year study related to factors impacting dropout rates in Philadelphia, Nield and Balfanz (2006) found that the greatest risk of dropping out is in the ninth grade, followed closely by tenth grade (p. 29). Many students who drop out of high school can trace some of their path to failure, if not the very trailhead, to their ninth-grade year. Successful high school completion is connected in a very large way to success in this *linchpin year* (Donnegan, 2008; Blankstein, 2004).

Applying Band-Aids When Stiches Are Needed

High School Principal Will Intendedefforts was looking at the current semester's F report on his desk. He noticed right away a significant spike in the number of failures at his high school and convened his department chairs to analyze the data and talk about possible strategies to address the issue. A quick analysis of the F report data showed the highest number of failures had taken place in required courses for graduation: health, algebra 1, and typewriting (okay, I had to see if you were paying attention—not typewriting, but English 9 and English 10). This was not only going to place some students in the at-risk category for potential dropout, but it was also going to cause a logjam in the master schedule as students would need to retake the classes they failed.

Principal Will opened the meeting by saying, "Many of these students who failed courses are now missing a graduation requirement and will likely need a change in their schedules. Many are also now behind in overall credits required for graduation. What should we do?"

(Continued)

(Continued)

A few department chairs voiced the need to look first at the possible reasons for the increases in failed classes rather than simply attempting to fix the problem after the fact. Their comments were met with eye rolls from some veterans who were more concerned with how the immediate logjam in scheduling would affect their class sizes for the upcoming semesters.

One teacher, Pam, in her analysis of the data, noted that four out of every five students who failed a course did so by less than 6%. Furthermore, she stated that almost 70% of the students who received an F in the course passed the end-of-course cumulative assessment or task with a C or better (over 35% with a B). Clearly, the students had some proficiency in the subject matter, and repeating courses would not make sense. Pam posed the possibility that perhaps some grading practice issues may be leading to the reasons for increased failure for at least some of these students. She questioned whether they could consider, for students who did show proficiency on end-of-course assessments, replacing some of the low grades on tests and assessments from earlier in the semester (over the same content) with the end-of-course assessment scores. "These students have shown enough mastery to at least pass the course, wouldn't you think?"

She also wondered out loud, "If students have a certain number of zeros for homework, could we at least offer a chance for them to make up these assignment instead of making them repeat an entire course?"

One vocal veteran, Paul, interrupted Pam. "Look, what this school needs to do is send a message to these lazy students so they understand why they need to do their homework during the semester and not after the fact!" Paul continued, "If we offer a chance to these slothful students to make up work and recover their credits, it should not happen during the regular school day or time frame." Several others echoed his strict standards.

During the summary discussion, Principal Will entertained the following possible strategies to deal with the spike in failed courses:

1. Increase the staffing and capacity of the summer school program in June to include more seats for students. This resonated with several in the group who would be interested a 4- to 6-week summer position at their daily rate of pay.

2. Offer a credit recovery program option (after school only) 3 days per week, in the form of both teacher-led traditional remediation as well as online programs that would be purchased and loaded onto the computers in the library. (One teacher said she recently saw an advertisement in a publication for some packaged online credit recovery courses for both algebra and health.)

While both of these options would cause the school to incur additional cost, and there has been a great deal of talk regarding budget issues in the district, Principal Will knew the superintendent had always seemed to find additional funds to support credit recovery to increase graduation rates. Will concluded the meeting by saying, "I feel there would easily be support for both of these ideas. Thank you all for your time."

As the meeting adjourned, Pam mentioned quietly to a peer, "Well, there's another Band-Aid idea for something that needs stitches. We did nothing to prevent this from happening again next semester!"

While the names in this scenario are fictitious, the example is quite real and has been lived out many times in middle and high school meeting rooms. Addressing the issue of student failure often comes after the students have already failed. I have personally been involved in discussions with middle and high schools trying to address high rates of student failure. Many times, they've focused on *reactions* such as finding additional financial and human resources to fix the problem after the failures had already taken place. Yet in almost every case, these same resources existed prior to the failures, but prevention was often not considered to be a wise use of them.

Making Failure a More Difficult Option

Many secondary schools have held to the tradition that to gain additional learning time, students have to fail the course first. Adding time to the learning process in a fluid way may be the most important action schools can take to prevent failure. This is a question that should drive all grading actions: What is more important—*when* students learn it or *that* they learn it well? The more students see failure as a path to dropping out, the more likely they will drop out if they experience failure. The more they can see a chance to get support early in the grading period, free from the destruction that zeros have on their grades, and the more they're given time to make up missed assignments and have stipulated second chances, the more they just might rise up instead of dropping out.

The grading practices or strategies outlined in this chapter may be different than some readers have considered previously. They are far from fool-proof. For each one, at least one middle or high school teacher may think, "I know a student that wouldn't work for!" My response is simply, "So do I. In fact, I know three who live in my own house!" Middle and high school teachers need to commit to actions to help prevent any unnecessary failures. Outliers and situations where a student figures out how to beat the system will happen, and it already happens every day. Schools and classrooms can make an immediate difference in reducing failure by using the strategies described below. Finally, wouldn't we desire fewer students repeating middle and high school courses? I mean, aren't these students who repeat entire 18-week courses just the most delightful and engaged students you have? (The sarcasm here is intentional.)

GRADING PRACTICES THAT PREVENT UNNECESSARY FAILURE

The example from *Switch* earlier as well as the vignette of Principal Will Intendedefforts provides the backdrop for secondary schools to implement grading practices to prevent failure. Middle and high school teachers must look to prevent avoidable failures and minimize the need for teachers and students to endure them. This chapter will provide tools to work toward these goals.

First, I encourage schools, professional learning communities (PLCs), and individual classroom teachers to consider the framework I provide, which offers schools specific elements to consider in preventing student failure: SI^{2}TE (*support, intervention, incentives, time, and evidence*; Figure 5.1). I share these specific grading practices, or actions, that can be implemented at the school or individual classroom level. None of them involve any level of calculation, mathematical formulas, or equations. In some cases, they may not even appear to be grading practices, as we traditionally know them. Each one provides schools and individual classroom teachers with actions that can drastically prevent student failure by shaping their paths to make it more difficult for them to fail.

The SI^{2}TE Model

Practices to prevent unnecessary failures in middle and high school classrooms should be as commonplace as hand washing in the cafeteria kitchen. It's a safety issue. They will not be employed, with rare exception, through mandates to implement one-size-fits-all practices or through changes to the grading scale. Middle and high schools are diverse learning operations where every discipline and even classroom has unique situations that call for grading practices to be malleable.

The SI^{2}TE model provides guidelines that every teacher can follow to help prevent unnecessary failure without mandating actions that stifle teachers' freedom to teach. The model is based on five key elements that provide a framework for teachers at the course, team, or individual classroom level and allows for adaptability and fidelity across classrooms. Each element provides a filter for teachers or schools to use in grading to allow practice adaptations across classrooms to better shape students' paths to success.

Figure 5.1   SI²TE Model

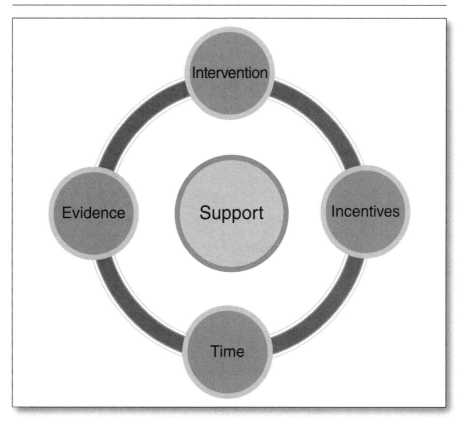

Support—Paramount to Everything Else

The first element of SI²TE is support. Preventing failure begins and ends with students knowing their academic struggles are not permanent. Learned helplessness is the result of looking at adversity as permanent or beyond the control of the teachers. Students who view their teachers as a support network will exert higher levels of effort and engagement and are less likely to even consider dropping out of school (Yazzie-Mintz, 2010).

Many students entering middle and high school have a history of academic struggles and failure. Lacking the grit to keep trying to learn when things get tough is common. If a middle school failure cycle reemerges in high school, students are likely to assume it is simply a way of life for them. For many students, once failure is probable, effort significantly decreases. Teaching stick-withitness is essential to help them develop the resilience they will need to succeed in high school and in life. Nan Henderson (2013, p. 24), president of Resiliency in Action, notes that providing "caring and support" is the single most important factor in building resilience in students.

Finally, distorting the accuracy of achievement levels and letting students pass classes without putting in the effort to demonstrate mastery diminishes their development of resilience (Perkins-Gough, 2013). Grading practices must support students and allow them to see that passing with hard work and effort is a real possibility.

(Early) Intervention

Schools and individual classroom teachers will have the best chance to prevent student failure by intervening as they see signs of it. Students' perception of being supported early is critical as well, because it relates to their motivation to learn. Ron Ferguson notes that increased self-efficacy in students can be increased with "high help" (Viadero, 2008). The National High School Center (n.d.) notes that failure of one class is a threshold indicator, meaning that failing even one course places students past the onset of potentially dropping out. It recommends that teachers evaluate grades between 20 and 30 days after the start of the semester to look for signs that intervention may be needed for some students (2013).

(Increasing) Incentives

When schools and classroom teachers implement grading practices that focus on incentives as opposed to consequences, they can significantly decrease unnecessary failure.

In a 2011 study, researchers Allan and Fryer examined the impact of teachers incentivizing student input (efforts) versus outputs (proficiency). They found that creating incentives is an effective way to counteract consequences like failing grades. The notion that low grades will teach students a lesson about the importance of effort on future assignments is unfounded. Conclusive studies proving punishing students with low grades will increase effort have not been found (Guskey & Bailey, 2010).

Time

Time is the one variable middle and high schools often forget they control when it comes to grading. Schools that focus more on students learning well as opposed to the time frame in which they learn can help avoid unnecessary failure. It's a basic concept that students behind in skill and knowledge need additional time to learn prior to being evaluated by a course grade.

Grading expert Ken O'Connor (2010) states that teachers create unnecessary problems by not offering students additional time, as that lack can "motivate the student to exactly the opposite behavior than intended" (p. 24). If students feel additional time will not be provided and points are deducted for lateness of work, many will cease attempting to complete it. O'Connor quotes Joel Barkey, who says, "It is best to do it right and on time, but it is better to do it right and late than the reverse" (p. 100).

Evidence

The final element of SI²TE is evidence. Teachers must use the best evidence when grading their students, especially when the possibility of failure is being considered. Failure can be dramatically decreased by allowing students to present multiple pieces of evidence of their mastery of essential content and skills.

To fully consider evidence, teachers may need to collect more evidence and offer students multiple chances to best show their level of skill and understanding. The less certain teachers are about a student's proficiency, the more assessment evidence they should collect and use (Marzano, 2006, p. 114). To prevent failure effectively, teachers must provide students with multiple avenues and opportunities to demonstrate evidence of their learning and achievement. In addition, evidence unrelated to academic achievement leading to unnecessary failure must not be included in assessing student achievement.

Each of these five elements of the SI²TE framework is a guide for secondary schools and individual classroom teachers to use and consider when creating or adjusting grading practices to prevent failure. Each element should offer teachers options in determining grading practices to prevent failure without lowering expectations or rigor levels.

Passing Students for Passing's Sake

Administrators' messages to teachers must never be "Thou shalt not fail a student or else!" A December 2013 article by Jay Mathews in the *Washington Post* highlighted a story of a teacher who resigned in part due to her belief that she simply could not fail any student, regardless of proficiency level or effort. She quoted her former principal telling her, "They are not allowed to fail. . . . If they have Ds or Fs, there is something that you are not doing for them."

This perception is all too real for many middle and high school teachers in an era of accountability. Hopefully, this was a rare case of an important message that was simply lost in translation. But the truth is, many schools struggle to successfully implement changes to their grading systems and practices because of miscommunication of

(Continued)

(Continued)

intent. Even the most well-intentioned grading change may not survive public opposition (Hanover Research, 2013). The intent of the strategy gets lost in translation when teachers are simply told to reduce failure without a system or framework in place to do so.

Student failure should alarm all adults in the system and cause us to search for and address reasons for the failure as well as to prevent them in the future. It is imperative that school building leaders communicate and work with teachers to make sure they are collecting the best evidence on whether students have acquired the essential skills to pass.

In addition to the SI²TE model, which offers loose guidelines, I present six specific grading practices that can help prevent student failure.

PRACTICE 1: EARLY FAILURE DETECTION

The strategy is simple: Notice and do your utmost to prevent failures as opposed to enduring them. Most secondary teachers and leaders intuitively know they should not wait until the end of the semester to identify student deficiencies and failures. Also, most teachers can tell you early in a semester which students are showing serious signs of potential failure. In a typical middle or high school, where the school year begins around Labor Day, most teachers can accurately identify students in danger of failure by October 1—often well before then. Teachers observing students demonstrating signs of potential failure, such as missing several assignments or lacking minimum levels of proficiency, are seeing an approaching failure funnel cloud and need to take action. Middle and high school teachers must have a system to detect failure early. This will allow them more time to intervene before failure becomes imminent.

There are a few steps to doing this well:

1. Every 2 to 3 weeks, teachers list every student who is in danger of failure as well as all possible reasons: attendance, missing work, lacking prerequisite skills, and so on.

2. Teachers record all contact with parents about students' danger of failure.

3. At subsequent professional learning community (PLC) meetings, teachers compile potential failure information with other teachers' information. Together, they analyze patterns, make inferences, and brainstorm and implement solutions.

See Figures 5.2 and 5.3 for useful charts to use in early failure detection.

Warnings Save Lives

Middle and high schools represent the hustle and bustle of a city where people are moving in countless directions for different purposes. In cities, alarms alert people to potential dangers with enough time for people to react to them and take action. Tornado warnings, for example, have become tremendously effective because of Doppler radar. One study cited that mean lead-time on warnings increased from 5.3 to 9.5 minutes. This directly correlated with a decrease in injuries and fatalities (Simmons & Sutter, 2004).

When high schools have radar on potential student failure, they can prevent credit casualties. Chicago Public Schools researchers Allensworth and Easton (2007) say that students with three or more semester Fs (in any grade) are not likely to ever graduate high school

Figure 5.2   Sample Early Failure Detection Form Used by PLCs and Course Teams

Department:	Teacher:	Semester: Fall/Spring, 20_____						
☐ 3 weeks ☐ 6 weeks ☐ 9 weeks/midterm		☐ 12 weeks ☐ 15 weeks ☐ 18 weeks/semester						
Students in danger of failing								
Possible reason(s) for failure								
Interventions attempted								
Parent contact (dates, whom spoke with)								
Eligible for extended semester?								

Figure 5.3   Sample Early Failure Detection Summary Report

Department: _____   **Chair:** _____

Course/department/PLC: _____   Total number of students served: _____

Number of teachers reporting: _____   Total number in danger of failure: _____   (% of total in danger: _____)

	Attendance	Low tests/ quizzes	Missing work/ assignments	Missing assessments (tests, quizzes, major projects)	Not working/ lack of participation	Specific skill deficiency (please list primary ones)	Not sure	Other reasons (please list)
Total #								
Total %								

Additional summary questions for the PLC: What courses have the highest failure rate? Lowest? What teacher interventions are having the most success? Which teachers need additional assistance?

(p. 9). They recommend that as soon as students acquire one F, adults must not wait to intervene (p. 11).

The National High School Center offers a free download of its Early Warning System (www.betterhighschools.org/EWSTool.aspx). This allows schools to input student data and track many risk factors, such as behavior, attendance, and, of course, grades and class failures. The system can be connected to a school's student information system, which allows the interfacing to be simple and data entry, pulling, and scrubbing to be more efficient.

Middle and high schools do not need to purchase an expensive instrument or technology for monitoring potential failures. They must, however, have a system that supports teachers in identifying potential failures early enough to intervene. An early warning practice allows teachers to work together to look for possible patterns in student failure to collectively determine the best approaches in addressing their needs.

Example

A math PLC team at Mason City High School, in Mason City, Iowa, identified early in the semester that a large proportion of student failure in algebra 1 was related to a lack of problem-solving skills. The teachers identified this as a significant skill gap, not a refusal to do work or attendance issues. They made the inference that pre-assessment had not taken place at the start of the semester. The teachers determined that potential failure for many students was due to their inability to set up the problem before being able to solve it. The teachers were able to focus their collaboration because of early identification and select specific instructional approaches for their coming unit. By doing so, they decreased their potential failure rate by 16% (Jumper, T. J.: personal interview, 2014).

Summary

The early failure detection model is an example of a team or school grading practice to identify potential failures. The conversation then shifts to collaboration related to adult actions to address potential failure and provide support for students. Middle and high schools implementing early warning practices don't rely on afterschool or summer school programs to intervene with students. Instead, they provide intervention and support *before* the number of potential failures gets too large to overcome.

Prior to reading Practice 2, please complete Part 1 of Activity 5.2 on pages 127–128 to determine the benefits and drawbacks of the early failure detection practice.

PRACTICE 2: MEAEC IT HAPPEN

While grading researchers have disagreed about the effectiveness of particular grading practices on student outcomes, they almost all agree on one specific point: The penalty for not doing the work should be doing the work (O'Connor, 2009, 2010; Reeves, 2011a; Wormelli, 2006).

MEAEC stands for *missing essential assignments or assessments extended chance*. The actual practice is much simpler than its name. Schools, PLCs, or individual classroom teachers provide scheduled time and locations during the school day (or in some cases, right after school) for students to complete important assignments or assessments that are either incomplete or below the quality necessary for proficiency. MEAECs become an opportunity for students to make up missing work as well as a forced choice for students to complete essential work.

Similar, but More ZAP

Many schools have ZAP (*zeros aren't permitted*) practices in place whereby students have a designated time during the school day or after school to complete missing work—a same-day work detention. ZAPs originated based on the premise that students will often avoid doing the work because taking a lower score or even a zero is easier. Just a few zeros factored into their grade can move students toward failure rapidly. Schools often utilize lunch, study hall, or advisory periods to intervene decisively by creating a structured environment for students to make up missed work right away and not get behind.

MEAECs can augment existing ZAPs in middle and high schools. ZAP programs often are focused on getting students to finish homework missed from the night before or from the previous week or even month. Not always is this work essential nor does it always provide the teacher with sufficient evidence to know where students' next learning steps are. MEAECs still help make sure students do not get too far behind in missing work, but the focus of MEAECs is to ensure the tasks are *important* for students to demonstrate mastery of essential content and skills. Schools must ensure assigned work in these settings is critical toward achieving the learning goals and objectives of the course; it must never be busy work. Also, teachers may determine that a previously missed assignment is no longer relevant to the student or his or her assessment needs. Applying the MEAEC principle, certain previously missed assignments would be replaced ones more aligned with current learning goals. Finally, some teachers will replace two or three lower or surface-level assignments with one that is more rigorous and allows the student to apply concepts and skills together. This may mean student makeup work in MEAECs is quantitatively less but qualitatively greater.

MEAEC systems can be implemented schoolwide or by individual teachers in their classrooms. Schools can get a bigger bang for their buck from their ZAP settings when they offer MEAEC opportunities specifically for essential assignments and assessments. They can then maximize learning while preventing failure at the same time.

Examples

At Cardinal High School, in Eldon, Iowa, school leaders acknowledged that Fs for missing work were only reinforcing the behavior of students avoiding doing rigorous work. They established what they called the Ketchup Room: study halls and advisory periods to provide students with support in completing work. Student eligibility for rigorous classes like zoology and advanced business increased as well as students' belief that they could succeed. The school also prevented a significant number of failures (138 down to 5) in one year (Reeves, 2012).

The Charter School for Applied Technologies (CSAT) has maintained graduation rates in the high 90s and even sometimes at 100% for several years in a row (see Figure 5.4). What makes these statistics even more impressive is the fact that the school pulls students from the same area of Buffalo, New York, where some graduation rates hover in the 50s (Tan, 2013).

The school adapted its MEAEC protocols by adding a 45-minute *flex time* period to the end of the day. When students get behind or miss needed and required assignments, support is available and provided immediately. Teachers can assign students to flex time for work makeup or proficiency catch-up for one day or several at a time. This holds students immediately accountable but also places the teachers on notice that immediate intervention is an expectation. Assistant Superintendent Eon Verrall states, "The key to our success is of course the dedicated staff but also the structure for a required remediation period every day" (personal communication). Flex time, a form of MEAEC, scheduled during the school day can have a dramatic positive impact on preventing failure (Nagel, 2010, p. 67).

During CSAT's first year of implementing flex time, students and parents viewed the intervention as punitive. The school day ended at 3 p.m., but flex time went until 4 p.m. In year two, the semantics changed. *Everybody* was scheduled until 4 p.m., but those who were proficient and had all of their work in left at 3 p.m. The intervention became less of a punishment. Students *asked* to stay for help or to improve grades even when not required (Nagel, 2010, p. 67).

MEAECs Increase PLC Effectiveness

Focusing on essential work moves ZAPs into MEAECs. PLCs are often where teachers collaborate and help determine the type of student work that should be expected. A middle school science PLC I was working with had implemented a ZAP program schoolwide. During a meeting, one of the teachers, Marcie said she had supervised the afterschool MEAEC (ZAP) room the night before and noticed that students assigned by her colleague were completing a crossword puzzle over the vocabulary for a current unit. She engaged her colleague, Beth, who had assigned the students to MEAEC (ZAP), in dialogue about the work they were doing. Marcie shared some more engaging and focused assignments she used to assist students in learning the new terms. These were at a much higher rigor level than the crossword puzzle. Beth was more than pleased to gain new ideas. She stated, "You're right. If we're going to hold students accountable for completing work, then we need to hold ourselves just as accountable to ensure the work is worth doing!"

MEAECs Actually Do Teach Responsibility

Some adults worry ZAP programs teach students to be less responsible, that to prepare them for the real world, it's better to let them accept the zero than to guide them into still doing the work.

Figure 5.4   CSAT Students Scoring 65 or Higher on New York State Regents Exams, 2007–2012

Subject	2007	Added end-of-day flex time intervention	2008	2009	2010	2011	2012
English	63%		91%	92%	93%	88%	94%
Algebra	64%		86%	97%	95%	97%	85%
Global History	55%		74%	87%	82%	80%	86%
U.S. History	76%		86%	93%	92%	87%	90%
Living Environment	70%		72%	94%	84%	91%	95%
Spanish	82%		91%	92%	86%	87%	89%
Graduation Rate	55%		94%	100%	100%	98%	98%

Recently, my wife and I were initially denied for a home refinance loan that we were well qualified for because of two late credit card payments totaling $37. I had stopped using the card and forgot to pay it when the statement came. In the real world, forgetting to pay the card off didn't make the problem go away—it made it worse. When students are allowed to just take a zero and not be given structure and accountability to complete missing work, we may instill the belief that tasks and responsibilities will just go away. People in trouble with the IRS for years of not filing taxes may have learned that behavior from their former middle and high school teachers letting them take a zero! We all doubt that, don't we? We must also doubt that giving them an opportunity to make up missing work would lead them there as well. (All of my credit cards are now paid electronically. Banks make it easier to make the payment rather than skip them.)

MEAECs teach students the valuable life lesson that you have to finish work that isn't always what you want to do. Yes, sometimes (and perhaps more than sometimes), high school students are far from exemplars in time management. However, many students simply need additional time and support to grasp the necessary concepts and complete work. When MEAECs allow or insist that students reattempt essential assignments that were either too difficult because of content or too big to squeeze in because of other obligations, students have a better chance to develop perseverance and prioritization.

Summary

When students complete their work in MEAECs—instead of never—teachers receive evidence that inform them of the students' current proficiency levels. The debate about whether we're teaching responsibility isn't and shouldn't be part of *this* dialogue.

Prior to reading Practice 3, please complete Part 2 of Activity 5.2 on pages 127–128 to determine the benefits and drawbacks of MEAECs.

PRACTICE 3: AMNESTY DAYS (PERIODS)

Amnesty Days could be accurately described as schoolwide MEAEC days. Amnesty Days, or periods, are scheduled instructional time devoted to supporting students who are behind or for students to make up missing work (regardless of the reason) without penalty. Granting someone amnesty means obliterating the ramifications of his or her offense. Implementing Amnesty Days as a grading practice, by definition, prohibits teachers from including any penalty or point deduction for student work arriving late. Middle and high schools implementing these days periodically can significantly reduce the negative impact of two root causes of course failure: students missing multiple assignments and students getting too far behind in content understanding.

Curriculum Benefits

Amnesty Days also provide considerable benefits for teachers. They are, in a sense, "buffer" days in the curriculum. Larry Ainsworth (2011, p. 81) recommends buffers, or scheduled breathing room for teachers, as designated days or weeks for reteaching critical content. We all know that, over the course of a 90-day semester, both teachers and students need a day or a few to reteach or get caught up. This scheduled time also allows students who need it to get support from teachers that addresses specific gaps that led to the potential failure. The intentionality of scheduling it and conveying to students that a lifeline is coming allows students to see hope.

Conception of Amnesty Day Practice

My late colleague Larry Hurt was an amazing educator who just happened to teach art. He came up with the idea of Amnesty Days. Our school leadership team was brainstorming about potential failure data and determined that large numbers of students were failing or very close primarily because of missing work. Lamenting, as usual, ensued. Most teachers were planning soon to move on in the pacing of their curriculum.

Larry, optimistic as always, said we could find solutions to these challenges. "I have an idea, folks," he said (his trademark statement). "Let's give students a full day to make up any missing work for full credit; no exceptions."

Several eyebrows were raised at the idea. We agreed, after discussing the logistics, to experiment with an amnesty day. The following Wednesday, in every classroom at Ben Davis High School, teachers focused exclusively on helping students with concepts they struggled with or any assignments that had been missed with no penalty.

Results

We tracked potential failure data after the amnesty day and found the number of students in danger of failure schoolwide decreased by 30%. Teachers also commented that almost all students who caught up were much more engaged in class and did not get behind again in the subsequent weeks after the amnesty day. Students recognized the positive impact on their grades and gained understanding and knowledge in content and skills needed for upcoming topics and units. One student commented on the semester-ending survey, "The amnesty day was the best thing that happened to me in chemistry this fall. Having a chance to get caught up, I was able to ace the next test and finally 'get stoichiometry.' I went from thinking I was going to fail, to having a B+!"

Pushback

Ben Davis is a large urban fringe high school on the west side of Indianapolis, with approximately 2,900 students in Grades 10–12. The school typically averaged around 94% attendance on any given day. During our first amnesty day, attendance was closer to 98%. That was a significant gain in the number of bodies walking the halls and sitting in the cafeteria. Several teachers approached me later that week concerned about having any future Amnesty Days. The issues raised were about the number of students in the cafeteria during lunch shift B and how full all six of their class periods were. Finally, there was fear that students may now wait for the next amnesty day and not apply themselves.

The fact that most students took full advantage of this opportunity was getting lost in the fear that some students might manipulate the system. I asked if any of their classes had students abusing the time and causing any disruptions. Their answer: no. I then stated matter-of-factly, "So, if I'm hearing you correctly, the concern is that too many students came to school today willing to do all of their work?" (I was not quite so sure that this was a bad problem.) While my comment was slightly sarcastic, by listening to teacher concerns about some of the drawbacks to Amnesty Days, we made the following adjustments to the practice:

1. Amnesty Days would be unannounced until the day of.

2. Each department would schedule two Amnesty Days per semester: the first between the sixth and eighth weeks, and second between the fourteenth and sixteenth weeks of the semester. This allowed course teams to determine, based on pacing of units, when it would make the most sense for them to build in a buffer day.

Practicality Point: Students Not Needing Amnesty

A common question is: During Amnesty Days, what happens to students who have completed all assignments? In most cases, they have the option to redo or improve any assignment to improve their grade. In some classes, these students work on an enrichment lesson or activity, or they gain the privilege that motivates most adolescents—freedom. Student behavioral expectations for arriving to class on time and following school and classroom rules do not change for students not needing the amnesty time or support.

Prior to reading Practice 4, please complete Part 3 of Activity 5.2 on pages 127–128 to determine the benefits and drawbacks of the Amnesty Days.

PRACTICE 4: EFFECTIVE USE OF HOMEWORK

Homework and its use in grading is an issue impacting all schools. Middle and high school students should be expected to complete homework. That said, the probability that teachers will have some students not complete some homework assignments on time or at all is high, like 100%. This often leads to zeros in the grade book. Very often, those zeros, if figured into student grades, are a leading cause of student failure.

The practice of effectively using homework to prevent failure has two key elements. First, schools and individual teachers simply cannot allow missing homework to be the sole reason for student failure. Second, teachers must use homework effectively to lead to student learning and achievement.

Missing Homework Causing Failures

Far too often, missing homework that gets calculated into students' grades leads to numerous unnecessary failures. In 2006, while I was serving as a building administrator at Ben Davis High School, we began providing students with stipulated second chances to recoup their credit after school or on Saturdays if they were close to passing. Prior to that year, these students would have had to retake the entire course to recover their credits. We analyzed the 341 grade sheets for students who would be eligible to attempt to recover their credit in the four core areas, and we found that 235 of these failures came directly from zeros that were predominantly on homework assignments (Figure 5.5; Nagel, 2008, p. 31).

Our further analysis of student grade reports revealed that a large number of students receiving failing grades predominantly from missing

Figure 5.5   Authentic Example of Impact of Homework on Grades

	Total students eligible to recover credits in the four core areas	Number of students just below passing due to missing work/zeros	Number of students who passed final with C+ or better	Number of students just below passing due to lack of demonstration of proficiency/skill
English	91	58	32	33
Social Studies	89	65	47	24
Math	87	62	12	25
Science	74	50	30	24
Total	341	235	121	106

homework had passed the comprehensive final exam with a C+ or better. We found that over 230 students, with a large number having shown at least some degree of proficiency based on their final exam, would have been taking entire core classes over the previous year. Prior to 2006, there was not any cap on what percentage of homework could be factored into a student's grade. After seeing the potential failures that could be avoided, teachers at Ben Davis agreed to implement a school-wide practice to cap the maximum amount of homework included in a student's grade at 10%.

Effectiveness of Homework

While capping the amount homework that can count toward a grade can prevent failure, middle and high schools should look to ensure effectiveness of homework as well. Secondary schools that implement policies and practices for effective use of homework can, just like with MEAECs, prevent failure and increase achievement at the same time.

Homework was one of the influences Hattie (2008) studied that had moderating effects, meaning differences were found in the evidence when comparing the effect between different student groups. Homework has shown to have a higher effect size for high school students as ($d = 0.64$) than for their elementary peers ($d = 0.15$; p. 235). Harris Cooper (1989), a leading researcher on the impacts of homework, found that for the most part, the more homework high school students do, the better their achievement. He adds, however, that there is a point of "diminishing returns" (p. 88). To consider the notion that the same level of learning can take place through homework in the absence of feedback and monitoring in the teaching cycle would tremendously devalue the role of the class-room teacher. Homework in which there is no active involvement by the teachers does not contribute to student learning (Hattie, 2008).

However, in many cases, teachers assign homework that is not viewed as effective or necessary, leading students to shirk the responsibility to complete it and receive zeros, which are then calculated into a final grade and can directly lead to unnecessary student failures.

In summary, Hattie's (2008, p. 235) synthesis on the effectiveness of homework on achievement found the following:

1. Homework had a greater effect for higher versus lower ability students.

2. Task-oriented homework had greater effects than deep learning or problem solving.

3. Rote learning and practice or rehearsal had the highest effects.

4. Project-based, higher level conceptual thinking had the least effectiveness.

5. For many students, homework simply reinforced their inability to learn by themselves and inability to "do school."

6. Prescribing homework "does not help students develop time management skills—there is no evidence this occurs."

Sampling of Homework Policies

I conducted an online random sampling of 100 school districts' grading policies on school websites, and I found the following summary highlights related to homework guidelines:

- 94 had specific guidelines and/or policies regarding homework.
- 63 had guidelines or recommendations for point values or percentage maximums.
- 39 had verbiage related to homework being specific to standards (state or Common Core).
- 86 had recommendations or policies for time limits for submission after which the teacher should or would not have to accept student work.

With rare exception, teacher discretion determined what types of assignments could be given for homework. Only 27 school districts had specific wording related to the types of assignments to be included for homework.

Example of Homework Policy

San Ramon Valley Unified School District in California has adopted a very specific and structured homework policy. It reads in part:

> Homework should be purposeful and meaningful to students. Legitimate purposes for homework include practicing a skill or process that students can do independently but not fluently, elaborating on information that has been addressed in class to deepen students' knowledge, and providing opportunities for students to explore topics of their own interest. Teachers are responsible for assigning homework that is appropriate and differentiated as needed.

This is an example of an effective policy that other schools could model new policies after. Additional guidelines and recommendations for parents, students, and principals can be found at http://www.srvusd.net/file/1276956734524/12757477929 62/2923794357213961669.pdf

Summary

Not providing guidelines about the types of assignments to use as homework is the equivalent of giving a new car buyer the recommendation to change the car's oil every 3,000 miles without any guidance on what type of oil to use, Quaker State or Crisco! Here are some guidelines that could help teachers determine what kinds of assignments to use as effective homework:

1. Create guidelines that are adaptable and monitored for their effectiveness by school evaluators and administrators.

2. Establish types of assignments that would be considered for homework or classwork. Practice work that is for skill refinement or rehearsal, whether it is taken home or done in class.

   a. Decide on types collaboratively in course teams or PLCs.

   b. Consistently apply differentiated homework (based on current skill level of student group) throughout the department.

3. Create a selection of choices based on students' current level of skill mastery.

4. If assigning point values, ensure the amount cannot drastically alter the accuracy of the overall grade.

   a. If teachers agree to 5% or less, this will significantly minimize distortion in the truthfulness of grades.

These guidelines are just a few examples. Schools and PLCs should strongly consider these as well as others that align with best evidence of homework use.

Prior to reading Practice 5, please complete Part 4 of Activity 5.2 on pages 127–128 to determine the benefits and drawbacks of adjusting the use of homework.

PRACTICE 5: INCENTIVES FOR EARLY WORK

In virtually every middle and high school classroom in America, teachers deal with students handing in work late or missing deadlines. Schools and classroom teachers often try to determine what the appropriate penalty that will trigger students to meet future deadlines as opposed to dealing with the consequences. This is similar to businesses that try to find the proper price point of a product to maximize profits. A strategy that can decrease the stress for both teachers and students is focusing more on creating incentives for early work submission.

Importance of Feedback

In E. B. Page's 1958 study, 177 high school English papers were scored and handed back to students. One group received grades, another grades and feedback in the form of predetermined comments, and the final group received detailed comments and a grade. Each group outperformed the previous.

Most teachers state that feedback from an administrator after a classroom observation is most useful if it is specific and they can apply it right away. The specificity and timeliness of the feedback is what makes it effective and useful. Teachers also often state that when feedback from their administrator either lacks specificity or arrives too long after the observation to be used or applied, it is then usually very ineffective and basically useless.

Feedback to students must be viewed the same way. Students crave feedback, and when effectively used in combination with secondary grading practices, feedback can have a tremendous impact on achievement. Feedback then can be used by teachers as an incentive for students to complete work early and ahead of deadlines. An incentive teachers can provide to students is that they will receive specific feedback for work submitted early to apply before resubmitting for a final grade. Students gain insights into how to improve their work, and teachers likely would deal with fewer missed deadlines and can intervene earlier through the use of formative assessment. Thus the incentive benefits both teachers and students.

Rigid Deadlines—Not Good for Teachers

As a former biology teacher, I understand and respect the challenge middle and high school teachers face when it comes to grading and providing feedback for up to 150 students. Delivering meaningful feedback to that many students is challenging, if not sometimes impossible. In addition, some students need more time because of learning gaps, while others above grade-level standards need more challenges. This, along with the day-to-day challenges of keeping up with the curriculum, can cause some middle and high school teachers to consider applying for a job as Wal-Mart greeter (absolutely no disrespect to them—they guide me in the right direction with a smile every trip!).

The challenge of providing quality feedback grows when student work is habitually late. This leads me to one question: Why would teachers encourage work submission by all students on the same day? By offering early submission incentives, teachers will likely see work and assignments come in waves instead of all at once, giving them a better chance to provide quality feedback to students.

Incentives Lead to Achievement

Mandy and Sandy

In Mrs. Smith's class, the following semester after Sandy received a D+, she implemented a practice to incentivize work, tasks, and assignments to be turned in completed prior to the agreed-upon deadline. If Mrs. Smith's students completed and submitted work prior to class deadlines, she gave them detailed and specific feedback to apply to improve their grade upon resubmission.

Sandy took full advantage of this. She prioritized her work to be able to complete and turn in her English 10 papers at least 2 days early. Sandy found the additional feedback tremendously useful for her rewrites and revisions. She ended up with an A− by the end of the semester. Mrs. Smith was confident this was a truthful, reliable grade, as her peers scored student work several times per month using the state-issued rubric. Sandy learned a critical life lesson that exceeding deadlines can actually offer more benefits than procrastination. Mrs. Smith found that more students were meeting early deadlines and seeking and valuing her feedback. This also minimized the overall volume of student work being submitted all at once.

Summary

Feedback is not the only incentive teachers can use to entice students to exceed deadlines. Here are a few others:

1. Choice of next assignment

2. Opportunity to revise previously submitted work or tasks for increased grade

3. Self-selecting the group for next collaborative learning project

4. Homework-free week (if all other assignments are turned in)

5. Additional peer review that students can apply before final submission

The more teachers use incentives instead of consequences in grading, the less students will view grades as punitive. This will allow feedback to become more of a tool for learning.

Prior to reading Practice 6, please complete Part 5 of Activity 5.2 on pages 127–128 to determine the benefits and drawbacks of creating incentives for students to submit work early.

PRACTICE 6: EARLY FINAL EXAMS

In Chapter 2, I addressed how traditions can prevent effective practice from being implemented. Final exams at the very end of the semester are one tradition that could use some adjusting. There are few benefits of final exams being administered at the very end of the semester. While they do allow teachers to use as much instructional time as possible and provide students with an incentive to behave and follow all school rules until the final bell of the school year rings, there are significant downsides. For example, students rarely if ever receive feedback on their performance, teachers are rarely able to use the evidence from the exams formatively, and teachers miss identifying student gaps in learning and understanding until it is too late to adjust instruction. The practice of administering final exams 1 to 2 weeks early can eliminate many of those drawbacks. Early final exams can provide middle and high schools with another tool in their arsenal for preventing failure.

Passing Early, Better Than Never

Schools may find that some people fear breaking the tradition of administering final exams in the last few scheduled days of the semester. This is often caused by the trepidation that students who pass early could become discipline issues and cause disruptions. Teachers may fear they do not have anything to incentivize good behavior if students ace their final and in a sense have already earned their grade and credit. This perceived drawback has prevented some schools from implementing early finals.

The question becomes, what would be a better challenge to have to deal with: the logistics of dealing with possibly more students passing early or the post-semester clean-up of students who fail? In addition, if teachers are aware of specific learning gaps earlier, they can make more decisive interventions from the data and evidence that early final exams would provide. In working with dozens of schools, in some of the most challenging environments, I've always seen positive results from early final exams; never have the patients begun running the asylum.

The primary benefit of the early final is creating a time buffer to intervene and assist students who have not mastered essential content and need specific support. At the same time, some students may have learned essentials in the class that they didn't receive credit for because their assignments were missing; to assume they don't have the skills is to rely on missing evidence. An early final may prove that these students do not need the additional support the teacher thinks they do. When this occurs, teachers could apply MEAEC principles and ensure that assignments missed that deal with concepts and skills the student already has already mastered will be replaced with more relevant ones for their specific learning needs. Additionally, the more some students demonstrate proficiency earlier, the more the teacher gains small-group time for students who need to go back over essentials. A teacher at a public high school in Chicago stated, "The early final parted the Red Sea at the end of the semester. I was able to see who was proficient and who was not—and what the biggest skill deficiencies were. My review and intervention at the end of the semester felt purposeful vs. frantic."

Actions for Implementing an Early Final

Here are some basic steps and guidelines that schools have used when successfully implementing an early final exam:

1. Develop two forms of the final—A and B—ensuring that both assess the same content and skills from priority standards at the same rigor levels.

2. Administer Form A one to two weeks prior to the regularly scheduled final date.

3. Determine the level of mastery that students must achieve on the early final to prove mastery.

4. Create a plan to identify and address the specific learning gaps for students not showing mastery on the first administration of the final exam (some schools have made that a C– or lower).

5. Create a plan for incentives or enrichment activities for students who complete requirements early.

6. For students who do not pass Form A, administer Form B on the regularly scheduled exam day.

Student Behavior Stipulations Between Finals A and B

Most schools create specific behavioral expectations for students who pass the final exam early. Most, if not all, students will still attend school until the very end of the year, as students passing one course early may not have passed them all early. Most students desire to finish the year on good terms and enjoy some of the celebratory event with their peers. The following are some guidelines schools have used effectively:

1. Students are required to attend class (on time) and follow normal day-to-day class and school rules.

2. To pass early means you must *pass by more.* Students must earn perhaps a B or B+ or higher on Form A, or they are required to continue to work on assignments and tasks and later take Form B.

3. Teachers can determine that students passing above a B on Form A must show a certain level of mastery. To earn their credit and not have to take Form B, students are then given the following options:

   a. An enrichment activity of their selection or from a predetermined list of tasks

   b. Providing focused peer tutoring for students still attempting to master essential concepts and skills with direction and guidance from the teacher

   c. Use and apply feedback from the teacher from the attempt on Form A to increase learning and the grade on the attempt at Form B

   If the student grade on the final and course is A or higher, some teachers provide options a or b above or students can have independent study time to work on appropriate school material for other classes.

4. Schools that have implemented the early final have also created stipulations for students to be eligible to take the final early:

   a. Specific attendance minimums

   b. Specific behavioral expectations

   c. No more than a predetermined number of assignments missing

   d. Current grade of C or higher

Summary

It's inevitable that some students will attempt use the early final to try to beat the system—just like many are beating the system now. Schools determining whether to implement an early final, or any other effective practice that could drastically reduce failure, should not worry that some students might try to manipulate the system. Yes, there is a chance that some students will apply themselves harder in the 2-week interval between final Forms A and B. This should not be a reason for dismissing it.

Discovery of Early Final by Accident

The concept of an early final exam was discovered by accident in the junior high school I was teaching at. In the fall of 2002, my biology teaching partner and I had a guest geneticist come and present to our students as a semester-culminating event in late December. The day of his visit happened to fall on the district-scheduled final exam date. With district permission, we drafted a plan to administer the final early to allow students to prove their proficiency and not miss the enrichment activity.

Our process looked like this:

1. We drafted a second version of the biology final that was approved by the district and covered all of the priority standards with different items, reference points, and examples.

2. We administered Form A of the final to all students 1 week early.

3. Students scoring 85% or better on Form A *and* having an overall grade of B or higher in the course were given their credit. They were required to complete an additional writing assignment on the genetics content related to the enrichment activity.

4. Students in the following two groups worked with their teacher on key content areas they were deficient in with specific instruction and practice.

Final	Overall grade
Below 85%	B (85%) or higher
Above 75%	Below 85%

Once students demonstrated mastery in these key areas, they conditionally earned their credit and moved on to the writing assignment. (We used the term *conditionally* with all students, as grades were not final until the end of the semester).

5. Students could demonstrate mastery anytime during the week and gain access to the enrichment project.

6. Students with 70% or below on Form A took Form B on the regularly scheduled final exam day, but before or after school so they could participate in the event if their effort and behavior were satisfactory. Students below a certain

(Continued)

(Continued)

level of mastery received an I for the course if additional proficiency demonstration was needed to receive a passing grade and credit. This ensured all students had access to the enrichment activity but proficiency was not compromised.

Figure 5.6 Results From Providing an Early Final

	Taking final exam Form A	Passing Form A with 80% or higher	Taking final exam Form B	Passing Form B with 80% or higher	Total passing with 80% or higher on either version
Number of students	324	217	107	82	299/324 (25 were eligible for credit recovery at the start of the second semester with very limited gaps because we had spent the week reteaching.)

Additionally, using an end-of-the-year final as a leverage point to hold over students' heads should not prohibit the implementation of an early final, either. Schools can and do set reasonable and normal expectations for student behavior prior to giving them an option of an early final. Finally, some schools have made the second version of the final more rigorous, requiring students to show deeper understanding of concepts and skills. This is a compromise many schools have made to ensure that students are not coasting to take the first version and then only applying themselves when they have only one shot left.

Please complete Part 6 of Activity 5.2 on pages 127–128 to determine the benefits and drawbacks of administering an early final exam.

CONCLUSION

As you probably noticed, not every grading practice mentioned in this chapter addresses all aspects of the SI²TE framework, with one exception—support. Supporting students by shaping their paths, through implementation of effective and practical grading practices, can not only increase achievement and decrease failure, but also provide a mechanism to teach responsibility and create resilience in students. Specific practices such as Amnesty Days and MEAEC don't teach students they can just slack off and wait for the extra chance. What they do teach is grit and perseverance.

Each practice comes with certain challenges that are either logistical or a derailment from traditional approaches to grading in middle and high school classrooms. Course teams, PLCs, or individual teachers should decide on the benefits and drawbacks of each and decide which of these might make the most sense for implementation. See Appendix B for a summary of the six practices outlined in this chapter.

Activity 5.2: Benefits, Drawbacks, and Committed Actions

As you finish reading about each of the various grading practices to reduce failure, please complete this activity. Determine the possible benefits of each and how they address some of the short- and long-term impacts of failure you identified in Activity 5.1. What are some of the possible drawbacks? Which ones would your team commit to try implementing this or next semester?

Grading practice to prevent unnecessary failure	Possible benefits	Potential drawbacks	Questions to consider	Committed actions to implement and monitor student results because of practice
1. Early Failure Detection				
2. MEAEC It Happen				

(Continued)

(Continued)

Grading practice to prevent unnecessary failure	Possible benefits	Potential drawbacks	Questions to consider	Committed actions to implement and monitor student results because of practice
3. Amnesty Days (Periods)				
4. Effective Use of Homework				
5. Incentives for Early Work				
6. Early Final Exams				

See Chapter 9 for guidelines to set up your action research project based on the implementation of any of these practices.

KEY IDEAS

1. Middle and high schools should use the SI^{2}TE framework for determining specific grading strategies and practices for reducing unnecessary failure. The SI^{2}TE framework provides a structure that individual schools, PLCs, and classroom teachers can adapt it to meet their specific needs.

2. It is far better to prevent failure than to endure it, and there are strategies to help make it difficult for students to fail without reducing expectations.

3. Addressing failure prevention at all levels is important, and it is most critical at the ninth- and tenth-grade levels. If students have success in earning credits and stay on track toward graduation early in their high school careers, there is a much better chance they will succeed in graduating.

4. Providing students with additional opportunities to complete work and reach proficiency is not going easy on them. In fact, it's just the opposite; it's helping develop resilience and stick-with-it-ness.

5. Warning systems to identify potential failures early are essential for high schools to know when and how to intervene.

6. The penalty for not doing the work is doing the work. MEAEC-It-Happen practices provide students with required time and do not allow them the ability to simply avoid doing their work. MEAECs also help teachers ensure any form of work (specifically makeup work) is targeted and essential for what the student's next learning need is.

Reflection questions for Chapter 5 have been replaced by Activity 5.2.

What Do We Do When Failure Does Happen?

6

Effective Credit Recovery

Last fall, I found out the importance of knowing which on- and off-ramps are the right ones to take. I was running late for a meeting at school, driving in rush hour traffic in downtown Chicago. Construction had shut down lanes and exits, and my car GPS was not providing me the kind of support $13.95 a day should. The principal and her administration team were expecting me. She was adamant her leadership team and I met prior to the all-staff meeting to make sure all of us were on the same page.

Feeling I may have missed my exit, and knowing I was pressed for time, I called the principal and reached her secretary, Jean. I first told her I was running late but I *was* on my way. When I asked her for some directions, Jean asked me what my location was. Jean informed me that I in fact had missed my exit and was now over a mile off course and heading the wrong way. I instantly began to feel that sensation of small beads of sweat on my brow and lower back. I needed to get back on track, and *fast* because time was becoming a serious issue.

Jean was great. First, she calmed me down—priority one! Then she provided me with very specific directions for which on- and off-ramps I needed to take to get to the school. I would have lost another 20 to 30 minutes had she not been as specific as she was, reminding me not to take certain exits that were closed or would have diverted me due to construction. I arrived just a few minutes late but still able to conduct the meeting, which led to a very successful day. Jean's specific guidance on which on- and off-ramps to take allowed me to get back on track and not lose valuable time.

CREDIT RECOVERY ON- AND OFF-RAMPS

Middle and high schools have some students in a similar predicament—they're lost, trying to find their way back toward graduation because of having failed required courses. Even schools that have implemented every failure prevention practice from Chapter 5 with fidelity will still have students who need help to find their on- and off-ramps. Which on-ramp students need to take will depend on the specific content they have yet to master or which course requirements still need to be completed. Today, we call what they need *credit recovery*. Students in credit recovery have most often failed a course and are attempting to retrieve the course credit lost by completing work missed or showing proficiency without repeating the entire course.

Continuing Need for Credit Recovery

A solid credit recovery system is likely to be needed even more in the very near future. Reports are plentiful highlighting where high schools specifically are and will continue to be in need of ways to deal with failures that weren't prevented. The *Washington Post* reported that 62% of geometry students and 56% of algebra students in Montgomery County, Maryland, failed either the class or the end-of-course exam (St. George, 2014). Another study from the Harvard Graduate School of Education noted that 60% of students who drop out within 6 years of starting high school didn't earn a full year's worth of credits as ninth graders (Symonds, Schwartz, & Ferguson, 2011, p. 10).

When students arrive for freshman year, their 4-year clock starts and it is full of diploma requirements that they must complete. But it doesn't always go according to plan. Secondary schools must have a solid plan to support students who fail classes that are required for graduation. Schools need to know how to help students find their on- and off-ramps by determining which essential skills and concepts they did not master and focusing on those instead of having students repeat entire courses.

Far From a New Concept

Credit recovery is far from a new or even recent phenomenon. Make-up tests, afterschool tutoring, summer school, and so on, one could argue, all qualify as examples of credit recovery. Giving students a chance to recover credits without repeating the entire course is perhaps one of the first examples of schools implementing stipulated second chances.

Secondary schools utilize a great deal of resources in implementing many different forms and variations of credit recovery. Success in helping students get back on track toward graduation in both recovering course credit and gaining skills needed for subsequent courses depends on many factors. As schools consider what to add to their resource options for students, they should look first at what *not* to do.

WHAT DOES NOT WORK

Schools can improve the effectiveness of their credit recovery by making sure that certain actions, including some traditions, are avoided when they provide middle and high school students with an opportunity to recover credits from courses failed. Two that are most often detrimental are retention and mandated seat time requirements. Both will hinder credit recovery effectiveness.

Retention

Retention has been shown to be one of the most deleterious influences on achievement, ranking behind only mobility (Hattie, 2008, p. 97). Retention, most often in the form of having students repeat an entire class already taken, is rarely effective. Students are usually taught the same content again in the same manner with the same teaching strategies as the previous year. This repetition fosters boredom while ignoring the fact that the students may need to be taught with a new approach in order to grasp the content. Furthermore, this repetition wastes valuable time. Students have a limited window to finish their requirements for a high school diploma in a 4-year period.

Robert Lynn Canady (n.d.) states, "Essentially we have institutionalized a 'take class, fail class, repeat class' model of instruction" (p. 2). Schools can avoid having students repeat entire courses unnecessarily by helping them find their on-ramps. Schools must have strategies to accurately determine which proficiencies students who are in credit recovery settings have not mastered and need to demonstrate.

Seat Time Mandates

A seat time requirement is the minimum number of hours, or class periods, students have to be physically present in a class to be eligible to earn credit. They were modeled after the Carnegie Unit, a timeline that colleges and universities developed for their guidelines for college-level credit (Shedd, 2003). Seat time requirements are created, in most instances, to provide *guidelines* for the amount of classroom instruction students are expected to be present for.

However, high schools provide additional obstacles for students trying to earn back lost credits by having unnecessary seat time requirements. Students who have failed a class, with rare exception, have very often met the requirements for being present the minimum amount of time required. That alone obviously did not equal proficiency. Mandated seat time requirements can hinder teachers and leaders, too, as they never take into account the varied pace at which students learn and master material (Darling-Hammond, 2010, p. 45). P. Vaughan, of America's Promise Alliance, sums up the little sense in the idea of requiring students who have sat for an 18-week course and failed to make up what they missed and what they didn't: "The notion that students should have to sit in a chair for a certain amount of time when it's only a certain aspect of algebra they didn't get baffles me" (quoted in Zehr, 2012).

Many States Loosen Seat Time Requirements

As of March 2012, 36 states had created policies to provide school districts with some flexibility for awarding credit to students based on mastery of content and skills as opposed to seat time (Zehr, 2012).

Oklahoma: High schools can allow students, upon request, to earn credits toward graduation based on demonstrations of mastery. Students can demonstrate mastery in multiple ways: submitting a portfolio of work, writing a thesis paper, doing other projects or performances, or passing a rigorous comprehensive test.

Ohio: High school students may earn credit through a variety of programs that have provided schools with offering "credit flexibility," including distance learning and expanded learning opportunities such as afterschool programs, summer programs, and internships.

New Hampshire: The state has taken credit flexibility a step further by requiring all public high schools to base credit attainment on student mastery rather than on seat time. Students in New Hampshire must still pass statewide standardized tests in literacy and math every year in Grades 3 through 8 and 11.

Retention and mandated seat time for students taking courses a second time can hinder how effective schools can be in helping students recover lost credits and develop missing skills. There are, however, specific effective strategies schools can implement to increase the effectiveness of

Activity 6.1: Assessment of Current School Seat-Time Reality

1. Does your school have minimum seat time requirements for earning a course credit? (If yes, go to question 2.)	2. Is this self-imposed? (If no, meaning it follows district or state guidelines, go to question 3.)	3. How can we avoid unnecessary seat time requirements for students in credit recovery?

their credit recovery programs. First I'll discuss the framework that supports credit recovery, and then I'll present five effective credit recovery strategies schools can implement.

A FRAMEWORK FOR CREDIT RECOVERY

Similar to the SI²TE failure prevention framework discussed in Chapter 5, middle and high schools can benefit tremendously from using a framework when they design, implement, and monitor adult actions to help students regain missed learning requirements and recover needed credits for graduation.

Eliminate Seat Time Requirements

Students who have failed a course, if seat time requirements are in place, have often already met them those requirements. The time mandate does not help students gain mastery of the content, so the first step is to eliminate the requirement. While recovering credits for these classes, effective use of time needs to be priority. Time is the variable; learning needs to be the constant for successful credit recovery.

Add Effective Elements

Once seat time is removed from the credit recovery equation, schools can effectively add the following five elements for best results (see Figure 6.1):

- **Support:** Schools must provide various forms of support to students when helping them regain proficiency and credits. Students in credit recovery have failed at least one course. Very often, these students have multiple academic and other challenges in the way of reaching the success of a high school diploma. Providing a lifeline for these students where credit retrieval is possible without repeating entire courses shapes their path toward graduation and success beyond high school.

- **Focus on priorities:** Students in credit recovery must concentrate on the most essential learning outcomes they have missed and need to prove proficiency on. These must be the essentials for the course for which they are working on recovering credit as well as what will lead to success in subsequent courses. Secondary teachers must ensure that they are assessing student mastery over prioritized standards in credit recovery settings. This will ensure that time will not be wasted on superfluous content.

- **Extend and utilize:** Credit recovery is one of the greatest examples of stipulated second chances. Often, schools must extend the opportunity for students to take advantage of earning back credits from failed classes. Schools must best utilize their resources of time,

Figure 6.1   A Framework for Credit Recovery Grading Strategies

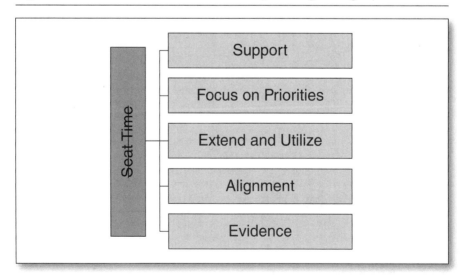

staffing, funding, and so on to maximize their potential in helping students develop essential skills when recovering lost credits.

- **Alignment:** Schools must ensure that essential curriculum objectives are vertically aligned in all content areas. This will better ensure that students earning proficiency in credit recovery are best prepared for the rigor of subsequent courses.

- **Evidence:** Students who are off track from graduation and on track to fail a class must be given the support to find their on- or off-ramp back to the highway as soon as possible. Schools must ensure credit recovery focuses on teachers using the most relevant evidence when determining student proficiency for earning back credits. This will prevent many students from going back and forth between failure and recovery.

CREDIT RECOVERY STRATEGIES

I have used the term *grading practices* throughout the book to indicate techniques teachers can use for the practical implementation of their school and district grading policies. Many of these practices could be applied similarly at the school or classroom level. For example, amnesty days could be implemented as a schoolwide practice or one that any teachers could execute individually in their classrooms. There would be little difference other than the number of students involved. The rest of this chapter will highlight several credit recovery strategies. The use of the term *strategy* here is intentional.

I have also attempted to present a compelling case regarding the need for increased teacher voice in grading changes at the middle and high school levels. Teachers can no longer have grading policy be *done to them* through edicts and noncollaborative mandates. However, once students fail a course and are lost in traffic headed toward not graduating, unless help is provided to find their ramp back, the voice of all adults in the school needs to be one. This may mean there is less input and need to push for buy-in. When studies have shown freshmen with one F are 15% more likely to drop out and multiple Fs raises the probability to 30% (Allensworth & Easton, 2007, p. 6), there is not time to make sure most people agree with the actions before schools take them.

The following strategies are described in more general concepts that could easily be included first in a school's yearly improvement planning process, perhaps aligned with a specific goal such as decreasing the number of credit-deficient students. Teachers and course teams would still be able to adapt specific practices from the strategies based on subject matter make-up and other factors. They are examples of actions secondary schools can take immediately to increase the quality and impact of their credit recovery systems. Each one ties back to the framework above, like the examples in Chapter 5 did for SI²TE. Furthermore, the strategies are more specific to high schools due to the fact that high schools deal much more with student credit recovery than most middle schools do.

Online Credit Recovery

In its report on credit recovery programs, the Center for Public Education (2012) defines three modes students can use to earn credit after failing a high school course:

- **Fully online:** Students recover credits from failed courses through fully online curricula, with software usually coming from multiple sources.
- **Blended:** Students experience a mixture of online/computer-based instruction and assessments combined with face-to-face teacher interaction.
- **In person:** Students recover credits in more traditional settings, with the support of classroom teachers or proctors and little to no online component.

The strategies in this chapter do not delineate any of these specifically. The actions are applicable and adapted to any of these settings. The online element of credit recovery is prevalent in many schools, and there is significant evidence regarding which actions and practices have shown to be more effective in assisting student learning—whether in recovery settings or for first-time learners.

Also, when it comes to online credit recovery, schools are faced with decisions such as whether to purchase courses or develop their own. I have not included much detail referencing specific online strategies for the examples in this chapter. Certainly, the level of online use for credit recovery in any school will dictate how these strategies are implemented. That is in fact why I have intentionally kept these as strategies instead of calling them practices. Specific recommendations, strategies, and guidelines for successful online credit recovery are included in Appendix C.

After reading about each strategy, please complete the corresponding activity. For the first strategy, bringing students back, Activity 6.2 is an action planning template for guiding actions related to that strategy. For the other strategies, please complete the corresponding part of Activity 6.3 on pages 161–162. This will help guide your course team's or entire school's actions related to implementing the strategy in whole or in part to increase the quality of your credit recovery programs.

STRATEGY 1: BRING 'EM BACK

Schools always have students who leave after their senior year without graduating or earning diplomas but are often just a few credits shy or have marginally missed passing proficiency exams. The first credit recovery strategy high schools can implement that will have a financial benefit as well as increase their graduation rate is to locate these students and give them an opportunity to finish their requirements for a high school diploma.

Financial and Graduation Impact

All schools these days are being more intentional at conserving financial resources. There are tremendous financial benefits for high schools that provide credit recovery for students who left after their senior year without a diploma. School districts can recover funding from state or national sources by getting students to enroll in credit-earning courses for completing their graduation requirements. Any cost related to doing so becomes more than justified. In addition, graduation rates can drastically sway one direction or the other based on the number of students who complete final credit requirements versus those who fall just short.

Examples

The Bridge Program, in Salem-Keizer School District, in Oregon, has proven to be worth its weight in recovered revenue. Each year close to 800 students in the district drop out and 450 are re-enrolled through the Bridge Program. That brings in over $2.7 million in funding directly tied to these students. The positive financial impact of having students stay in school, recoup credits, and get back on track to graduation far outweighs any cost of running the Bridge Program.

The Pharr-San Juan-Alamo Independent School District, in Texas, reduced its dropout rate by nearly 90% in just over 4 years while its graduation rate moved from 62% in 2006–2007 to almost 88% in 2012. This was due in part to its Countdown to Zero plan, implemented by Superintendent Daniel King. Many of the now graduates were potential dropouts who had left their senior year falling short of a diploma by just a few credits. King initiated Countdown to Zero, which was a block-by-block and door-to-door campaign to bring students who had failed to graduate back to the school. These students had walked away once, so offering them something different or in addition to what their previous experience provided them was essential. King and his team set up a partnership with a community college so students could earn their final high school credits as well as college credit toward an associate's degree or certification. The school also provided support to pass the Texas state high school exam for those who needed it (Maxwell, 2013).

Action Planning

High schools can benefit by creating an action plan for how to locate and bring back students who have not completed requirements, similar to the Bridge Program and Countdown to Zero. This will help focus their actions and monitor how they are bringing students back to earn their diplomas one dropout-turned-graduate at a time.

Activity 6.2: Creating a Plan for Bringing Back Students for Credit Recovery

Use this chart to create an action plan for your school's credit recovery program. The first row is filled in with an example.

Planned action	Current strategies	Current evidence of successful implementation	New or adjusted strategies	Evidence of successful implementation of strategies (word pictures of success)	Dates for monitoring successful implementation	Primary person(s) responsible
Develop or improve plan to connect with our students who left without a diploma (and do not attend another school)	School registrar sends quarterly report of students who have withdrawn (WD) and have not had a request for transcripts from other schools in 2 weeks. Letter is sent to try to reach out to them.	We had 15 students last semester. We connected with 8. Five are recovering credits for graduation and 3 are in a GED program.	Generate weekly list of these students. Phone calls and specific visit to home for each student by social worker, counselor, or administrator to encourage they attend our Night School Diploma program. (GED as last resort.)	Monthly: we should be able to account for every WD student, and 90% are enrolled in Night School Diploma program.	First Wednesday of the month cabinet meeting	Graduation coach (Cass); guidance director (Bruce) associate principal (Dave)

STRATEGY 2: EXTEND SEMESTERS

Schools can increase students' opportunity to recover credits quickly by extending time at the end of the semester for students to demonstrate proficiency in essential content knowledge and skills. Extended semesters resemble MEAECs (*missing essential assignments extended chance;* see Chapter 5). Schools indicate a specific setting and time where students who have failed courses, sometimes by only by a few percentage points, can complete missing essential and relevant assignments or assessments needed to earn their credit.

Example

In January 2007, Ben Davis High School, in Indianapolis, began extending the deadline after the semester ended for students to meet passing requirements in failed courses. During the first offering of extending the semester, students who had failed a course by 6% or less could attempt to recover their credit. School counselors, teacher leaders, and administrators analyzed electronic grade sheets and identified all eligible students. Students were placed into two categories based on how they could recover their credit:

1. Need to complete required missing assignments

2. Need to demonstrate proficiency in essential content and skills

The school made eligible students and their parents aware of this new opportunity to recover credit and avoid repeating failed courses. Letters and contracts were sent home for parents and students to sign acknowledging the stipulations as well as the potential consequences of not meeting the requirements: students were required to attend at least two help sessions after school or a Saturday morning help session in January. This provided them with their stipulated second chance.

Teachers met with students individually during these help sessions to make them aware of the specific requirements for recovering their credit. Teachers were also available during help sessions to assist students who needed individual support to master concepts missed. Students had until the end of February to complete specific assignments or demonstrate proficiency to earn their credit. Students who were not meeting these deadlines but were showing improvement and effort garnered an additional extension.

Example of Parent Letter

Dear Ben Davis High School Parent:

Your child, _Blake Morgan_, did not pass _Chemistry 1-A_. This was due to either missing required assignments or tasks, or not showing enough mastery of essential content. At this time, _his_ grade is considered **failing** and his permanent transcript will reflect that.

However, Ben Davis High School is committed to increasing the opportunities for students to master essential content and skills toward a high school diploma. Since _Blake's_ grade was within 7% of passing, _he_ is being offered a chance to earn _his_ credit in our *extended semester* program. On January 15, students eligible and wishing to recover their credit are required to attend a mandatory help session after school from 3:30 to 5:30. Counselors or teachers will be on hand to show _Blake_ what _he_ needs to accomplish to master the material or which assignments _he_ needs to complete to earn his credit. _He_ will be required to attend at least one other 2-hour session after school or one of the Saturday morning help sessions (9 to 11 a.m.). Additional help sessions will be offered every Wednesday from 3:30 to 5:30 p.m. as well. _He_ may attend as many as he needs. Once _he_ demonstrates proficiency, or completes required work, _he_ will earn his credit up to a C+.

Should _he_ decide not to work through the extended semester program or fail to make adequate progress by February 28, _Blake_ will receive an F on _his_ transcript and will need to make up the course in summer school or next fall.

Parent: _____

Student: _____

☐ We agree with the stipulations and plan to complete requirements for credit recovery in extended semester:

☐ We forgo this opportunity and understand the course grade will be an F, and the course may have to be repeated in summer school or next fall:

Help sessions: Every Wednesday, 3:30–5:30 p.m., Cafeteria

Saturday sessions: January 16, 23, 30, (9–11 a.m.)

Student and Culture Benefited

The entire school benefited and transformed tremendously from this first attempt at extending the semester. Students recovered 312 credits that spring in the four core areas (English, science, math, social studies).

This was the equivalent of two full-time teachers (156 students each) if all these students had all repeated these courses. Individually, students went from being way off track to back in the correct traffic lane toward graduation. One student mentioned after credit recovery allowed her to get back on track, "At the start of my junior year, I felt I was just passing time—waiting to drop out. Because of the learning center and credit recovery, I am now filling out college applications for the fall!"

The school's culture also transformed somewhat during this process. Teachers and administrators who proctored the help sessions would have up to 15 students recovering credit in the same course. Many students either had missed assignments or didn't show proficiency on similar standards. There was neither time nor logistics to have every student complete a different task from her or his first semester teacher, so department chairs led professional learning community (PLC) meetings early in January to generate common assignments and assessments. These were linked to specific priority standards that all students who had failed their course would use.

For example, a student who needed to recover credit in English 10 for Mrs. Smith may have missed several written assignments on *To Kill a Mockingbird*, while another student in Mrs. Mitchel's class may have missed written assignments on *The Kite Runner*. The primary standard being addressed in both teachers' classes was to evaluate interactions between characters in a literary text and explain the way those interactions affect the plot (see Figure 6.2). Neither text is mandatory for students to master that standard. They could demonstrate proficiency with virtually any grade-appropriate fiction text.

Students were given a great deal of choice and freedom in many cases. Their motivation increased significantly, and many students produced work at levels well above what they had done during the fall semester. This culture change impacted how teachers viewed the importance of student evidence instead of insisting students had to complete their specific assignments. Teachers realized that not every assignment students missed needed to be made up, nor should there be only one assignment or assessment students could complete to demonstrate proficiency of specific standards.

Success Breeds Success

This simple strategy, which of course took a great deal of hard work, created ripples at Ben Davis High School for years to come. Figure 6.3 highlights the success in credit recovery from the extended semester strategy. From 2005 until June 2013, students at Ben Davis High School recovered 1,994 credits.

Figure 6.2 Example of Agreed-Upon Assignments Linked to Standards for Credit Recovery

Course	Standard	Common assignments agreed
English 10	10.3.7 Evaluate interactions between characters in a literary text and explain the way those interactions affect the plot.	Write an expository essay clearly delineating how specific interactions of three characters impacted the plot. Also, include two examples where a change in a character's action could have significantly changed the plot.
Algebra	A1.2.6 Solve word problems that involve linear equations, formulas, and inequalities.	Task(s): Students are given a variety of math word problems to select a certain number to complete. Some examples: Steve can clean an office complex in 5 hours. Working together, Dave and Steve can clean the office complex in 3.5 hours. How long would it take Dave to clean the office complex by himself? An office has two envelope-stuffing machines. Machine 1 can stuff a batch of envelopes in 4.5 hours, while Machine 2 can stuff a batch of envelopes in 3.5 hours. How long would it take the two machines working together to stuff a batch of envelopes?
Biology	B.1.13 Know and describe that within the cell are specialized parts for the transport of materials, energy capture and release, protein building, waste disposal, information feedback, and movement. In addition to these basic cellular functions common to all cells, understand that most cells in multicellular organisms perform some special functions that others do not.	Tasks: Students created a model of the cell (paper-and-pencil or use of online program). Students then had to complete a detailed five-paragraph essay comparing the functions of a cell to that of a city or factory, with detailed and accurate example comparisons for 10 organelles.
U.S. History 1	Social studies U.S. History CORE Standard 2 Reform Movements: Describe the conditions that led to the reform movements. Identify important reform leaders and the principles for which they fought. Examples: Compare the reform policies of Theodore Roosevelt, William Howard Taft, and Woodrow Wilson. Give examples of legislation and Supreme Court cases that addressed issues of the reform movements.	Task(s): Students could select any Supreme Court cases dealing with reform movements (any era). Students developed an argument through writing an essay or developing a presentation and shared key events that led to the case coming before the high court, what the opinion was, and what the ramifications are today. Students did not have to be locked into cases at the start of the 20th century.

Figure 6.3   Credit Recovery Success Evidence

	Fall 2006: credits recovered/eligible through extended semester (students within 6% of passing)	Spring 2007: credits recovered/eligible through extended semester (students within 6% of passing)	Fall 2007: credits recovered/eligible through extended semester (students within 6% of passing)	Spring 2008: credits recovered/eligible through extended semester (students within 6% of passing)
English	81/91	65/72	70/76	49/51
Social Studies	84/89	61/71	33/39	31/36
Math	78/87	54/63	57/61	31/37
Science	69/74	48/53	28/32	19/24
Total	**312/341**	**228/259**	**188/208**	**130/148**

Canadian Extension of Semester

Derrick Cameron, former principal of Goose Lake High School, in Roblin, Manitoba, and now curriculum coordinator of Prairie South Schools, in Moose Jaw, Saskatchewan, implemented an extended semester at the start of the 2011–2012 school year. Similar to at Ben Davis High School, Prairie South provided students within a certain percentage of passing courses at the end of the previous school year with a chance to demonstrate proficiency within the first 2 months of the new school year. Derrick used a MEAEC format in which students attempting credit recovery did so during lunch study hall daily over critical tasks linked to essential standards. Students had 2 months at the beginning of any new semester to demonstrate proficiency, so credit recovery, in essence, ran 4 months out of the 10 (2 at the beginning of semester one and 2 at the beginning of semester two). Student attendance was mandatory until proficiency was met, and only absences accompanied by a note from a professional were accepted.

The staff felt that if students were committed to giving up an hour every day away from friends and socializing to earn their credit, they should be afforded the chance to so. MEAEC always occurred at lunch so students would not miss additional classes on the timetable and get further behind. However, teachers believed that if students were sporadic in attending these sessions, this might indicate a lack of work ethic and perhaps repeating a course would be necessary. Students with two consecutive unexcused absences from lunch credit recovery were removed and had to repeat the course.

Derrick stated, "Our students now realize accountability comes from having to do the work. Students realized they do not get an easy way out by just taking the zero. Also, our staff bought in to providing students structured chances

> to earn proficiencies and began to believe that if students hadn't failed every aspect of the course, there was no reason they shouldn't be given the opportunity to make up those deficiencies."

Source: *Used with permission from Derrick Cameron, M.Ed.*

Purdue University Grade Change Policy: Incomplete Grades

Some people question the effectiveness of extending the semester for students. The argument is that when students arrive in college settings, they will not be given additional time after a semester to complete work and earn their credit. The only option will be to repeat a course after failure. That's not necessarily true anymore.

Purdue University, a highly reputable, research-based, state school, has a policy that students (even in college) will still have *stipulated second chances:*

A student who receives a grade of I, PI, or SI [see grade key below] in a course and who successfully completes his/her work in the time interval specified by the instructor, but no later than one academic year after the I grade was given, will receive from the instructor whatever permanent grade his/her work would have deserved if it had been completed on time regardless of the student's enrollment status. The value of the final grade resulting from the late completion of the course requirements shall be incorporated in future cumulative GPAs. If the student fails to achieve within the specified time a permanent grade in any course for which he/she received a grade of I, PI, or SI, the registrar shall record a permanent grade of IF, IN, or IU for the grade of I, PI, or SI, respectively. The value of an IF grade shall be incorporated in future cumulative GPAs.

To meet the extended semester requirements, Purdue students have to meet with their professor and devise a plan that may involve more work or more time than if they had met the requirements previously. The focus is on learning *well*, not just on *when* the learning happens.

Grade Key

I: Incomplete; no grade; student enrolled in credit course under regular grade option

PI: Incomplete; no grade; student enrolled in a credit course: pass/not-pass option

SI: Incomplete; no grade; student enrolled in a zero-credit course

IF: Incomplete—failing; credit course student received I grade; record of student's failure to achieve permanent grade before end of one year after Incomplete was given

IN: Incomplete—not passing; credit course-pass/not-pass option student received a PI grade; same as an IF grade except that it does not affect GPA computations

IU: Incomplete—unsatisfactory; zero-credit course student received SI grade; same as an IF grade except that it does not affect GPA computations

Source: www.purdue.edu/studentregulations/regulations_procedures/grades.html.

Prior to reading about Strategy 3, please complete part 1 of Activity 6.3 on pages 161–162 to determine questions, current level of implementation, and short- and long-term actions needed related to extending the semester.

STRATEGY 3: RE-CULTURE SUMMER SCHOOL AND INTERSESSIONS

The term *summer school* evokes many negative emotions in both teachers and students. Students fear the loss of not only freedom but also time with friends and the ability to just be a kid during the warm weather months. Many teachers desire, and need, a break from the day-to-day grind they just endured from August until June. Students most often view summer school as a punishment, and many teachers fear having to deal with students who are disruptive behaviorally because they feel they are being punished. A Dallas, Texas, school recently experienced a significant summer school teacher shortage. Teachers voiced strong concerns about not wanting to address academic challenges but more so behavioral challenges of students who did not want to be there (Parker, 2013).

Clarity of Terminology: Summer School Synonymous With Intersessions

A growing number of schools have moved from a traditional school year to a more balanced calendar. Instead of the longer and traditional 11- to 12-week summer break, several 2- to 3-week breaks occur throughout the year. Some schools call these intersessions. During intersessions, many schools schedule intervention days for students needing to improve their skills, very similar to summer school. The same evidence applies for practices to help students recover credits and proficiency in either summer school or intersessions that may occur in the fall or spring. I will use the terms *summer school* and *intersession* interchangeably.

Summer School Impact

The impact of summer school on achievement has shown to be relatively average at best ($d = 0.23$). This does not seem to matter whether teachers are the same ones that students had during the regular school year, whether students are fed meals, or whether the curriculum of the summer matches the curriculum of the regular school year (Hattie, 2008). Some school systems have abandoned summer school programs because they haven't seen the necessary return on their investments of time, effort, and financial resources.

Re-Culture Instead of Abandon

For failing students, supplemental instructional intervention during the summer may be their only option for getting back on the path to graduation. Summer programs specifically designed for remediation or to address course failure have shown significant gains in test scores in reading and math (Cooper, Valentine, Charlton, & Melson, 2003). Hattie (2008) even makes the point that while the effects of summer school have not been as high as we would hope, "it is difficult to ignore even these small gains if they are critical to students who may already be marginal" (p. 77). Middle and high schools can build on of the notion that summer school *can* be effective for some students and maximize its impact when it comes to credit recovery.

Increase Motivation, Increase Impact

Secondary schools can maximize the impact of intersessions and summer school by increasing student motivation by giving students more control of their learning. Daniel Pink (2011), in *Drive: The Surprising Truth About What Motivates Us*, tells us we cannot underestimate the power of autonomy in increasing people's productivity. When students have a sense of control over their own learning needs, it is a tremendous motivator (Yazzie-Mintz, 2010). Student motivation is highest when teachers provide them with a level of independence in their learning. Students gain this when they set worthwhile goals and receive effective feedback from teachers as they progress toward meeting goals. Schools must create these conditions if they hope to make students see extended learning environments as something other than punishments.

Rehabilitation vs. Incarceration

The more students view intercessions and summer school as punishments and serving time for someone other than themselves, the less likely they will be motivated to put forth the necessary effort to learn. The more they view these sessions as opportunities for them to gain and benefit personally, student effort grows exponentially.

Schools can more effectively address both academic and behavioral issues by shifting the structure in extended learning sessions to proficiency-based credit recovery. Here, summer school no longer has a minimum seat time requirement. Students stay until they complete proficiency requirements for courses they previously failed. Instead of the traditional 4-week prison term, students earn *early parole* for quality time served. In a proficiency-based model for intersession credit recovery, once students demonstrate proficiency for a course they are recovering credit in, they either move to work on another previously failed course or simply leave and move on with their break. This provides students with motivation and purpose because they have greater autonomous control of their own learning.

Example

Matt Smith, interim chief of schools for Des Moines Public Schools and former principal at North High School, in Des Moines, Iowa, had been focusing his efforts on raising both achievement and expectations. He also knew students who are behind in credits and academic skills do not have time to waste on tasks or assessments not linked to state academic standards. Summer school at North has focused exclusively on credit recovery for the past several years. In 2012, 29 seniors attempted credit recovery toward graduation requirements in summer school, and more than half of these attempts were successful. This led directly to 16 more graduates that June, and several more students completed diploma requirements before September by focusing only on specifics missed in previous attempts.

Matt placed School Improvement Leader Jessie Van Der Wall to oversee summer school as a credit recovery model. Van Der Wall said, "Moving to a proficiency-based summer school focusing on credit recovery has allowed specific and decisive teaching and intervention to take place. Students are getting exactly the support they need. We aren't going easy on students. If anything, we are challenging them even more—just focusing the challenges we provide to meet their needs."[1]

Prior to reading about Strategy 4, please complete part 3 of Activity 6.3 on pages 161–162 to determine questions, current level of implementation, and short- and long-term actions needed related to re-culturing summer school and other intersessions.

---

[1]Used with permission from Matt Smith, Jessie Van Der Wall, and Mike Vukovich of North High School.

Credit Recovery Contract: Summer School Example

Summer school at Nagel High School is set up exclusively as a credit recovery program. We offer students an opportunity to regain lost credits due to failing grades in the core academic classes: English, math, science, and social studies.

Students may sign up for only two classes at a time. Once proficiency is met in any course, another may be added. To make up one credit in one class, students must complete the requirements based on their current proficiency level in the course they are attempting. Students must attend at least two summer school sessions per class they are attempting. Sessions are from 9 to 11:30 a.m. and 12:30 to 3 p.m., Monday–Thursday, June 2–20. Students may attend either or both sessions, but they may not leave and come back during the same session. Students more than 15 minutes late for any session are not allowed to enter the lab on that day. They will be allowed to attend the next scheduled session. Students should plan to leave early during any session only if they have successfully completed all the lessons or requirements to earn their credit. Students are finished as soon as they satisfactorily complete the lessons, as there is no specified number of lessons. Students must be on time, follow all school rules, and complete and only work on the one or two courses they are signed up for. Students must provide their own transportation, and there is no charge for credit recovery.

Student name _____

Grade 9 10 11 12

Student ID (lunch #) _____

PIN # _____

Class needed _____

Phone numbers _____

I, _____, agree to all of the stipulations for credit recovery at Nagel High School. I agree to follow rules and apply myself in the courses I am working on to earn back my lost credit. I understand I must be on time and complete and pass all assigned work. I also agree to provide my own transportation. I acknowledge that any major disruption and/or noncompliance with teacher rules and regulations will result in immediate dismissal from the program, and I may lose my privilege to earn my credit back through recovery and have to repeat in the fall.

_____ Parent Signature

STRATEGY 4: ALIGN OBJECTIVES IN CREDIT RECOVERY TO DAY SCHOOL CLASSES

Schools can increase the success of their credit recovery programs by ensuring there is direct curriculum alignment between credit recovery and day school classes. The same standards and assessment expectations for meeting these should not be different for students in the same school or school district. Credit recovery in most schools has some version of a technical or online component. Students taking courses for credit must have similar assessments for critical course objectives. For example, students working on cell functions in room 217 first period for biology with 30 other students should have virtually the same content objectives and assessments of required skills as students in the credit recovery computer lab during study hall. The teaching approaches and support may be different, but expectations must be the same. This allows tighter continuity for students who may complete credit recovery in a learning center lab or summer school/intersession and then be back in the flow of courses in the same subject for the following semester. If a student does not master requirements in a course during the traditional or day school setting, then specific priority concepts and skills should already be defined for him or her to do so in credit recovery (online or otherwise).

Focus on Critical Standards

What will better ensure alignment between credit recovery and the day school course is identifying critical standards. When students have failed a course or proficiency has not been demonstrated, the focus needs to be on the most essential content. As middle and high schools look to build, plan for, or improve current credit recovery practices, ensuring students spend credit recovery time and effort on the most essential learning outcomes is critical. The more that standards and curriculum are prioritized, the better chance schools will have to ensure that the time students spend in credit recovery is related to the essentials, and the better chance that students will succeed.

In his book *Rigorous Curriculum Design: How to Create Curricular Units of Study That Align Standards, Assessment, and Instruction,* Larry Ainsworth (2011, p. 56) shares that all schools must come to consensus when identifying critical and essential outcomes of courses. Here are a few questions middle and high schools teachers and teams should consider when designing what outcomes are essential for students to recover their credit:

1. Are credit recovery standards essential for readiness of the subsequent coursework in the discipline?

2. Are the standards (work related to it) enduring?

3. Are the standards important in relation to state, provincial, or other external assessments?

4. Does the standard relate to other disciplines?

These questions should drive which standards are essential and thus should be the basis for students retrieving credits from failed courses. This will ensure that the time invested for students to recover credits is focused on critical concepts and skills they will need for success in future courses.

Prior to reading about Strategy 5, please complete part 4 of Activity 6.3 on pages 161–162 to determine questions, current level of implementation, and short- and long-term actions needed related to aligning credit recovery objectives to day school classes.

STRATEGY 5: USE BEST EVIDENCE FOR ALL CREDIT RECOVERY DECISIONS

Each time a student loses a credit from failing a course, her or his chances of becoming a dropout increase. Meanwhile, schools cannot lower standards and issue course credits to students who have not demonstrated mastery. Students recovering credit, online or in traditional settings, must demonstrate the same level of standards-based proficiency expected in every classroom.

Accurately Weighing Evidence

Teachers use various forms of assignments and assessments when determining student grades. They often have a lot of evidence they have collected over the course of a semester. When a student does not have a passing grade at the end of the 18-week semester, it is critical that schools and teachers use the best evidence available to make valid, reliable inferences to know where to find the on-ramp.

When a student does not pass a course, specifically in Grades 9 through 12, teachers must determine if the student has gained enough skills to be successful in the next course or level of learning. This is independent from whether the student is offered a chance to recover the credit. Evidence from different assessments or tasks students completed is not always of equal value or rigor. Middle and high school teachers, especially of like courses, must collaborate effectively to ensure they are making quality inferences from the evidence in student work when determining if students should be entered into a credit recovery program after failing a class or repeat the course.

Example

Kristen, after first semester, has received a failing grade in Algebra 1-A of a yearlong Algebra 1 A-B course worth 2 credits. She has missed earning credit in Algebra 1-A. Her school is faced with two decisions:

- *Option 1*: Change her spring schedule, remove her from Algebra 1-B, and replace it with Algebra 1-A again. Hopefully she can earn the Algebra 1-A credit and gain proficiency in foundational algebra skills for success in Algebra 1-B the following year. (She will be behind in credits, but it may be necessary for her to gain essential skills.)
- *Option 2:* Kristen's teacher, Miss Petroff, determines she has shown enough mastery of foundational skills that with support, effort, and diligence Kristen could likely gain the proficiencies missed and still keep up with the new content material in Algebra 1-B. Her schedule is not changed. She is not given a grade or credit for Algebra 1-A until she shows the level of mastery needed. She then could receive both credits in June, not needing credit recovery or a change in her schedule.

Let's look at an example from Miss Petroff's class with Kristen and three other students' summary grades (Figure 6.4).

In Figure 6.4, we can see all four students have earned a failing grade in Algebra 1-A. Miss Petroff must determine whether each student has demonstrated enough mastery to move onto recovery or might need to repeat the course. She must look much deeper than the final average grade. (We will discuss more on averaging in Chapter 7.) Miss. Petroff and her other Algebra teaching peers focused on eight standards during the semester. The percentages for each student indicate their mastery of concepts and skills addressing each particular standard over the course of the semester.

Miss. Petroff has also noted the amount of work completed and submitted for each standard. She did not simply count zeros or take away points for missing work. She determined inferences from the evidence students produced on standards-based assignments, tasks, and assessments. Finally, Miss Petroff has indicated that standards 1, 3, 4, and 5 are the critical foundation standards for Algebra 1-A. She and her peers who teach Algebra 1-A and 1-B determined this collaboratively. Miss Petroff must also collaborate with her peers to determine the type of evidence students must provide to show mastery of key concepts and skills that would afford them a recovery opportunity, but also to show signs of being successful in the next course while doing so. (This example would apply to any high school course.)

Figure 6.4 Example: Weighing Evidence for Repeat vs. Recovery of Credit

	Standard 1*	Standard 2	Standard 3*	Standard 4*	Standard 5*	Standard 6	Standard 7	Standard 8	Final grade (%)
Kristen	80% all work completed	78% missing three assignments	No evidence	80% all work completed	80% all work completed	No evidence	75% missing four assignments	80% missing three assignments	F (50%)
Mark	No evidence	No evidence	90% missing four assignments	No evidence	No evidence	85% all work completed	78% all work completed	No evidence	F (30%)
Samantha	No evidence	No evidence	No evidence	45% missing three assignments	No evidence	80% all work completed	No evidence	No evidence	F (30%)
Brittany	30% all work completed	20% all work completed	19% all work completed	45% all work completed	10% all work completed	43% all work completed	35% all work completed	20% all work completed	F (30%)

* Priority and foundation for next level of course.

154

Kristen: For standards 1, 4, and 5, she has completed all work and demonstrated 80% proficiency. For standards 2, 7, and 8, her work is proficient, but she hasn't provided enough evidence yet that she has mastered the standard, missing several assignments. She has not demonstrated any evidence for standard 3, which was one of the four critical and foundation standards determined by the Algebra 1 teachers. Kristen has likely provided enough evidence of potential proficiency for Miss Petroff to allow her to recover her credit while moving into Algebra I-B. Miss Petroff will need to provide Kristen with support and perhaps stipulate she complete additional work to provide evidence in standard 3 before or as she begins the next level of course.

Mark: He has mastered only two standards with all work in (6, 7) and one that needs more evidence but indicates he is close (3). For the other five standards, no evidence is present. Mark is showing, just from this evidence, strong signs of proficiency but there are issues. He is missing a great deal of work. Is this possibly boredom, or is he in need of serious behavior interventions? This should be a PLC decision, but strong inferences could be made that credit recovery would suit this student well, and repeating the course entirely would be unnecessary or perhaps even detrimental.

Samantha: Similar to Mark, Samantha has gaps and multiple standards with no evidence. But hers are even more extensive, with only one standard having been met. Unless Samantha can truly demonstrate that she has mastered certain content and skills, Miss Petroff might infer that her gaps may be too large for recovery.

Brittany: I think most of us can picture Brittany. She has submitted all work for all standards. However, she has not come close to demonstrating potential proficiency for any. Miss Petroff will need to consider whether Brittany can survive academically next semester in Algebra 1-B without some serious gain in concept/skill proficiency or some intense intervention in addition to the time spent in her class. *How many Brittanys do you have in your class? How many of them end up passing with a D?*

Practicality Points

If a student has missed a great deal of work and not demonstrated mastery of the essential content and skills of the class, that might be where the teachers would start in building a plan for the student to demonstrate proficiency in an extended semester situation. Students repeating courses like English 9, for example, often do so while also taking another English course during sophomore or junior year. Taking multiple courses of the same content, especially core content, is usually if not always a recipe for disaster.

School-level grading practices of collaborative scoring and analysis of student work are essential for making these decisions. Grade differences between A or B+ can impact class rank and grade point averages and thus college admissions and scholarships for students. Collaborative scoring of anonymous student work increases the fairness, reliability, and impartiality of grades. However, when teachers are considering whether a student should repeat an entire course or be allowed to recover the credit, collaborative scoring and analysis become even more imperative to ensure students are not unnecessarily being retained, even just for one course. We have to look seriously at any reason and rationale to make a student repeat an entire course. Retention of any kind significantly increases the chance of students dropping out, and repeating a course at the high school level is a *form of retention*. Schools at any level must take caution in using any form of retention.

Relying on Parameters

Schools that have created parameters (see Chapter 4) for grading decisions can rely on them to generate questions when considering recovery versus repeat situations.

The questions in Figure 6.5 can effectively and efficiently guide teachers when making the decision about repeat versus recovery. Again, whether

Figure 6.5   Grading Parameter Filters for Credit Recovery Decisions

Parameters on which to base questions	Primary questions	Supporting questions
Mission Use grading and reporting methods to enhance, not hinder, teaching and learning (Guskey & Bailey, 2000)	Did the grading decisions we used to consider possible repeat or recover align with our school's mission for grades?	Will this recovery be to the ultimate long-term benefit of the student? Will repeating this course allow the student to gain the skills necessary to increase both confidence and ability to succeed in the subsequent course? Or will having to repeat this course be another push for the student to consider dropping out?
Truthfulness	Are there clearly defined priority objectives and standards for the course?	Did the assessments we used for determining students' grades provide evidence toward these?

Parameters on which to base questions	Primary questions	Supporting questions
	If the assessments we used allowed students to provide evidence of priorities, were they at the appropriate rigor level?	Did the assessments we used allow students to demonstrate progress toward learning evidence?
Reliability	How many priority standards did the students in question demonstrate proficiency on?	Were they all of equal value and importance? Were some more foundational than others? Did each teacher weigh his or her assessment similarly?
	How much collaborative scoring was done?	Were we in agreement consistently regarding student proficiency and/or progress toward standards?
	Did some teachers average grades and include zeros for missing assignments and assessment, thereby distorting the average?	If so, can the missing assignments be completed through credit recovery rather than repeating the course?
Impartiality	Did teachers equally provide students with multiple opportunities and stipulated second chances?	Were expectations related to proficiency of priority standards the same between teachers of like courses? If not, did teachers collaborate for agreement on necessary student evidence demonstrating mastery, or if determining repeat vs. recover, what constituted sufficient progress?
Understandability	Did all teachers share and compare their grading systems and practices with each other before the semester to look for enough commonalities?	Did we communicate to parents and students clearly what level of demonstration of skill and content knowledge (not percentage of total points) would determine repeat vs. possible recover in a failure situation?

students need to complete work or show mastery when they haven't is not on the table—they do it to receive credit. School leaders must challenge teachers to provide clear evidence of why they feel repeating the course, which is a form of retention, is the best possible option for their students.

Example

The New York State Department of Education has some very specific guidelines in its *High School Academic Policy Reference Guide*, which was updated in April 2014, related to how schools can provide credit recovery to students.

Students eligible to recover credit must

- have attended two thirds of class time of the failed course,
- attempt to recover credit during the semester or summer immediately following the failed course. (After, students must repeat the course.)

To provide students with a credit recovery opportunity, the school must

- form a panel to consult with the teacher of the failing student (if she or he still teaches at the school) to determine
  o whether the student should repeat the course or earn credit through targeted credit recovery,
  o the scope and content of the targeted learning plan for the student,
  o how the original failing course grade will be reconciled with the targeted credit recovery grade in accordance with the school or course's grading policy.

Pre-Assess Before Credit Recovery Starts

Finally, where students should start when they are recovering credits is just as essential as whether they should be recovering or repeating courses. Middle and high schools offering any form of credit recovery for a failed course should have a pre-assessment prior to beginning to determine what content has already been mastered. They need to find where the student's on-ramp is. There is a very good chance that students mastered material in certain areas but simply did not complete work.

Let's go back to Mark from our algebra class example (Figure 6.6). Mark's course average of 30% is very likely because of all of the missing work. At his first credit recovery session, he was given a comprehensive assessment that included rigorous items and tasks for each of the eight standards that were covered during the course. Mark was proficient on seven, but only on two did he show exemplary performance. He is obviously proficient enough to earn his credit based on this one assessment. Just as his average of 30% should not be the only piece of evidence used to

Figure 6.6 Single Student Analysis of Repeat vs. Recovery

Student: Mark   **Course: Algebra 1-A**

	Standard 1*	Standard 2	Standard 3*	Standard 4*	Standard 5*	Standard 6	Standard 7	Standard 8	F (30%)
Grade/evidence produced	No evidence	85% missing three assignments	90% missing four assignments	No evidence	100% missing three assignments	85% all work completed	78% all work completed	No evidence	F (40%)
Credit recovery pre-assessment	Non-mastery	Proficient	Proficient	Proficient	Proficient	Exemplary	Proficient	Non-mastery	6 of 8 proficient

* Priority and foundation for next level of course.

determine if he should complete the entire course, neither should this one assessment be viewed as the only piece of evidence to provide credit—yet. He is obviously not like our AP chemistry student in Chapter 2, who received a 5 on his AP chemistry exam. Mark still has some areas in which he can improve.

When he did not master standard 1 or standard 8 on the credit recovery pre-assessment, neither of which he'd showed any evidence of mastering during the semester either, Miss Petroff provided him with six essential assignments: four on standard 1 and two on standard 8. Standard 1 is a foundational standard for Algebra 1-B, which his teachers felt will provide him with a chance to work on the most important skills during his stipulated second chance. In a sense, he received a credit recovery MEAEC.

Quality credit recovery pre-assessments provide teachers with the type of evidence to guide students to their proper on-ramp. These are essential to avoid disengaging students by having them complete assignments and tasks they have already proven they know how to do and miss extra opportunities to work on objectives that they need more support with. Schools where students complete end-of-course exams that feel they are aligned and provide the kind of evidence to make accurate inferences can analyze results from those related to standards. This would avoid having student reassess again. If the end-of-course assessment perhaps isn't geared to provide that information, a credit recovery pre-assessment may still be required. Deciding what students should have to demonstrate proficiency on in order to earn credit should start with eliminating anything they have already provided evidence of mastery on.

Please complete part 5 of Activity 6.3 on pages 161–162 to determine questions, current level of implementation, and short- and long-term actions needed related to making credit recovery decisions.

CONCLUSION

Students who have failed courses have placed themselves on the highway to dropping out. Some are driving faster to that destination than others. High schools must ensure that they have a plan in place to implement various strategies to support students in recovering credits while gaining essential content and skill mastery. Teachers must have a voice related to changing grading practices, but credit recovery decisions must have a different level of accountability. Schools must ensure the best evidence is being used to make decisions related to helping find students- on-ramps back on the highway toward high school graduation.

Activity 6.3: Credit Recovery Strategy Action Planning

Strategies to help students recover credits and increase quality of credit recovery	Questions to ask	Where is our school, course, or department related to current implementation?	What are our short-term steps (next 3 months)?	What are our long-term steps (next 4–9 months)?
Strategy 1: Bring 'Em Back (completed in Activity 6.2)				
Strategy 2: Extend Semesters (see Activity 6.2 on page 140)	Does our school have a specific system in place to give students needed time after the semester to make up work or show proficiency? Do we provide support for learning (teaching) that some students need? Is it currently enough? How do we know?			
Strategy 3: Re-culture Summer School and Intersessions (see Activity 6.2 on page 140)	Do we currently have a summer school or intersession program? Does it allow for credit recovery? Does it allow for students to focus only on material not mastered?			

(Continued)

(Continued)

Strategies to help students recover credits and increase quality of credit recovery	Questions to ask	Where is our school, course, or department related to current implementation?	What are our short-term steps (next 3 months)?	What are our long-term steps (next 4–9 months)?
Strategy 4: Align objectives in Credit Recovery to Day School Classes	Are the expectations (standards) the same for credit recovery as they are for day school? Are we consistent in how we assess student learning and proficiency in both?			
Strategy 5: Use Best Evidence for All Credit Recovery Decisions	How are we currently assessing whether students need to repeat a course vs. recover credit? What learning evidence are we looking for? Are we consistent? Is moving students through a credit recovery program of support—knowing they may struggle at the next level of learning but that we will offer support—a better option than a full repeat of a course?			

KEY IDEAS

1. Credit recovery is not at all a new phenomenon. Many different aspects have been in place for many years.

2. Retention and mandatory seat time requirements are obstacles for effective credit recovery.

3. Similar to failure prevention, secondary schools can use a framework when considering school-level credit recovery decisions.

4. Providing support and extended time are essential elements for effective credit recovery.

5. Summer school and other intersessions can be excellent places for schools to use a proficiency-based credit recovery model.

6. Semester-long assessment information and inferences related to specific standards mastered or not should drive decisions for recovering credits versus repeating courses.

7. Pre-assessment prior to starting a credit recovery plan is essential for schools to know where students are in terms of content and skill mastered. Students' credit recovery plans should be shaped around the gaps presented in pre-assessment evidence.

REFLECTION QUESTIONS

1. What credit recovery systems are formally in place at your (middle) high school?

2. What individual forms of classroom and team credit recovery practices are occurring in your school that could be made more holistic?

3. How could summer school and other breaks (winter, spring, fall) allow for specific credit recovery practices?

4. How are we determining whether students should repeat a course or recover credit?

5. What evidence are teachers using collaboratively to determine whether students have shown mastery in essential content to be able to move on to the next course and be successful (even if they still are in credit recovery)?

Standards-Based Grading

7

In a quick Internet search of *minimum standard*, I found that there are minimum standards published for child care facilities, bachelor's and master's degree programs in most states, and even wildlife rehabilitation. For each one of these and countless other processes, programs, and entities, there is a grade, so to speak, that people or groups earn based on performance against specific criteria. These standards help with quality control, safety, and also consistency. The consistency is what many of us expect in our lives and take for granted almost everywhere, except across classrooms. A Big Mac from McDonalds is expected to be the same in Chicago, Cleveland, and Cheyenne. If we were to order one and not have "Two all-beef patties . . ." (I won't type the entire jingle), we would demand another be made as to our expected consistency or a refund of our money. My question is: Do we even consider making a fuss when Mandy gets a B+ and Sandy a D for virtually the exact same work in the same school? Maybe we should, don't you think? This is what standards-based grading is all about.

WHAT STANDARDS-BASED GRADING IS

Standards-based grading simply means emphasizing established criteria for grade reporting focused on student proficiency in relation to a standard (Guskey & Bailey, 2000; Sadler & Tai, 2007). Standards-based grading is not a new concept, and numerous researchers have indicated that it leads to higher levels of achievement than traditional grading practices (Guskey & Bailey, 2000, 2010; Marzano, 2006; O'Connor, 2009, 2010; Reeves, 2004, 2011b). Teachers using standards-based grading practices determine student grades with minimal to no inclusion of any process or progress skill information.

WHAT STANDARDS-BASED
GRADING IS NOT (NECESSARILY)

A common misconception is that standards-based grading is 100% synonymous with having a standards-based report card (SBRC). Yes, schools implementing a standards-based report card have moved away from reporting student grades traditionally (A-B-C-D) to reporting students' achievement levels on specific benchmarks. These are most often reported to students and parents with an anecdote, such as mastery proficient, below standards, well below standards, or perhaps they just replace the letters with numbers: 1, 2, 3, 4 (Guskey & Bailey, 2010). Schools desiring to move to more standards-based grading do *not* have to implement a complete overhaul of their current report card.

Heflebower, Hoegh, and Warrick (2014, p. 3) specifically mention that often standards-based grading is confused with standards-referenced grading. They note that most schools actually engage in standards-referenced grading, where when students meet or master a standard they are not necessarily moved forward to different levels, standards, or courses based on their performance.

Secondary SBRC Challenges

SBRC implementation is much more of a challenge at the secondary level than in elementary school settings. Middle school but even more so high school teachers, parents, and other stakeholders often fear that colleges will not be able to decipher anything other than letter grades on their students' transcripts (Hanover Research, 2013, p. 4). Standards-based report cards are not unheard of at the high school level. Guskey and Bailey's (2010) masterful work in *Developing Standards-Based Report Cards* outlines a very clear process for any school (elementary, middle, high) that is considering implementing an SBRC and provides an excellent example of a high school SBRC. There is a picture of the teacher and an overview of the course focus. Each teacher reports separate grades for achievement, participation, homework, punctuality, and effort (Guskey & Bailey, 2010, p. 152).

While Guskey and Bailey's example displays a very personal tone and offers a great deal of targeted feedback for both academic and behavioral elements, the challenges of implementing a reporting mechanism as they describe it are vast. Hanover Research's (2011) study notes that for schools to implement standards-based grading reporting systems, the professional development for teachers and communication with stakeholders to understand both the purpose and the information conveyed on the report card itself may require up to 4 years of investment (p. 4).

Middle and high schools often abandon the idea of SBRCs early in the discussion. The time alone required to develop teachers' expertise around accurately determining and reporting standards-based evaluations for 150 students on multiple standards prohibits implementation before it even starts. But that doesn't mean schools have to stay away from standards-based grading, which is much simpler to implement and very effective for achieving consistency in grading across classrooms.

STANDARDS-BASED (STANDARDS-REFERENCED) GRADING STRATEGIES

As I've mentioned, teacher voice is critical as middle and high schools look to make adjustments in grading practices. However, when schools determine that one of their parameters in guiding both grading policy formation and grading practice implementation is truthfulness, then grades must be determined principally on evidence students provide related to academic standards. This can be accomplished without abandoning letter grades and still allow flexibility in grading practices across different subjects. Similar to credit recovery, school leaders may build into their improvement plans specific overarching strategies/standards referenced that will increase the quantity and effectiveness of standards-based grading in all classrooms. Implementing schoolwide strategies can guide course teams and individual teachers' to implement specific grading practices that will lead to grades that are more truthful, reliable, impartial and understandable. I highlight the following five school-level strategies along with specific practices that teachers and courses teams can implement that are directly aligned with these strategies:

Strategy 1: Focus on Academic Standards

- Example Practice: Use Priority Standards and Learning Objectives
- Example Practice: Use Learning Progressions (Spiraling of Common Core State Standards)

Strategy 2: Implement Mastery Grading

- Example Practice: Provide Effective Feedback

Strategy 3: Minimize What Is Actually Graded

- Example Practice: Use Training Assignments Early in Units

Strategy 4: Ensure Accurate Weighting

- Example Practice: Use Depth of Knowledge Rigor Level
- Example Practice: Use a Selection Syllabus

Strategy 5: Eradicate the Average (Once and for All)

- Example Practice: Use J Curve Grading
- Example Practice: Removing Extreme Scores

Some practices address multiple strategies. A summary box is provided in Figure 7.21.

STRATEGY 1: FOCUS ON ACADEMIC STANDARDS

For any standards-based or standards-referenced grading system, teachers must focus their grading on student work directly tied to priority academic standards. (My dad would call that a blinding flash of the obvious.) Final student grade determinations cannot include extraneous non-academic factors such as effort, behavior, and attendance. Teachers must use evidence from assignments, assessments, tasks, and student performance that are directly linked to learning standards and benchmarks.

Example Practice: Use Priority Standards and Learning Objectives

Secondary schools can increase the truthfulness of their grades by determining the academic standards most important for teachers to monitor. Ainsworth (2003) calls for schools to have *priority standards*—the benchmarks most vital for students to master in their current course and those foundational for the subsequent course in that discipline. Teachers should focus their grading not just on standards but also on these priority standards.

For each priority standard, teachers keep track of how students have fared and determine final grades from evidence students provide of each of these (see Figure 7.1). Teachers determine one student grade for each priority standard. Similarly, Ken O'Connor (2009) suggests teachers select 7 to 15 learning goals and that final grades be based exclusively on student mastery toward these (see Figure 7.2).

In both Figures 7.1 and 7.2, student grades are determined by the teacher focusing on how students fared on each essential priority standard or learning objective of that course. The teacher keeps track of the grade students received as well as the evidence from specific assignments and tasks they submitted for each standard or objective.

Figure 7.1 Example of Priority Standard Grading

Standards	9.1.2	9.1.3	9.1.5	9.2.7	9.3.1	9.5.3	9.7.1	9.7.2	9.7.4	9.10.1	Final Grade
Student grade	B	C	A	C	B	A	B	C	D	C	B−
Evidence collected	2 performance assessment tasks	2 quizzes	1 major project	4 assignments, 1 quiz	2 quizzes, 1 performance task	3 quizzes, 1 short essay	1 presentation, 1 short essay, 1 long essay	1 report, 3 performance tasks	1 quiz, 2 essays	4 short essays	

Figure 7.2 U.S. Government Grade 12

Learning objective	Compare various types of government	Explain early founding civic life in America	Describe fundamental principles of the constitution	Explain why U.S. government is defined as federal, presidential, constitutional, and a representative democracy	Compare and contrast branches of U.S. state government and enumerated, implied, and denied powers	Analyze processes essential to functioning of federal and state governments (e.g., the process of how a bill becomes law)	Explain electoral process at the national, state, and local levels	Explain various points of view associated with different political parties and contemporary public issues
Grade	C	B	D	A	A	B	C	B
Evidence collected	2 short essays, 1 quiz	1 short essay, 1 presentation	2 performance tasks	1 long essay, 2 quizzes	4 performance tasks	2 performance tasks, 1 quiz	1 presentation, 1 long essay	3 performance tasks

Example Practice: Use Learning Progressions (Spiraling of Common Core State Standards)

The Common Core State Standards have provided teachers with a rigorous road map for guiding students toward college and career readiness. The Common Core State Standards have a spiral design. This means for every standard, students are expected to master everything from previous grade-level expectations, plus what is added for the current grade level. These serve as learning progressions for teachers to use as a guide for how students progress in their learning at deeper levels of rigor. Learning progressions are a foundation of standards-based education (Mosher, 2011; see Figure 7.3).

The three Common Core standards in Figure 7.3 are from the Reading for Informational Text strand (RI). The number (e.g., RI.6.1) indicates the grade level (6) and the standard (1). Seventh-grade students in language arts classes are expected to be able to quote accurately from a text when explaining and drawing inferences as well as refer to details from the text (sixth-grade expectation). When they arrive in eighth grade, they will be expected to still demonstrate proficiency in the skills from lower grades as well as now cite textual evidence to support their analysis of what they read.

Teachers can use the spiraling of learning progressions embedded in the Common Core State Standards to determine the learning targets students need to master at their current grade levels. They also can see what the previous and subsequent grade-level targets are for each standard. These provide teachers with targets for determining how they will weight assignments based on point values if students reach mastery related to the concepts or skills above *or* below current grade level. This gives teachers a better chance to increase the understandability of their grades on student work for parents and students.

Eighth-Grade English Language Arts Example

In the example task displayed in Figure 7.4, Mrs. Hatcher's eighth-grade language arts students were asked to analyze the central idea of a passage from Fredrick Douglas through a multi-paragraph essay. Mrs. Hatcher is

Figure 7.3   Eighth-Grade English Language Arts Common Core Standards

RI.8.1 Cite textual evidence to support analysis of what the text says explicitly as well as inferences drawn from the text.
RI.7.1 Quote accurately from a text when explaining what the text says explicitly and when drawing inferences from the text.
RI.6.1 Refer to details and examples in a text when explaining what the text says explicitly and when drawing inferences from the text.

intentional in determining the point allotment she will give students based on the evidence they provide in their essay addressing standard RI.8.2.

The bold wording in standard RI.8.2 (see Figure 7.5) demonstrates the Common Core spiraling effect of rigor levels increasing from one grade

Figure 7.4   Eighth-Grade Task Linked to Specific English Language Arts Common Core Standard

Reading passage: Douglass, Frederick. (1845). *Narrative of the life of Frederick Douglass an American slave, written by himself.* Boston, MA: Anti-Slavery Office.

Task to students: After reading the passage from Fredrick Douglas, determine and analyze his central idea regarding the evils of slavery he conveyed through supporting ideas and developed over the course of the text. Then provide an objective. For additional points, state at least two points at which you feel Douglas used specific details to refine, polish, and perfect his argument.

(Text and tasks retrieved and adapted from Common Core Standards Initiative, n.d., pp. 91, 93.)

Figure 7.5   Common Core State Standards Aligned in This Task

Grade/mark (range)		Corresponding Common Core State Standard
A+ (75–71 points)	This means I have met the following standard	RI.9-10.2 Determine a central idea of a text and analyze its development over the course of the text, **including how it emerges and is shaped and refined by specific details**; provide an objective summary of the text.
A or A− (70–66 points)	This means I have met the following standard	RI.8.2 **Determine a central idea of a text** and analyze its development over the course of the text, **including its relationship to supporting ideas**; provide an objective summary of the text.
B or B+ (65–60 points)	This means I have met the following standard	RI.7.2 **Determine two or more central ideas in a text and analyze their development over the course of the text; provide an objective summary of the text.**
C (59–53 points)	This means I have met the following standard	RI.6.2 **Determine a central idea of a text and how it is conveyed through particular details; provide a summary of the text distinct from personal opinions or judgments.**
Not yet passing (No points yet)	Here is a starting standard-target for me	RI.5.2 **Determine two or more main ideas** of a text and explain how they are **supported by key details**; summarize the text.

level to the next within the same standard. Mrs. Hatcher will use these as guides for scoring her students' papers in terms of both the feedback she will give them and the amount of points possible.

Mrs. Hatcher brings home five student essays to score this evening:

- **Kristen's** paper met the standard at the eighth-grade level as expected. Her essay had a clear analysis of Douglas's central idea with specific supporting details from the text, and she provided an objective summary. Kristen earned an A, which garnered her 70 points.

- **Brittany's** essay did not include evidence of Douglas's central idea. Instead, she addressed two main ideas that were related and included details to support them. She did include an objective summary. Brittany's performance on this assignment wasn't proficient at the eighth-grade level, but showed progressing mastery at the seventh-grade level. She earned a B, and 63 points.

- **Mark's** essay was accurate in determining Douglas's central idea, and he provided a few examples from the text. His summary was not tied objectively to the text, nor was it aligned to the central message. Mark is on track for potential proficiency, as he is demonstrating mastery at the sixth-grade level for this eighth-grade standard. For this assignment Mark earned 57 points, a C.

- **Samantha's** essay demonstrated a basic understanding of what Douglas was saying, but she included little specificity in her details and her summary was very basic. While her effort was obvious, she was well below eighth-grade proficiency. She will not receive any points at this time. Samantha will receive feedback and additional time to work on this essay. Mrs. Hatcher plans to work with Samantha, and students with similar issues, during intervention time on Tuesday.

- **Gabe's** essay exceeded all of the eighth-grade objectives and included clear examples based on choice details Douglas provided to sharpen his argument. Gabe's paper conveys mastery at the ninth-grade level, based on the Common Core learning progressions. He received **80 points;** 5 above the maximum allotment for this assignment.

Mrs. Hatcher uses a slight range in points to allow her to reward neatness and diligence, but nothing that would render grades untruthful. Also, for students who are proficient, Mrs. Hatcher provides standards-based targets for them to shoot for in their assignments. If they exceed and meet the next grade-level standard, she rewards them in an accurate manner, with a point increase aligned to the standard. She calls this *standards-based extra credit.*

Figure 7.6   Summary of the Five Students' Essay Performance

Student	Essay evidence	Points	Grade
Kristen	Clear analysis of Douglas's central idea; supporting details provided, objective summary	70	A
Brittany	Addressed two related main ideas; included support details and an objective summary.	63	B
Mark	Douglas's central idea provided with few examples from the text; summary not tied objectively to text or aligned to central message	57	C
Samantha	Basic understanding of Douglas's speech; little specificity; summary was very basic	Nothing Yet	I
Gabe	Exceeded all eighth-grade objectives; included clear examples of choice details that sharpened Douglas's argument	80	A+

Teachers can increase student and parent understanding of proficiency expectations for grades by using learning progressions from the Common Core State Standards. The differences between the student grades on individual assignments can be referred back to actual standards. Also, when students are not mastering grade-level standards, their grade becomes a guide as to how far from grade-level standard they are—or where their on-ramp is.

> **Reflection:** What units do you teach that would lend then themselves to grading students, based on the grade-level standards they are demonstrating for a unit?

STRATEGY 2: IMPLEMENT MASTERY GRADING

Middle and high schools can move quickly from traditional to a more standards-based grading approach by ensuring *mastery grading* practices take place in every classroom. Mastery grading is a scoring method that incorporates a standards-based approach with a pass/fail system (Guskey & Bailey, 2000). Teachers using mastery grading practices establish a cutoff, or threshold, between student product submissions that demonstrate mastery of essential objectives and those that do not. Mastery grading thresholds give students minimum targets to strive for in their work submissions to earn the minimum amount of points possible. Anything less in quality is considered non-mastery and students do not receive any points or grade. Instead of assigning a lower grade for these submissions, teachers provide written or verbal feedback to guide students to the specific elements in their work needing improvement before their next revision.

When schools or individual teachers implement the practice of mastery grading, teachers simply do *not* accept student work that is less than proficient for grading purposes. Student products must be progressing toward proficiency to have any value for a grade. Researchers Kris Green and W. Allen Emerson (2007) call this approach a *categorical objective grading system*. In their description, a student's work is scored at either the expected level or an impressive level. These levels equate to some predetermined point value used for grade calculations by teachers.

Teacher Benefit

Middle and high school teachers who implement mastery grading strategies remove themselves from a common grading quandary: They no longer have to lament the decision of how many points to give to wretched work turned in (even if by hardworking, likable students). When teachers are presented with student work that is well below proficient, they don't consider points at all; they focus on providing feedback to students about the learning process. Teachers using mastery grading can focus more on helping students learn and improve rather than trying to gauge what point value is sufficient for the effort, when work may still be at the *despicable stage*! At the same time, students who may complete all lower level or less rigorous assignments but cannot demonstrate proficiency related to key concepts and skills at certain levels are unable to receive high or inflated grades.

Example Practice: Provide Effective Feedback

Standards-based grading will not lead to increases in student learning unless students are made aware of what their next learning step is. Once the standard or learning objective has been made clear to students, it becomes both a grading target and a feedback target. Hattie (2008) describes an instructional model for feedback that involves four levels: task, process, self-regulation, and self (p. 176).

The effectiveness of feedback is determined by using the appropriate kind for the current level of performance being demonstrated by the learner. Task feedback is used when learners are at an emergent or novice level. It is directly related to the task at hand. Feedback here is often provided to students relative to correctness or incorrectness of answers when they are not showing the ability to move toward the learning goals on their own. Task feedback is usually very specific. Process feedback is applied when learners show some degree of proficiency or when they have demonstrated proficiency previously. Self-regulation feedback is applied when learners are at a proficient level and are monitoring their own learning processes. Self-regulation feedback enhances students' ability to evaluate their own learning and should give them confidence to engage in the task at hand at a deeper level (Hattie, 2012, p. 120).

The fourth type of feedback is called self-feedback. Often, this comes in the form of praise (e.g., "You are so smart," "Great job"). While there is the perception that praise is a necessary element of a teacher's repertoire of tools to motivate students and increase their self-esteem, rarely has research demonstrated this to be true. Hattie (2012, p. 121) cites Kessels, Warner, Holle, and Hanover's (2008) study in which providing feedback with praise led to lower levels of engagement and effort because students focused on the praise rather than what needed improvement.

Figure 7.7   Classroom Examples of the Types of Classroom Instructional Feedback (Self-Feedback Intentionally Left Out)

	English	Math	Science	Social Studies
Task	"You have stated the events from the text in the correct order, but haven't correctly stated key inferences from how their sequence impacted future impacts. Include that specific point in your rewrite."	"You are getting the order of operations wrong right from the start. Let's try this one again, and let's use your reference chart."	"You are getting phenotype and genotype mixed up. Which one conveys the physical display of the trait?"	"Your timeline is not scaled properly. Let's start again."
Process	"You have aligned your three main points in your opening paragraph, but your next two paragraphs seem to lack focus. What could we do to tighten them up?"	"How could you complete this proof in fewer steps? Tell me the strategies you were using. Which ones might be the most effective here?"	"You have correctly come up with a solid hypothesis, but I am not sure you have identified the controlled variable. How do we determine the difference between the two types of variables?"	"You are correct about two benefits of the balance of powers related to the three branches of government. What are a few others or maybe a downside?"

(Continued)

Figure 7.7 (Continued)

	English	Math	Science	Social Studies
Self-regulation	"How might you condense your summary into a headline in a newspaper?"	"You have solved the problem correctly and identified the best plan to build the bridge to withstand seismic waves up to 7.0. How could you explain your conclusion to a novice?"	"What recommendation would you make to these two parents related to their probability of having a child with that disorder? What tools would you give them to help weigh their decision?"	"How could you teach another student to come to the same conclusion about the real causes of the Civil War? What questions might you ask them if they get stuck?"

Activity 7.1: Mastery Grading With Effective Feedback

Upcoming student assignment or task (one that you have done before)	Evidence students must produce for partial proficiency	For students close to proficiency but not quite there, what errors might you expect in their work? (These may indicate learning progressions.)	Instead of fewer points, what specific feedback might you give these students?

STRATEGY 3: MINIMIZE WHAT IS ACTUALLY GRADED

Secondary teachers face a daily challenge of trying to provide quality feedback consistently to all of their 100+ students (for some it's closer to 150). One solution is to minimize the amount of work they actually grade. Teachers can provide more effective feedback to students by eliminating nonessential tasks from any grading. Teachers must view work they assign students for practice—such as most homework, classwork, or first attempts at mastery—as *non-gradable*.

Avoid ALL Grading Early

In order to minimize what is actually graded, teachers should avoid grading with points during the beginning stages of a unit. When students are beginning to learn new concepts or skills or to develop mastery, they need practice—the deliberate kind. Teachers need to cultivate deliberate practice, in which students refine their skills and make connections from repetition and feedback. We all learn more from errors and disconfirmation than from getting things right the first time. Students who do not fear that their early mistakes will count against them permanently in lost grade points develop better assessment capabilities.

When teachers grade specifically on the correctness (or lack thereof) of answers early in a learning cycle, they are encouraging students to focus more on the immediate goal of acquiring a certain number of points and less on the strategies they are using for learning (Kluger & DeNisi, 1998). Secondary teachers use mastery grading when they grade only the core essentials and do not tabulate everything students do.

Example Practice: Use Training Assignments Early in Units

Mr. Jones, a biology teacher, has created six tasks for his unit on heredity. He has determined that understanding probability is a key learning progression that students must have to be successful in the later, more rigorous tasks. The first two tasks are for students to practice and master this essential learning progression. If students show proficiency of this learning progression on the first two tasks, they can skip the third and move onto the more difficult material that will be graded.

Mr. Jones kept records to know which students were proficient or not on each task. Students did not receive any grade on Tasks 1, 2, and, if needed, 3; they received only feedback related to their proficiency level. Kristen and Brittany opted out of the third task, while Mark and Samantha needed to still practice probability crosses. Tasks 4, 5, and 6 progressed in rigor and difficulty as well as in the weight possible.

Figure 7.8 Mr. Jones's Use of Training Assignments Early in a Unit

Task	1	2	3	4	5	6
	Training task Probability lab (coin flipping)	**Training task** Genetic cross lab	**Optional training task** (if not proficient on task 2) Double trait cross-probability lab	**Heredity task** 50 points (M) 35 (SPG)	**Genetic disease essay** 90 points (E) 80 (M) 70 (SPG)	**Summative performance assessment** Design campaign for or against pre-birth genetic testing 120 points (E) 100 (M) 80 (SPG)
Kristen	M+	E	N/A	(M) 50	(E) 90	(M) 100
Brittany	M−	M	N/A	(SPG) 35	(M) 80	(E) 120
Mark	NME	NME	SPG	(SPG) 35	IP → feedback	(SPG) 80
Samantha	SPG	NME	M−	IP → feedback	(SPG) 70	IP → feedback

Note. E = exemplary, M = mastery, SPG = significant progress. NME = no mastery evidence, IP = in progress.

Description: Mr. Jones will use training assignments early to help determine how students are developing skills on essential learning progressions in his high school biology class. He determined his students needed deliberate practice to develop mastery in math probability skills before being able to progress to more challenging tasks during his unit on genetics and human heredity. Mr. Jones developed two training tasks that were not graded at all with any points. He provided specific feedback to students below mastery to help them hone their math skills. He also included a third training task for students who still needed practice. Once students demonstrated enough proficiency they moved on to the first of three larger tasks (4, 5, and 6). Finally, Mr. Jones implemented mastery grading for all tasks. Students received points for submissions only at the mastery or significant progress level. Student work below mastery for tasks 4, 5, and 6 received the grade of IP (in progress). Students and parents knew that students could apply the feedback Mr. Jones provided and resubmit. Also, Mr. Jones included a target for students to strive for in their performance that was a level above mastery for Tasks 5 and 6.

Activity 7.2: Determining Essential Learning Progressions

For an upcoming unit of study, determine the essential learning progressions. Then decide what training tasks would allow students to practice those, which will be non-graded, and summative tasks students would be working towards, which would be graded.

Essential learning progressions needed to build towards summative task	Tasks to allow students to practice and refine (will not grade, provide only feedback)	Summative task students are building towards (will be graded)

STRATEGY 4: ENSURE ACCURATE WEIGHTING

Whether or not schools will weight their grades for Advanced Placement (AP) or honors courses is a significant decision related to standards-based grading.

Research on Weighted Grades

While weighted grades appear to have benefited students in most cases, un-weighted grading systems have placed students at a disadvantage when applying for college admissions and scholarships. Paul Sadler looked at rigor levels in high school courses and their impact on achievement when students attend college. He found that for every increasing level of rigor in high school science classes students obtained, college course grades rose by an average of 2.4 points on a 100-point scale. Translating those numbers to a typical high school grade scale, Sadler and Tai (2007) estimated students taking an honors science class in high school "ought to get an extra half a point for their trouble" (p. 7); the grade of B in an AP science course should be considered an A for the purpose of high school grade-point averages (p. 16). The College Board, which administers the AP program, stated that Sadler and Tai are probably right on that point, but makes no specific recommendations for schools regarding increased bonus points, mark, or weight for AP courses.

High schools have most often implemented weighted grades to incentivize learning for their academically capable students. Anne M. Cognard (1996), a researcher at the University of Connecticut studying the impacts of weighted grades, found that most if not all high schools that weighted grades had one commonality: a commitment to defining "excellence" (p. vii). David Lang (2007), from the University of California at Sacramento, determined that weighted grade point averages have two objectives:

1. Provide colleges with a measure of class standing between students

2. Provide students with extrinsic incentives to take appropriately challenging courses

He states, "These two objectives are very closely tied together. If the incentives are not properly constructed, students may not take courses that would best prepare them for college and therefore, Class Rank would be a far less accurate depiction of class standing" (p. 45).

The research on weighting grades for courses at the school level can be applied at the classroom level. Teachers can use *depth of knowledge*

(DOK) levels in determining weight values for grades on individual tasks, similar to using Common Core learning progressions. When students demonstrate understanding and cognitive rigor above grade-level standards, teachers can weight grades within their own classrooms. This will lead to more truthfulness in their standards-based grading.

Cautions to Consider

There are many benefits documented in literature for schools to weight grades of more rigorous courses. Weighted grades also have some possible negative consequences to consider, though. Schools have seen increases in unhealthy student behaviors due to implementation of weighted grades. Some students have engaged in cheating, attending only classes with grades, taking easier courses, and ignoring feedback that wasn't the actual grade on assignments in grade-weighted classes (Gillespie, Kim, Oswald, Ramsay, & Schmitt, 2002, p. 119). In addition, students who are overly concerned about earning good grades avoid difficult courses altogether to maximize their grade point average (Vickers, 2000, p. 147).

Teachers implementing the Common Core State Standards have likely heard of the pedagogical shifts needed to take place in classrooms for successful implementation (see Figure 7.9). A shift needed in middle and high school classrooms implementing standards-based grading practices is aligning grading with accurate weighting to the DOK level demonstrated in student work.

Introduced by Norman Webb, depth of knowledge measures the degree of knowledge that is prompted from students on tasks or assessment items, comparing it to what standards expect students to know and be able to do. Students will need to prove mastery of Common Core State Standards through demonstrated proficiency of concepts and skill attainment at deeper levels of rigor than ever before (EngageNY, 2012).

Example Practice: Use Depth of Knowledge Rigor Level

Eleventh-grade English teacher Mrs. Tonkovich's lesson is focused on Standard RI.11-12.1: "Cite strong and thorough textual evidence to support analysis of what the text says explicitly as well as inferences drawn from the text, including determining where the text leaves matters uncertain." The task she developed for her students (Figure 7.11) focuses on a particular portion of the standard: "determining where the text leaves matters uncertain." Mrs. Tonkovich selected a text that aligns with junior- and senior-level text complexity from Appendix B of the Common Core State Standards (Common Core State Standards Initiative, n.d.), John Keats's poem "Ode on a Grecian Urn."

Figure 7.9   Instructional Shifts in English/Language Arts Called for by Common Core

Shift 1	Balancing Informational and Literary Text	Students read a true balance of informational and literary texts.
Shift 2	Knowledge in the Disciplines	Students build knowledge about the world (domains/content areas) through TEXT rather than the teacher or activities
Shift 3	Staircase of Complexity	Students read the central, grade appropriate text around which instruction is centered. Teachers are patient, create more time and space and support in the curriculum for close reading.
Shift 4	Text-Based Answers	Students engage in rich and rigorous evidence based conversations about text.
Shift 5	Writing From Sources	Writing emphasizes use of evidence from sources to inform or make an argument.
Shift 6	Academic Vocabulary	Students constantly build the transferable vocabulary they need to access grade level complex texts. This can be done effectively by spiraling like content in increasingly complex texts.

Instructional Shifts in Mathematics Called for by Common Core

Shift 1	Focus	Teachers significantly narrow and deepen the scope of how time and energy is spent in the math classroom. They do so in order to focus deeply on only the concepts that are prioritized in the standards.
Shift 2	Coherence	Principals and teachers carefully connect the learning within and across grades so that students can build new understanding onto foundations built in previous years.
Shift 3	Fluency	Students are expected to have speed and accuracy with simple calculations; teachers structure class time and/or homework time for students to memorize, through repetition, core functions.
Shift 4	Deep Understanding	Students deeply understand and can operate easily within a math concept before moving on. They learn more than the trick to get the answer right. They learn the math.
Shift 5	Application	Students are expected to use math and choose the appropriate concept for application even when they are not prompted to do so.
Shift 6	Dual Intensity	Students are practicing and understanding. There is more than a balance between these two things in the classroom —both are occurring with intensity.

Figure 7.10   Depth of Knowledge Chart

Depth of knowledge level	General description	Detailed description	Tasks or product examples
1	Recall—Facts, information, procedure	Working with facts, terms, or use of simple procedures and/or formulas. Limited transformation or extended processing of the target knowledge required by the tasks at Level 1.	Vocabulary quizzes Fact sheets Matching with one correct answer Creating an outline of main points Basic one-step tasks
2	Skills and concepts—Requires some decisions about how to approach a question	Some mental processing beyond recalling or reproducing a response. Comparing or contrasting places, events and concepts, or people. Converting or classifying information from one form to another or into meaningful categories. Identifying issues and problems, patterns, cause and effect, significance or impact, relationships, points of view, or processes.	Simulations Classifying steps in a process Applying rules or protocols Recognizing concepts and ideas in terms of how they appear
3 (multiple right answers)	Strategic thinking—Reasoning, developing a plan	Higher order thinking processes. Analysis and evaluation, solving real-world problems where outcomes are somewhat predictable. Stating reasoning and rationale, and requiring coordination of knowledge and skill from multiple subject areas to carry out processes and reach a solution in a project-based setting.	Forming reports and conclusions Determining uncertainties from text Conducting an investigation to support a view Proposing solutions or making predictions
4 (multiple right answers)	Extended thinking—Investigation, collection of data, analysis of results from multiple sources	Extended use of higher order thinking processes. Solving a problem or question that is a key feature of curricular objectives that are assigned to this level. Synthesizing, reflecting, making new determinations from multiple sources or pieces of evidence.	Projects and essays with detailed and synthesized conclusions Written tasks that can argue or strongly persuade because of evidence and citations

Mrs. Tonkovich determined the DOK of this task at a Level 3 (strategic thinking) because there will be multiple correct answers from students as they analyze and interpret Keats's poem.

She also added an elective task (Figure 7.12) designed at a higher level of rigor for students who have either the ability or the desire to attempt to go beyond grade-level standard to a depth of knowledge Level 4. Her scoring rubric for both is listed in Figure 7.13.

Figure 7.11 Task for All Students

Read "Ode on a Grecian Urn," and note where Keats left you wondering about the urn and its decoration. Write 1–2 paragraphs citing specific examples about why you feel Keats left readers to ponder what happened.

30 points possible

Figure 7.12 Challenge (Weighted) Task

Students wanting a greater challenge for greater possible reward . . . In addition to citing the uncertainties in "Ode on a Grecian Urn," cite from at least 2 additional John Keats poems listed below specific examples where he left matters open to interpretation for readers across multiple poems. This task carries a weighted bonus of 10 points for possible 40 out of 30.

- Addressed to Haydon
- A Thing of Beauty (Endymion)
- Imitation of Spenser
- Ode on Melancholy
- To Autumn

For the additional points, you must score a 2 on the 3-point rubric to earn any points.

Grade Weighting Between the Two Tasks

Examining Figure 7.14, you can see how five of Mrs. Tonkovich's students did on the tasks and their corresponding grades.

- Kristen attempted the general task and demonstrated proficiency on rubric. She earned 30/30.
- Brittany attempted the more rigorous task and scored 2 based on the rubric. She also earned 30/30 on the rigorous task, equivalent to Kristen's attempt on the more general task.
- Mark attempted the more rigorous task and scored a 3, exceeding grade-level expectation in rigor. He was awarded an additional 10 points above standard.

Figure 7.13   Example Rubrics for Both Tasks

General task rubric (all students)		Elective (weighted) task rubric	
Rubric score	Point total	Rubric score	Point total
3	30/30	3	40/30
2	20/30	2	30/30
1	None (Feedback and re-attempt)	1	20/30 (Feedback and opportunity to re-attempt) Students may keep the score
		0	Feedback and have to attempt to demonstrate mastery on Task 1 before attempting elective task

Figure 7.14   Sample of Student Grades on the Task

Student	Task performed	Demonstration of skill	Grade
Kristen	General task	3	30/30
Brittany	More rigorous task	2	30/30
Mark	More rigorous task	3	40/30
Samantha	More rigorous task	1	20/30
Gabe	General task	1	No points yet (feedback)

- Samantha attempted the more rigorous task but scored only a 1 on the rubric. This was equivalent to a 2 on the general task. She earned 20/30 points and can apply the feedback from Mrs. Tonkovich and try again.
- Gabe attempted the general task and scored only a 1 on rubric. Like other students falling below threshold, he will not receive any points yet. He received feedback from Mrs. Tonkovich to use and apply later in resubmission of work.

Students like Brittany, Mark, and Samantha who attempted the more rigorous elective task had to apply interpretations from multiple poems by John Keats. They had to synthesize examples and find common uncertainties across several of his poems. Here are a few arguments for justifying more points to these students for demonstrating proficiency at a higher level of rigor:

- Students demonstrated higher levels of skill in understanding poetic vernacular at levels well above the grade-level standard and task.
- Students who could or would be interested in attempting this task might be driven away if there is not a possible reward of additional points/grade weighting (Lang, 2007).
- This is akin to a mini AP lesson—one specific rigorous assignment assembled into a regular/non-AP classroom.

Practicality Points

Not all students will want, or have the ability, to complete ever more rigorous tasks in non-honors and non-AP courses, but some likely will. Teachers who offer students optional challenging, more rigorous tasks that they have a keen interest in will likely increase engagement and motivation (Csikszentmihalyi, 1990). Secondary teachers who teach the regular version of courses are likely to have students who would or could take AP courses, but for various reasons did not. Mrs. Tonkovich may not have a large number of 11th-grade students with an insatiable desire to dive into multiple poems by John Keats. If she has only one, it is worth the time and effort for her to develop optional tasks at high rigor levels to provide that student with a challenge that she or he is interested in.

Example Practice: Use a Selection Syllabus

The use of a selection syllabus is a standards-based/standards-referenced grading practice that combines accurate weighting, minimizing the amount of student work teachers grade, linking students' grades directly to academic standards, and offering teachers an excellent opportunity to provide effective feedback to students. It's like Prego spaghetti sauce: *It's in there!*

A selection syllabus provides clear and defined guidelines for assignments and tasks students have to complete during the course of a semester, equating performance levels to grades. Similar to a course syllabus in college, students are shown which standards all graded tasks and assessments will address as well as point values for each. Finally, as the name implies, students are given some degree of choice for determining how to demonstrate mastery of essential standards and objectives. Secondary teachers can increase student motivation and effort a great deal when they provide them with options for assignments and tasks that will eventually be graded

(Guskey, 2011; O'Connor, 2009; Stiggins, 2005; Wormelli, 2006). Reeves (2011a) describes an overall point system as way of offering students choices for their assignments (p. 100). What a selection syllabus provides at a deeper level than just student choice is clear alignment to standards and objectives of the class and intentionality in terms of accurate weighting of tasks.

Mr. Self and his ninth-grade U.S. history professional learning community (PLC) at Upper High School collaborated and designed a selection syllabus (Figure 7.15) for their students entering in the fall. For each unit, they determined specific student tasks, assessments, and assignments that directly align with Indiana Academic Standards for U.S. history and Common Core literacy standards for history, science, and technical subjects.

Weighting Considerations

Mr. Self and his U.S. history peers invested a great deal of time to accurately determine the weight values for each task based on its rigor level. The teachers determined that students critiquing peers' arguments (Task 4) is a worthwhile assignment and should be included in students' grades if the critiques are done well. This task linked to the Common Core speaking and listening standard: "Assess the extent to which the reasoning and evidence in a text support the author's claim or a recommendation for solving a scientific or technical problem." Mr. Self's PLC felt that compared to other more important standards in the course, this is of less overall importance and should be of lesser point value. They limited the amount of points a student can earn for completing up to three of these at 45 points maximum.

The write-up of a current event connecting to historical context (Task 1, 75 points maximum for the semester) is similar. Mr. Self and his PLC felt this task was not equal in importance or rigor level to the analysis of Supreme Court decisions (Task 18, up to 100) or the track selection project for the period of 1960 to 1980 (Tasks 12–14, 350 points possible). Finally, Mr. Self and his colleagues felt that for some assignments or tasks, they would provide students with two levels as targets to reach (proficient and progressing), for others, three was more appropriate (exemplary, proficient, progressing). For these tasks, students would be given criteria to go above and beyond within the content and apply ideas and concepts at deeper levels. This would allow students to challenge themselves at times when their interests drove them. They would in a sense have a chance at standards-based extra credit. None of these point values for any one assignment would allow students to have their grade

Figure 7.15 Selection Syllabus for Ninth-Grade U.S. History

Unit of study or overarching topic	Primary standards assessed	Assignments/assessments/ performance tasks	Point or mark values	Total possible
History Repeating Itself—Lessons to Be Learned	Multiple social studies: Applying historical thinking to present-day issues. CCSS.ELA.W.11-12.1.A and B	1. Current event write-ups: 3/4 of a page that states the event and argues its significance to historical context	Up to five 15 points for mastery	75
The United States in WWII (1939–1945)	USH 5.1-5.6	2. Vocabulary assessments	Two: 40 for mastery; 30 for significant progress	80
	USH.5.2 CCSS.ELA.W.11-12.1.C	3. Looking through another's lens. Create written (1–2 pages), oral (5–8 minutes), and/or visual comparisons of views of two different pairs of world leaders from their perspective	Two: 75 for exemplary; 50 for significant progress	150
	CCSS.ELA.W.11-12.1.C	4. Written critiques of peer comparisons of former world leaders	Up to three for 15 points apiece	45
	USH.5.6 CCSS.SL.11-12.1.B CCSS.SL.11-12.5	5. Collaborative task: Sharing their voice: Student teams create a virtual and social media presence to describe and promote the message related to how certain ethic groups in the United States were treated and viewed their situation during WWII. Choice element: Teams can select any of the following: Japanese Americans, African Americans, Native Americans, Hispanics, and women.	115 for exemplary 100 for mastery 85 for significant progress	100*

188

Unit of study or overarching topic	Primary standards assessed	Assignments/assessments/ performance tasks	Point or mark values	Total possible
	A = USH.5.8; B = USH.5.9 CCSS.RST.9-10.1, 9-10.2, 9-10.5	6. Essay: Student choice: One of the following Roar of Guns and Rivets to the Roar of the 1950s: Explain and argue how American culture was shaped by the events of and end of WWII. From Friend to Foe: Explain and argue how World War II led to the rise of the United States and the Soviet Union as rival superpowers.	165 for exemplary 150 for mastery 120 for significant progress	150*
	USH.5.7 Summarize the efforts the national government made to regulate production, labor, and prices during the war and evaluate the success or failure of these efforts. (Government)	7. Bonus/optional tasks: Short essay or multimedia presentation forming an argument related to the success/failure and long-term impact of regulation of production, labor, prices, etc. during WWII and its continued impact (regulation) today.	50 for exemplary 40 for mastery	*50
Postwar United States (1945–1960)	USH.6.1-6.4	8. Vocabulary assessment	40 for mastery 30 for significant progress	40
	USH.6.1	9. Domino or No-Domino: Analyzing the beliefs and ideas that formulated the belief in the "domino effect."	65 for mastery 45 for significant progress	45

(Continued)

Figure 7.15 (Continued)

Unit of study or overarching topic	Primary standards assessed	Assignments/assessments/performance tasks	Point or mark values	Total possible
	USH.6.3	10. Constitutional and societal effects for civil rights through education: Analysis of one of the following: *Brown v. Board of Education* Supreme Court case Little Rock Nine (Little Rock High School) Optional methods for demonstrating mastery: Essay, presentation, multimedia. Student choice with teacher approval.	110 for exemplary 90 for mastery 75 for significant progress	*100
America in Troubled Times (1960–1980)	USH.7.1-7.11	11. Vocabulary assessment	Two: 40 for mastery; 30 for significant progress	80
		Track selection: Students select from one of the following tracks to focus on during this unit: Civil rights Vietnam War Education reform Developing trends in science (progress) Political issues and scandals	Group task: Students investigate their area in detail. (Some mandatory resources will be provided.) Their task is to design several tasks that demonstrate understanding of the major elements of this focus area, events that happened, significant individuals, and impact both short and long term. Their product must include impact seen within the last 5 years.	

Unit of study or overarching topic	Primary standards assessed	Assignments/assessments/ performance tasks	Point or mark values	Total possible
	Depends on track	12. Quiz/test assessment: Over major aspects of track (50 questions, 10 of which are short answer)	90–100 for mastery 75–89 for significant progress	100
	Depends on track CCSS.SL.11-12.6	13. Individual 4-minute argumentative speech	50 for mastery 40 for significant progress	50
	CCSS.SL.11-12.1.B	14. Group product/performance of evidence of mastery: Convey individual and group solid understanding of what the most significant events were and their short and long term impact. Optional methods for demonstrating mastery: Essay, presentation, multimedia. Student choice with teacher approval.	Individual grade: 165 for exemplary 150 for mastery 120 for significant progress Group grade: 65 for exemplary 50 for mastery 30 for significant progress	*200 (20 points max bonus for individual or group)
	CCSS.W.11-12.1	15. Written critiques of peer products and individual speeches	Up to four for 15 points for mastery	60
Contemporary United States (1980–Present)	USH.8.1-8.9	16. Vocabulary assessment	40 for mastery 30 for significant progress	40
	USH.8.5	17. How the Cold War turned warm: Analyze events and argue which were most significant in reducing tensions between the United States and the Soviet Union.	60 for exemplary 50 for mastery 40 for significant progress	*50

(Continued)

Figure 7.15 (Continued)

Unit of study or overarching topic	Primary standards assessed	Assignments/assessments/ performance tasks	Point or mark values	Total possible
	USH.8.7	18. Supreme Court analysis: Explain the constitutional significance of two the following landmark decisions of the U.S. Supreme Court: *Westside Community School District v. Mergens* (1990), *Reno v. American Civil Liberties Union* (1997), *Mitchell v. Helms* (2000), *Bush v. Gore* (2000).	120 for exemplary (60 per case) 100 for mastery (50 per case) 80 for significant progress (40 per case)	*100
	USH.8.8 Multiple ELA Common Core	19. 9/11 analysis: Argue with evidence of three major changes in U.S. society and culture and three changes that didn't happen because of American resolve.	115 for exemplary 100 for mastery 85 for significant progress	*100
Speaking and listening/ participation	CCSS.SL.9-10.1d	20. Engage in weekly discussions that propel conversations	5 per week for 18 weeks (up to 90)	90
Total possible points/ grade distribution			Total possible: 1,705 (bonus not included) *Total possible bonus: 155 (Tasks listed with * are ones for which students can earn more than the possible point total.)	1,575 1,400 1,225 1,224 or less (Feedback and chance to improve grade with resubmissions of tasks or assignments)

Note. This example is one I have modified from several versions I personally observed teachers implementing. I have aligned standards for tasks with Indiana Social Studies Standards for U.S. History 1939–present: http://www.doe.in.gov/sites/default/files/standards/socialstudies/ss-2014-ushistory-20140325.pdf.

become inflated or dishonest. Finally, as recommended by O'Conner (2009, p. 52), the PLC for the most part avoided any large amount of group grades and scores. Only on Task 5 (sharing the voice, up to 100 points) and the product for the track selection (Task 14, 50 points) were students' score at all related to those of any of their peers. Also, Task 14 was more heavily weighted individually in terms of achievement and evidence of learning.

Demystification of the Grading Process

When most middle and high school students are asked, "Why or how did you get that grade on your report card?" they most often retort, "I dunno." Frequently they're not lying; they really don't know! When teachers provide students with a selection syllabus, students check the number of points they have accumulated throughout the semester. There is full disclosure for what students have to do to earn an A, B, C, and so on. This practice demystifies grading by dramatically increasing understandability for both students and their parents.

Only Quality Work Accepted

A selection syllabus is also a great tool to focus and guide teachers in helping students realize the importance of certain tasks and why their weight value is critically important. This will help teachers guide students to focus their efforts and time on the most essential and graded content. Students will be less likely to try to gather all of the low-hanging fruit, and points, on tasks that are less essential to the course. They learn that if it's worth more weight, it's worth more effort.

Considerations in Developing a Selection Syllabus

A selection syllabus is a useful tool, but it's not foolproof. Two considerations to keep in mind when developing one are that accurate weighting is essential and that providing choice—in moderation—supports success.

When it comes to weighting, teachers must examine all course objectives and standards, and then assign tasks that can assess student performance on them. A well-designed selection syllabus will make it mathematically impossible for students to acquire a passing grade, let alone an A or B, without demonstrating proficiency at high levels on essential standards.

Choice offers an antidote for disinterested and unmotivated students. Indiana University Researcher Ethan Yazzie-Mintz (2010), in surveying over 50,000 high school students with his High School Survey of Student Engagement, found that a main reason students feel boredom in high school is that the material is not interesting or relevant. Students show higher levels of engagement when they have more freedom to express their ideas on topics (p. 22). Teachers can minimize apathy and increase engagement by including multiple options for students for certain assignments. "Every classroom teacher knows that in order for students to be successful academically, we must employ methods that engage students' bodies and emotions and not just their brains" (Qualia & Corso, 2014, p. 43).

Teachers must be cautious in providing too many choices for students, however. Researchers Patall, Cooper, and Robinson (2008) found a solid connection between giving students choices and their motivation and performance. They found that teachers offering more than five choices led students to struggle in determining which options to take. This led to a decrease in student performance. Patall et al. recommended three to five as ideal (p. 298). Mr. Self and his PLC felt they provided enough choice to better engage students, but not so much as to lead to paralysis in students determining their path.

Activity 7.3: Benefits and Drawbacks of the Selection Syllabus

List some potential benefits and drawbacks of using a selection syllabus in your classroom. Are there certain units more aligned with the use of a selection syllabus than others?

Benefits	Drawbacks	Specific units that you teach that may lend themselves more to the use of a selection syllabus than others

Conclusion on Weighting

Not all student tasks or assignments are of equal rigor levels. The weighting of student work must be accurate and proportionate to the rigor level of the course standards. When teachers are not accurate in the weighting of student tasks and assignments compared to their rigor levels, grades become distorted and lack truthfulness. Teachers who overly weight certain assignments can unknowingly inflate grades that are not indicative of students' proficiency levels. When students do not complete overly weighted assignments, they are penalized disproportionately.

PLCs must engage in the core practice of collaborating to determine accurate and consistent weighting of their assignments. Teachers providing the same assignments and the same level of grade weight are headed in the direction of ensuring truthfulness and reliability in a standards-based grading system.

STRATEGY 5: ERADICATE THE AVERAGE (ONCE AND FOR ALL)

As the World Health Organization did for smallpox in the 1970s, teachers and leaders could do as much for grading health by finally eradicating once and for all the practice of averaging students' final grades. Many researchers have discarded the idea that averaging should play any role in determining grades (Guskey & Bailey, 2000, 2010; Kirschenbaum, Simon, & Napier, 1971; Marzano, 2006; O'Connor, 2009, 2010; Reeves, 2004, 2009, 2011b; Wormelli, 2006).

In *Understanding by Design*, Wiggins, McTighe, and McTighe (1998) express that averaging one's initial versus final understanding would be a questionable measurement. Students who show mastery of a standard on their first of 15 attempts have still demonstrated mastery. A standards-based grade must convey where students are currently in demonstrating mastery, not the path they took to get there. Academic standards do not ask teachers to include the number of attempts a student needed to determine the central ideas or conclusions of a text.

Tom Guskey and Jane Bailey (2000) eloquently challenges the idea of averaging with a series of questions:

> Learning is a progressive and incremental process. Recognizing this, most teachers agree that students should have many opportunities to demonstrate their command of the subject. But should all of those learning trials be considered in determining the grade? If at any time in the instructional sequence students demonstrate that they have learned the concepts well and mastered learning goals, does that not make all previous information on their learning of those concepts and goals inadequate and invalid? Why then should such information be "averaged in" when determining students' grades? (p. 140)

Example Practice: Use J-Curve Grading

Teachers using a J-curve grading model determine student grades based solely on the level of mastery of priority standards or learning objectives at the end of the semester. The number of attempts are not averaged. This practice has a great deal to do with teacher beliefs. In a J-curve system, all students are expected to be proficient during the semester, with time being the variable that separates them.

A Bell Curve and a J-Curve

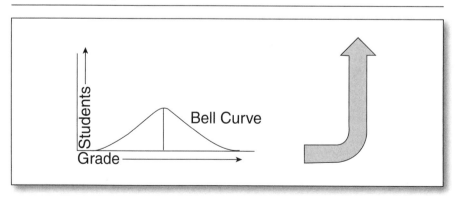

Imagine the scenario of four students in a typical high school class-room, as laid out in Figures 7.16 and 7.17. As John Lennon said, "It's easy if you try."

Figure 7.16   Classroom Application of J-Curve Grading

Student	Likely traditional grade (based on averaging)	Description of performance over the semester	Grade using a J-curve
Kristen	A	Enters course on grade level. Applies effort consistently throughout semester, demonstrates work at standard on virtually all assessments and performance measures. *At semester end she demonstrates mastery of all course objectives.*	A
Brittany	B	Enters class one grade level behind. Applies more effort than in previous years, applies feedback, addresses gaps, demonstrates work at standard on virtually all assessments and performance measures. *At semester end she demonstrates mastery of all course objectives.*	A
Mark	C– or D	Enters class significantly behind. Needs intense instruction and intervention. Shows a linear progression toward the mastery of standards. By late semester starts to demonstrate proficiency on assessments and proficiency measures. Final work submission and final exam/project demonstrates proficiency. *At semester end he demonstrates mastery of all course objectives.*	A
Samantha	D or likely F	She is an anomaly. Though she starts off well below grade level, she demonstrates solid proficiency early in the semester, followed by a lack of proficiency. Teacher is unsure if it was lack of effort or rigor difficulty. Finally, student is able to demonstrate expected mastery of concept and skills. *At semester end she demonstrates mastery of all course objectives.*	A

Figure 7.17   Further Classroom Application of J-Curve Grading

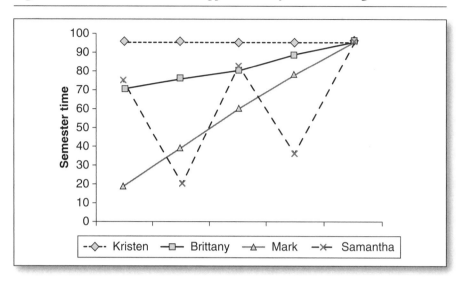

The challenge to J-curve grading is often about perception of fairness. Is it fair that Kristen gets the same grade as Samantha if Kristen didn't make as many mistakes throughout the semester? That is a fair question. Should Brittany, Mark, and Samantha be punished when, at semester end, they can demonstrate the same level of skill proficiency as Kristen but perhaps had less support at home or maybe less quality instruction in previous years? That's a fair question also. The debate about whether Kristen's grade should be slightly higher than Samantha's is not as relevant as ensuring that Samantha's grade is not lower because of her lack of initial proficiency. Students earning an A, or even a B+, in any course should convey that they have mastered all (or most) key concepts and skills, whether they took 15 tries to do so or just one.

In *Leading and Managing a Differentiated Classroom*, Carol Ann Tomlinson and Marcia B. Imbeau (2010) note:

> The J-Curve represents the theoretical distribution of grades in an educational system that believes most students are capable of doing well in school. It is the opposite of the classic bell curve, the theoretical distribution of grades in an educational system that believes most students are NOT capable of doing well in school. The J-Curve concept for grading and supporting students to achieve advocates work on changing the system until all or most students learn at a high level. (p. 56)

Teachers using a J-curve determine grades based on how they feel students would demonstrate proficiency on their next attempt at course objectives, not on failed attempts from 3 months earlier.

Activity 7.4: Consider Using J-Curve Grading for an Upcoming Unit

Consider a unit in which students have to put multiple pieces of information together to produce a product or demonstration of skill.	What are essential learning progressions that multiple attempts would be expected as students connect ideas to new learning?	What evidence (success criteria) would you look for to determine if students are progressing toward new learning targets?	How might you adjust your grading of student attempts to determine their final unit grade based on performance at the end of the unit?

Example Practice: Remove Extreme Scores

Often in many middle and high schools, the decision to continue averaging grades or not comes down to tradition. As we talked about in Chapter 2, traditions are hard to break. So then I, as your colleague, request that if you are still going to average and calculate grades to come up with the mean score, at least drop the lowest score first.

Averaging Zeros Obliterates Truthfulness

The issues related to zeros in grading are less about the zero itself than many people think. It is when teachers *average* zeros into a student's grade calculation that the grade is rendered untrue, unreliable, and not at all understandable. These two traditional practices, zeros and averaging, are the true villains that can drastically prohibit standards-based/standards-referenced grading from taking place in their presence.

Let's examine Figure 7.18. Regardless of one's belief about the merit of using zeros, one can accurately say that Brittany is a C student. If assessment 2 was a critical piece of evidence that her teacher needed to determine her overall mastery of course objectives, and no other assessment addressed that particular standard, then she should not yet have a grade. She should receive an I for *incomplete information*. She could then be given a stipulated second chance to make up that assessment or demonstrate proficiency in an alternative method, and not be given a grade that is distortedly inaccurate.

Kristen, on the other hand, if traditional grading methods are in place like in many middle or high schools, might be required to repeat the entire course, attend summer school, or perhaps even be retained another year. However, it would be hard to say that she has failed to demonstrate enough mastery to pass the class. She is also showing significant improvement and perhaps learning on a J-curve.

Rick Wormelli (2006) has pointed out that students, like all of us, have bad days, and perhaps dropping a students' lowest grades would allow for more accuracy of their true performance and not overly penalize them. If, as in our example here, both students have their lowest grade dropped, their grades become an A for Brittany and C for Kristen. If all assessments directly relate to the academic standards of the class, most teachers examining their assessment scores would deem the new grades much more accurate and truthful.

Figure 7.18   Standard Grading Example With Averaging Zero

	Assessment							Mean or average	Letter grade
	1	2	3	4	5	6	7		
Brittany	90	0	85	95	90	100	95	79	C
Kristen	60	0	66	73	70	82	90	63	F

100–90: A, 89–80: B, 79–70: C, 69–65: D, 64–0: F

Just Like the Olympics

In Olympic competitions, where judges' subjective scores determine gold, silver, and bronze medals, both the highest and lowest scores are eliminated from the calculations to ensure that no individual judge can have too much influence over an athlete's score. When I share with secondary audiences the example in Figure 7.19, where the lowest score from a student's grade was dropped, some challenge that if we drop the lowest then we should drop the highest as well, like they do in the Olympics. It's a fair statement. If we apply the idea of dropping *both* the highest and the lowest scores and then attempt to find the mean, we get the results for Kristen and Brittany shown in Figure 7.20.

By dropping both the highest and lowest scores, the impact on the final grade is much less than dropping only the lowest when a zero was calculated. The zero was, and always will be, so disproportionate mathematically to the other scores. The impact of the zero is much less significant on the final grade if we drop both the highest and lowest scores. We now add a minus to their grades of A and C, respectively, which perhaps offers the kind of truthfulness grading parameters call for.

Middle and high schools beginning to implement standards-based/standards-referenced grading on any level but still planning to average grades and include zeros could apply this example of dropping both the highest and lowest scores. Schools would then at least be closer to having more accurate student grades based on proficiency of standards demonstration. However, it needs to once again be emphasized that it is the averaging of a student's attempts that often distorts any form of standards-based grading—not the zero alone.

CONCLUSION

Standards are what we expect of virtually everything we interact with in our lives. We count on minimum standards for food, sanitation, and behaviors of others. We must demand the same of our schools in all that they do for the future thinkers and leaders of our country. Grading practices must be held to acceptable standards. This chapter outlined strategies and practices teachers and course teams can implement immediately that will lead to more standards-based/standards-referenced grading without abandoning letter grades. Each one asks teachers to determine versus calculate final grades.

Figure 7.19 Grading Example Dropping Lowest Score

	Assessment							Mean or average	Initial letter grade	New mean or average (drop lowest)	New letter grade
	1	2	3	4	5	6	7				
Brittany	90	0	85	95	90	100	95	79	C	92.5	A
Kristen	65	0	70	73	70	78	85	63	F	73.5	C

100–90: A, 89–80: B, 79–70: C, 69–65: D, 64–0: F

Figure 7.20 Grading Example Dropping Both Lowest and Highest Scores

	Assessment							Mean or average	Initial letter grade	New mean/ average (drop lowest only)	First new letter grade	New mean/ average (drop lowest and highest)	Final new grade
	1	2	3	4	5	6	7						
Brittany	90	0	85	95	90	100	95	79	C	92.5	A	91.0	A–
Kristen	65	0	70	73	70	78	85	63	F	72.3	C	71.2	C–

100–90: A, 89–80: B, 79–70: C, 69–65: D, 64–0: F

Figure 7.21   Summary of Standards-Based Grading Strategies and Practices

	Strategies				
	Focus on Academic Standards	**Implement Mastery Grading**	**Minimize What Is Actually Graded**	**Ensure Accurate Weighting**	**Eradicate the Average**
Practices	Grading only priority standards and learning targets Spiraling of Common Core (learning progressions) Selection syllabus	Selection syllabus Training assignments	Training assignments Spiraling and learning targets Selection syllabus	Selection syllabus Depth of knowledge levels Spiraling and learning targets	J-curve grading Dropping low scores (or low and high scores)

KEY POINTS

1. The evidence tells us that standards-based report cards and standards-based reporting of grades equates to higher levels of student achievement than more traditional reporting of letter grades alone.

2. At times, moving to a complete or even modified standards-based report card is not an option for some schools because of cost, time needed for professional development, and other factors.

3. Schools can implement standards-based/standards-referenced grading strategies that guide teachers in implementing classroom grading practices that will increase the amount of standards-based/standards-referenced grading. This can be done without an overhaul of the current report card or moving to a standards-based reporting card.

4. From school-based grading strategies, specific grading practices that can lead to more standards-based/standards-referenced grading (without the need to abandon the letter grade) are developing a selection syllabus, eradicating the average, using J-curve grading, using Common Core spiraling and learning progressions as guides for weighting assignments and tasks, and applying weighting of grades for higher levels of depth of knowledge demonstration.

5. Additional weight in grades can and should occur when demonstrations of higher levels of rigor do as well.

REFLECTION QUESTIONS

1. How can you ensure grades represent how students demonstrate mastery of standards regardless of your school's overall reporting method?

2. How could you increase the amount of mastery grading in your school, department, team, or classroom immediately?

3. What units, tasks, or assignments lend themselves to mastery grading more than others?

4. How can mastery grading become an approach to better teach resilience in college and life readiness?

5. How can you begin to apply more effective feedback for less-than-proficient work instead of scoring with low points?

6. Which classes currently grade on some form of a J-curve model? How can other classes emulate their grading practice?

7. How could you offer students a high level of depth-of-knowledge task for grade weighting on an upcoming unit of study?

PART IV

Elements for Successful Implementation

Determining What (Could) Change 8

In their masterful work *Switch: How to Change Things When Change Is Hard,* Chip and Dan Heath (2010) provide readers with simple and evidence-based tips for getting humans to accept the need to change our behaviors. One tactic they refer to often is to shrink the change by breaking it down into smaller and more manageable parts so the modification does not appear to be insurmountable. The less people are worried about the size of the change, the more likely they are to give it a chance.

The same simple idea can be applied to making sure middle and high school teachers and parents of their students are aware of aspects in the current grading system and practices that are *not* going change. When the discussion about changing grading practices begins, some people perceive that this will mean the abandonment of every current policy and practice related to how grades are determined, calculated, and distributed to students. This perception and fear can build unnecessary anger and backlash if schools don't address early on what will still be their *grading givens.* By determining early what grading related changes are *not* on the table for discussion, there is a strong possibility to minimize some initial pushback related to the discussion as a whole.

Think back to the example of 10-year-old Jack who had the cavity (Chapter 5). His dad knew that Jack needed to become more consistent with brushing his teeth, and toothbrushes in the downstairs bathroom were only part of the solution. He provided Jack with a challenge that had incentives built in. He gave Jack a punch card with 20 punch points. He told Jack he or his mother would punch a spot on the card every time Jack brushed his teeth during the school week (Monday morning to Friday evening). If Jack got to 18 punches in a week, he would earn an increase in his allowance. He got excited at the chance. When his Dad also told him if he had less than 15 by Friday night that he would be grounded for the weekend, Jack's excitement changed to feeling defeated. He was less confident of reaching 15, let alone 18, and 14 or less brought a very undesirable consequence. Jack's dad knew that if Jack got to 15, that was brushing three times per day—more than what the dentist said would remedy the problem. He also knew that when Jack got close to 15, the desire to get to 18 and earn the extra $5 would be good motivation.

On the first Monday morning of the challenge, when Jack got his punch card, his dad started him with 2 free punches. Jack still had to get to 18, but this was actually now only 16. Jack's confidence jumped as he ran into the bathroom to get to 3 before the week really even started. The change that seemed hard had been shrunk to appear much more manageable. Jack met his goal every week, and although his dad gave out over $250 in extra allowances over the course of a year, he saved money on dentist bills and instilled a health life habit in his son.

DETERMINING GRADING GIVENS

Middle and high schools can employ the same strategy when they are going to engage in discussions with teachers and parents about grading changes. School leaders will have much better success at initial and long-term implementation of adjustments in grading practices if they *shrink the change*. They do this by first establishing their grading givens. These are current grading policies or practices at the classroom level that are not going to change anytime soon. This allows everyone to feel more at ease knowing that whatever changes are going to take place, certain decisions are currently not on the table.

Figure 8.1   Grading Givens

Examples of secondary grading givens

1. There will still be letter grades and report cards.
2. We will still recognize excellence: honor roll, National Honor Society, etc.
3. We will maintain the current system of grade point averages and class ranking.
4. Teachers will have the final say in grade decisions.
5. Homework will still be an accepted practice, and at least some will count toward grades.

Reasons for determining your grading givens

1. There is currently not enough evidence in the literature to support change.
2. There are significant logistical roadblocks to change.
3. The school culture is not ready to tackle all aspects of specific grading changes. (Some givens can be tabled for later discussion that would be in the school or district's best interest.)

Secondary schools and districts can help teachers know what aspects of grading freedom in their classrooms they are not going to lose by determining and communicating grading givens early. This alone can move grading discussions away from defensiveness toward reasonable dialogue.

Activity 8.1: Determining Your Grading Givens

List some possible grading decisions that currently are not on the table for change in your school or district. What roadblocks to change would be removed by taking these givens out of the discussion?

Your school's current grading givens	Reasons for having them (lack of research, current logistics, more time and discussion needed, etc.)

Vignette: Part 1

Westeast School District in lower-upstate middle America wasn't sure where it was going: directionally or with some of its grading decisions related to grading policy and practice changes. The district had one sixth-grade center, two traditional junior high schools made up of seventh and eighth grades, and one high school of ninth through twelfth grades. The high school had about 1,600 students.

In February 2011, Superintendent Rick Barnes determined it was time to make some changes in grading policies and practices. Rick commissioned a broad-based grading task force made up of students, parents, administrators, teachers, and members of the community at large. They were charged with gathering research on best practices and surveying all stakeholders regarding their beliefs, feelings, and opinions about current grading structures in the four secondary schools. They utilized several listening posts to offer all constituents a chance to share their thoughts and ideas in person. Once these were complete and data were collected, the task force planned to meet twice monthly to examine evidence, facilitate discussions, and make recommendations to the school board about changes to the current grading structure in Westeast schools by the end of the 2013 calendar year. This allowed the task force two full years to be thorough and intentional in any recommendations they would make to the board.

March–May 2011

During the first task force meetings, the group determined the district's grading givens: what was not going to change, at least for the next two school years. This allowed the district to revisit these again in 24 months, but teachers could feel less anxious about the change knowing these at least would stay steady for now. The group reviewed all information from surveys, listening posts, and other meetings with teacher representatives from all four schools. They determined the grading givens. These were posted on the district website as well as the website for each school to allow for clear communication to all stakeholders heading into the summer break.

Grading Givens for Westeast Schools for the Next 2 Years

1. *Letter grades will stay as the basic structure for reporting student achievement.*

2. *Report cards will still be distributed, with a few changes in distribution. They will now go home (email and hard copy) every 6 weeks versus every 9 weeks. (Every 3 weeks an emailed progress report will go out to all parents unless they opt for a hard copy to be mailed.)*

3. *Teachers will have the final decision for grades on report cards and transcripts.**

4. *Current honor roll recognition, GPAs, and method for choosing valedictorian/salutatorian would stay the same for the next year. A subcommittee was established to study possible changes to the current system for the 2012–2013 school year.***

*The committee noted to the board that there was a strong desire from both teachers and parents for more collaboration in grading decisions. This would be investigated throughout the coming year.

**There was strong sentiment that choosing one student as the ultimate academic winner (valedictorian) was perhaps not in the best interest of all Westeast. The task force did not feel they could make any recommendations for changes with class rank for the upcoming school year.

The task force planned to meet in the high school library on the first and third Thursday of each month starting in September. They would submit their notes after every meeting to the four school principals, to be shared with all faculty and staff members. This was to ensure full transparency and open, honest communication with all stakeholders.

Once your school or district's grading givens have been determined and communicated clearly to all necessary stakeholders, the school or district needs to move to discussion on deciding some of the larger considerations related to grading practice and policy changes: letter grades versus standards-based report cards or a hybrid version, how to include and report student progress on non-academic skills, and whether to keep the current system of valedictorian versus moving to high honors.

CRITICAL GRADING DECISION 1: LETTER GRADES VS. STANDARDS-BASED REPORT CARDS OR A HYBRID

Whether or not secondary schools should move to a standards-based report card (SBRC) is often a point of contention with many teachers and parents who've experienced only traditional A-B-C-D grading in their school careers. Moving to an SBRC should be an early grading given decision.

Determining what the letter grade really conveys is a crucial next decision for any middle or high school looking to transform its grading practices. How much of the letter grade is academics versus other important attributes such as collaboration and other college and career ready skills? Chapter 7 demonstrated that letter grades can become more standards based through school and classroom practices that focus specifically on reporting academic demonstration of standards. Guskey and Bailey (2010, p. 180) remind us, however, that a single letter grade simply cannot provide enough sufficient detail to give parents a clear picture of how their child is doing and what specific supports are needed.

I look forward to middle school parent conferences for my son Zachary (6), because based on current evidence, it is very possible his teacher will tell me he is disorganized, at times disrespectful, ignores deadlines, and is often lackadaisical in effort. I will then simply retort, "I know. I live with him. Please tell me what he knows about math!"

Secondary SBRC: No Easy Task

Guskey and Bailey's (2010) masterful work *Developing Standards-Based Report Cards* offers numerous concrete reasons in support of grade reporting that moves away from hodgepodge grading where teachers often combine student process, product, and progress into a single letter grade. Moving to an SBRC in secondary schools, while doable, is a difficult task. Schools must take into account the professional development needed for creation of the actual report card, the collaboration needed to determine standards to be reported, increased collaborative scoring and use of rubrics, and so on. These are all needed for any semblance of successful implementation.

Communication with members of the community also is a challenge for most schools. Most parents have been accustomed to a letter grade–based system for their whole lives, and misunderstanding the purpose of an SBRC can lead to incivility. I'm not advocating against secondary standards-based report cards, but I do recommend that school-level decision makers make the determination on whether to use them early in the discussion. If plans to move toward an SBRC are imminent, communicate with stakeholders often and clearly. For those who choose to make this change, *Developing Standards-Based Report Cards* (Guskey & Bailey, 2010) is an excellent resource.

Vignette: Part 2

When the Westeast grading task force reconvened in September 2011, they conducted a thorough review of the research related to best practices in grading while comparing findings to their existing grading polices and classroom grading practices. Two major issues surfaced about which they would need to made recommendations to the board during the coming year:

1. *If the current system for letter grades was not going to change, how would teachers communicate to parents and students about specific learning gaps and successes?*

2. *How would teachers report to parents about students' progress on important non-academic skills (responsibility, effort, homework completion, etc.)?*

The task force planned to tackle these one at a time.

September–October 2011

In their meetings during this time, the task force focused on survey data from parent and student groups. The evidence showed an overwhelming desire by both groups to maintain the current letter grade system (A-B-C-F; they had eliminated D several years earlier), but both groups felt the letter grade wasn't providing enough information about specific academic performance. Parents and students wanted more information and better feedback to know how to guide students to improving their performance. This was reflected in the research on evidence of best practices as well.

The task force felt there was not yet enough desire or structure in place to move the district to a more standards-based report card. Most task force members noted that current roadblocks included logistics to plan for professional development, time and collaboration to create the structure for the reporting system itself, and the level of communication needed to work with parents and students on understanding a new system like this. There was some strong feeling that if both quantity and clarity in communication with parents and students increased over time, a change to an SBRC might be possible in just one year's time. The task force agreed to have a subcommittee look into whether a pilot version of a standards-based report card could be implemented as a possible option for a few teams of teachers in the coming year. They used Guskey and Bailey's (2010, p. 24) work and recommendation to plan for this.

In the meantime, the task force agreed on a hybrid version of a standards-based report card. Teachers would write several handwritten comments to accompany letter grades; these would be related to specific behaviors they were seeing in students related to standards and skills in class as well as anything pertinent related to behaviors that were contributing positively or negatively to their progress. Teachers would be given an additional half-day of professional work time to complete their report card comments, which would be emailed to parents as well as attached to the report card and placed in students' permanent files and transcripts. The task force agreed to the following expectations for reporting to parents:

- *one or two paragraphs of narrative (more would signal the need for a parent conference)*
- *two or three specific feedback targets related to content and skills of the class*
- *one or two specific feedback targets related to behaviors and process criteria that would lead to success in the class*

Committee members provided this example of comments about a middle school science student:

Dave's grade of B directly reflects his proficiency of skill and concept mastery demonstration on the following units during this 6-week period: rocks and minerals, ocean currents, and weather patterns. Dave also continues to show mastery in two of the three core focus skills this semester: determining and testing hypotheses and writing informatively for all science reporting. His growth area for improvement during the next 6-week period is safety and accuracy in lab skills. Dave continues to engage well in class, although less time spent socializing before and at the beginning of class will help him know what's going on later during lab activities.

The committee made this recommendation to the board November 5, 2011, and scheduled their next meeting for the following Thursday.

Example Hybrid Report Card: Aurora Public Schools

Aurora Public Schools implemented a modified standards-based report card while maintaining traditional letter grades (see Appendix F on pages 276–277). The desire was to provide more and specific information to parents related to how academic letter grades were derived. The district provided some detail in its description of how academic performance levels led to determination of letter grades. For example, in English 9, Jack Jones received a C and a B in the first and second quarters, respectively. In quarter one, he needed more teacher support on benchmarks than he did in quarter two. While multiple standards were the focus for these quarters, the benchmarks and comments offer parents more specific feedback regarding his strengths when wrestling with complex texts and the stamina he is demonstrating leading to his success.

The district also created simple but specific criteria for reporting student proficiency around the process elements of effort, engagement, homework, and responsibility. While Jack met or exceeded expectations in all four of these areas in English 9, Physical Science, Integrated Algebra, and Geometry in quarter one, he needed improvement in engagement and responsibility in Geography, Word Processing, and French 1. Jack improved in all three classes in responsibility, which was defined as "Follows rules and directions; manages time; advocates for self." He moved from 2s to 3s in these areas in all classes.

Source: Used with permission from Aurora Public Schools.

Deciding whether current grade reporting in the form of letter grades will stay the same or be adjusted needs to be an early decision for any high school embarking on changing grading practice. Choosing between letter grades or standards-based report cards, as the examples above highlight, does not have to be an either-or decision, but it is still one that schools must agree on early in the change process.

Before moving on to Critical Grading Decision 2, please complete the first part of Activity 8.2 on pages 230–232.

CRITICAL GRADING DECISION 2: REPORTING STUDENT PROGRESS ON NON-ACADEMIC SKILLS SEPARATELY VS. COMBINING INTO ONE GRADE

Schools with and without grading task force committees often struggle to determine how best to include student progress related to non-academic skills (responsibility, work ethic, participation, effort, etc.) into student grades. Leaders in secondary schools need to tackle the issue head on and raise an important question that should lead to specific decisions: Is the letter grade an academic grade or not? If it is, then really *none* of these factors should be figured into a single letter grade (Guskey & Bailey, 2000, 2010; Marzano, 2006). The conversation should move to decisions about how these skills are going to be reported to students and parents related to their progress—not just averaged into the current academic grade. Affective behavioral skills such as homework completion, effort/work ethic, participation, and collaboration are often at the forefront of the discussion.

Too Worried About Effort and Work Habits

Sometimes well-intended teachers desire to include all factors of student performance and behavior into a final grade to make sure they are providing the most accurate picture possible. This can cause some teachers to lose their sense of direction and definition of terms. If letter grades are to be maintained while still using standards-based grading, even with more detail being provided to students, middle and high schools must remember the dangers of hodgepodge grading. If letter grades are to be the sole reporting mechanism, then some aspects of student performance simply cannot be included in the determination of the grade. The following is from an actual district grading policy:

> The purpose of the Effort/Work Habits grade is to communicate to parents/guardians and to the student how much effort the child is putting into the class and how well he/she is completing assignments. *Please remember that 10% of the academic grade is work habits.*

This is a perfect example of the school having good intentions and obviously trying to make its grades more understandable to parents and students. But we cannot ignore the oxymoron of having one tenth of an academic grade be based on *perceptions* of factors such as work ethic. This renders the grade reasonably untruthful if it is now called an academic grade.

Separate Academic and Work Ethic Skills

When middle and high school teachers separate reporting how students meet deadlines, collaborate, complete homework, participate, and so on from the academic letter grade, they significantly reduce the hodgepodge nature of their grades. Researchers have characterized this happy medium as essential for schools to have any level of standards-based grading (Guskey & Bailey, 2010; O'Connor, 2009, 2010; Reeves, 2011a; Wormelli, 2006). One fear that teachers have is that this will cause extra work. However, this is not always as true as some think. Guskey and Bailey (2010) note that

> providing separate grades or marks for product, process, and progress goals on a secondary report card offers an efficient and effective intermediate step. . . . It always seems to result in wonderful and highly professional conversations among teachers. (p. 156)

Perception of Homework Effort

Homework completion is a very common non-academic factor included in grades. Teachers often judge, inaccurately, student effort based on how much homework students complete and how long they take to do it (Jussim & Eccles, 1992). Many teachers believe that unless homework counts for points, students will not do it, and parents generally agree. Hattie (2008, p. 235) notes that many parents judge their children's schools by the quantity of homework students bring home.

Cathy Vatterott (2009), in her excellent book *Rethinking Homework: Best Practices That Support Diverse Needs* discusses the following five unexamined beliefs about homework, children, and learning and how those beliefs drive actions about traditional grading of homework (see also Figure 8.2).

1. The role of the school is to extend learning beyond the classroom.

2. Intellectual activity is intrinsically more valuable than non-intellectual activity.

3. Homework teaches responsibility.

4. Lots of homework is a sign of a rigorous curriculum.

5. Good teachers give homework; good students do their homework.

Here are a few arguments *against* including homework grading (at any level that would distort grades) as part of a district's policies:

1. **Evidence:** To be effective, homework should be a risk-free chance to experiment with new skills (Carr & Farr, 2000; Marzano, 2006; O'Connor, 2009).

2. **Who did the homework?** Very often teachers lament defending the decision of whether or not to grade homework. They state that as a student turns in completed homework, they never can be 100% assured that the student did it independently.

Figure 8.2   Beliefs About Homework and Challenges to Them

Beliefs	Challenges to these beliefs being 100% true
1	If learning occurred from simply assigning work, the role of the teacher would be diminished, if not potentially eliminated.
2	Many experts tell us that a balance of leisure, family time, and work are essential for physical and mental health.
3	Not doing homework will not cause us to skip jury duty, fail to file taxes, or never arrive to work on time.
4	Larry Ainsworth and Heidi Hayes Jacobs would make this a strong recommendation for implementation in their curriculum models versus the strong recommendation to avoid it. LA and HHJ would make a strong recommendation that quality of work and evidence produce and purposeful practice in their curriculum models vs. recommending simply the quantity of any work students complete.
5	Good is relative. Many effective teachers assign necessary practice work for students, and many ineffective ones do not.

3. **Potential abuse and minimizing student choice:** The High School Survey for Student Engagement data are clear that irrelevant work is a major reason for lack of student engagement and high levels of student boredom in high school classrooms, and a strong "motivator" for students to start considering dropping out (Yazzie-Mintz, 2010). Having non-academic factors account for more than 10% of the total grade significantly diminishes student voice for how the grade is earned. O'Connor (2009, p. 128) quotes Patterson's (2003) response about why teachers grade homework: "Because it's the only leverage they have to get students to do it."

4. **Poor use of assessment for learning:** If students are not ready to apply skills and concepts taught in class at the independent level, then teachers need to allow for guided practice. Hattie (2008, p. 207) notes that during guided practice, a specific step in direct instruction ($d = 0.59$), it is essential that students practice doing it right so the teacher can gauge when the students understand before they start to practice. This is the heart of formative assessment. Teachers must allow for students to perform at the independent level on a task before assessing them at all for a grade.

There are, however, reasons *for* including homework grading (at some level less than 10%) as part of district policies:

1. **Evidence:** Homework can and does have a positive effect on achievement, especially for middle and high school students (Cooper, 1989; Hattie, 2008). In 1989, Cooper found higher effects for science and social studies, followed by English and then math.

2. **Common sense:** Time spent on a task matters, especially if deliberate practice is taking place. Students need effective teacher feedback to grow and develop skills, but grading homework alone should not be confused as effective feedback. Grading some aspects of homework will not render grades completely inaccurate and may provide a rationale for some students to put forth necessary effort to do the work.

Policy Application

The School District of Waukesha, Wisconsin, published clear grading guidelines for teachers in its district policy in 2007 and again in 2009. The policy strategies included detailed evidence from research that was conducted as the district formed the grading policy.

The policy outlined clear expectations related to how homework should be used in Waukesha classrooms. It defined four types of homework:

- **Homework for practice:** Should occur when concepts taught in class can be practiced and expanded upon through homework to enrich students' knowledge base and inform their continued learning
- **Homework as preparation for learning:** An opportunity for students to share prior and background knowledge and to build new information into their long-term memory and later retrieval of meaningful information
- **Homework as an extension of learning:** Serves to solidify concepts taught in the classroom and provides students with an opportunity to expand on the learning they participated in during class
- **Homework as true assessment:** Homework used as a true assessment of learning and for learning to shape instruction. (The policy specifically stated that the word *assessment* should not require teachers to assign a grade, but if homework is graded, it should be included along with other pieces of student evidence.)

The January 2007 policy stated, "Best practice documents indicate that homework for practice or preparation should not include more than 10% of the grade."

In September 2009, the policy was updated. The district used evidence to build an exemplary model of a policy for grading practice expectations for all classrooms in Waukesha. The policy included specific expected practices for teachers related to homework:

- Teachers should let students know when homework is for practice or assessment.
- Homework should be directly related to instructional objectives and concepts.
- Homework should be viewed as formative, allowing for practice of new skills and knowledge without penalty.

Source: Used with permission from School District of Waukesha.

Vignette: Part 3

November 2011

Westeast reconvened its grading task force in November to tackle the final two issues: how much homework could count toward the letter grade and how progress on other non-academic skills would be reported to parents. After reviewing the research on best practices and survey data responses from students, teachers, and parents, the task force agreed on recommendations that they would make to the board.

Homework Recommendations

The task force recommended that the weight of homework in overall grading should decrease and be capped. Based on solid evidence, they considered recommending the elimination of homework being included as part of any student's grade. They felt, however, that it would cause far too much backlash from teachers. The task force compromised by not eliminating grading of homework completely but minimizing its potential for making grades untruthful. Their recommendation summary stated, "Homework completion alone should never prohibit a student from passing a course, nor should a student's grade become inflated due to accumulating an inordinate amount of points from homework or classwork completed with support." The cap on the maximum percentage of homework counting toward a grade would come in phases over the coming years. The task force felt that since schools did not currently have consistent policies, teachers would need time to adapt and experiment with how to adjust their classroom practices regarding homework.

The task force recommended the following:

- *Starting the spring semester of 2012, no more than 15% of a student's grade in any course could be counted from homework in Westeast secondary classrooms.*
- *In the fall of 2012, this cap would be reduced to 10%.*
- *In the spring of 2013, the cap would be reduced to 5%.*

Their final charge was how to report student progress on non-academic skills to parents. The task force agreed that teachers' use of a rubric for parents and students to refer to would provide more consistency across schools and classrooms. A 4-3-2-1 system was recommended to the board, which would be added to the report card in the areas of participation, meeting deadlines, homework, and collaboration. The committee felt the term responsibility was far too subjective to be applied across classrooms.

Also, the group felt that while collaboration was an important 21st century skill that all students needed for success in life, collaboration might look very

> *different from one classroom to the next and across subject areas. Collaboration between students was just as important as between student and teacher. Many Westeast teachers used blogs and other Internet-based tools for students to collaborate after school hours with them and with other students. Proficient growth in collaboration skills could be observed by teachers' classroom discussions, in group class work and projects, and through online communiqués.*
>
> *Westeast was also in a state that had adopted the Common Core State Standards. The Common Core speaking and listening standards (SLS) would be implemented in all classrooms and could be used for academic grading purposes in the coming year. The task force recommended that course professional learning communities collaborate and determine consistent success criteria for students to meet learning targets for specific activities and projects aligned with the SLS. (See Appendix D for an example of grading using the SLS.) It was recommended that some teachers and departments consider piloting this in the spring of 2012, as it would not become policy for expected practice and implementation districtwide until the start of the 2012–2013 school year.*
>
> *Figure 8.3 shows the draft rubric the task force submitted to the school board.*

Before moving on to Critical Grading Decision 3, please complete the second part of Activity 8.2 on pages 230–232.

CRITICAL GRADING DECISION 3: KEEPING VALEDICTORIAN VS. MOVING TO HIGH HONORS

Another important grading decision high schools must wrestle with is whether to keep their current grade point average (GPA) ranking systems. These will determine how to address what is an emotional topic at most secondary schools: the selection of a valedictorian and salutatorian.

Few students, parents, teachers, or community members have any recollection of *not* recognizing the top one or two students on commencement day with honors, speeches, and so on. My dear mother-in-law, Nancy, talks of my wife's anguish from coming up just short of being #1 in her class. Nancy also still expresses overwhelming pride when she recollects watching her daughter offer the salutatorian speech at commencement. (Yes, my wife is much smarter than I am!) The notion that a high school would not recognize the one student with the highest GPA is blasphemous to some and intriguing to others.

Doesn't Resemble College

Preparation for college is often the filter for many decisions made about how high schools operate. However, having one student recognized

Figure 8.3 Westeast District Process Skills Rubric to Be Included on or With Report Card

Participation	Meeting deadlines	Homework	Collaboration (These were left more subjective due to each class having different levels of collaboration possibilities)
4: Contributes significantly; positively impacts other students' learning	4: Work is always on time or exceeds deadlines	4: All assignments are turned in on time	4: Exceeds collaboration standards (benefits other students)
3: Consistently participates and contributes to class	3: Work is consistently on time (less than 10% of assignments are late)	3: No more than two homework assignments are missed	3: Meets collaboration standards of the class
2: Participation is sporadic	2: Work is often handed in past assigned deadlines	2: Three to five homework assignments are missed	2: Is inconsistent related to the collaborative aspect of the class
1: Participation is extremely limited or reduces learning opportunities for others	1: Work is rarely if ever completed within time guidelines	1: Five or more homework assignments are missed	1: Diminishes others' learning opportunities because of a lack of proper collaborative skills

Note: The committee felt this alone could take care of homework and teachers' need to include more weight in the final letter grade.

above all others by perhaps a 10,000th of a decimal point difference in her or his final GPA is incongruent with anything that will happen at the university level. True, some colleges share how students in a particular program compare to their peers in that tract, but few have a race in which only one student wins. Most colleges recognize levels of high achievement such as magna cum laude, summa cum laude, and cum laude. They recognize the excellence of everyone who achieves above a common criterion-based reference point. They do not set the bar in relation to how well someone performed compared to other students.

High schools and districts should deliberate around several key considerations if they are looking at moving away from their current ranking system. These include current college acceptance criteria, state-level benefits for students, impact on student decision making, and community mores and traditions.

Current college acceptance criteria. The overall ranking of a student's GPA in relationship to his or her peers has become greatly reduced in selection criteria for many colleges and universities. In 2013, the National Association for College Admission Counseling (NACAC) submitted its ranking of top factor considerations for college acceptance, summarized in Figure 8.4.

According to NACAC (2013), the quality of the education students have received is most important when it comes to accepting incoming students. In surveys administered by NACAC, only 19% of colleges placed considerable importance on class rank, compared to 42% in 1993. "[The valedictorian title is] a strong indication of an academically talented student, but the honor is losing some of its luster," says Michael Reilly, executive director of the Washington-based American Association of Collegiate Registrars and Admissions Officers (quoted in Kurutz, 2013).

State-level benefits for students. Students' class rank can significantly influence their acceptance and tuition aid at many state-funded universities. For example, state-resident students in the top 10% of their graduating class receive free tuition at the University of Alaska. In Texas, high school students in the top 10% of their graduating class are promised admission to the state school of their choice, excluding the University of Texas (UT). (UT allocates only 75% of its incoming freshman class seats to students in the top 8%.) Texas high schools that would abandon completely their GPA ranking system would probably garner more consternation than did a truth-in-grading law (see this book's Introduction), and rightfully so. Each school and system should look at these types of ramifications before completely eliminating their current GPA ranking system.

Impact on student decision making. The ranking system for valedictorian in most high schools is typically based on a mathematical formula that is inherently vague and ambiguous. This frequently promotes unnecessary competition between students. My wife still talks about decisions she made or didn't make related to the courses she took in an effort to keep up with her closest valedictorian competitor. High

Figure 8.4   Top Factors for College Acceptance

Considerably important	Moderately important
1. College prep courses 2. Strength of high school curriculum 3. College prep course grades 4. Standardized test scores 5. Overall grade point average	6. Admissions essay 7. Letters of recommendation 8. Demonstrated interest in the school 9. Class rank 10. Extracurricular commitment

school students every year divert their own path or desires for course selection in an effort to beat the system and maybe just one other student. In countless cases, students stress over courses they should take, many that are unrelated to their desires or strengths but would impact their GPA related to competition with their peers for the top spot. Students close to the top spot will throw their own game to preserve a high GPA. Instead of taking classes that are more challenging and that will allow them to grow and develop skills, they select classes at lower levels of rigor to maintain their stellar GPAs. Students are using calculus formulas to determine the best path to the highest possible GPA when they are not even taking calculus. (Weighted grades can prevent some of this; see the discussion of weighted grades Chapter 7.)

Community mores and traditions. High schools adjusting from valedictorian to a more college-based, high honors approach, in which more students are recognized for excellence, often find that parents raise the most questions. These usually come from parents who have envisioned their son or daughter wearing the sash and addressing the school and community as the top scholar. Based on the amount of pushback on the issue, schools may decide that even engaging in the conversation is too difficult. Tradition, as we have learned, is so hard to change. Schools that want to honor many students for outstanding academic success over their 4-year career instead of recognizing one student above the rest might not be able to make that change in some communities, at least not at this time.

Some Adjusting, Some Eliminating

The long-honored tradition of naming a valedictorian *is* starting to lose its value in many communities, which is a good thing, as college admission counselors have informed us. Instead of eliminating valedictorian altogether, some schools have adjusted how the top-rated student is selected, when she or he is selected, and if there may be more than one. Schools must remember that when they are adjusting the valedictorian selection process, or possibly eliminating it, parents, teachers, students, and community members must be involved in the discussion.

When a practice based on tradition is hurting achievement, school and community leaders must abandon tradition. New Trier Township High School, near Chicago, eradicated its student ranking system in 2008. Teachers and officials were seeing academically solid college-bound seniors, with diverse experiences and virtually flawless academic records, being ranked lower than 50 of around 1,000 students. Counselors and parents believed this was negatively and unjustly impacting their college admissions process. The school found college admissions officers were taking a longer

224 • Part IV   Elements for Successful Implementation

look at the entire body of work that students had produced over their high school careers after it eliminated class rank. This made that application process much more objective. New Trier students are aware of their own grade point averages but not those of their peers. All students wanting to deliver the keynote at commencement can submit an application to do so ("Valedictorian, You're Retired," 2012).

When traditions are too hard to break, then adjusting them is the next best option. Wickenburg High School, near Phoenix, decided that valedictorian was a tradition that was so dear to the community that it could not just abandon. In 2012, the school devised a complicated new formula that took up several pages in the school handbook. Knowing that the race for valedictorian causes some students to shut down in their last semester after the final calculations are determined, leading to senioritis in top students, the school now factors in grades from the final semester. Students are unaware of each other's grade point average, just like at New Trier. Students and parents do not find out who actually wins until just before graduation (Wang, 2012).

Finally, it is not the ranking differences between students that many parents and even students care about. Who provides the commencement speech is really the tradition many cling to. North Side College Prep High School, an academically competitive school in the Chicago Public School System, eliminated class rankings in 2006 but still awards one student with the title of valedictorian. Principal Barry Rodgers commented on why the school still determines a valedictorian based on grades: "I think we still have to acknowledge those students who have demonstrated an incredible amount of effort and scholarship. We have a unique environment where it's very success-driven" (quoted in Fergus, 2008).

Before moving on, please complete the third part of Activity 8.2 on pages 230–232.

Case Study: Tri-Creek Schools

Dr. Deb Howe became superintendent of Tri-Creek Schools, in northwest Indiana, in 2011. She was determined to take a school system that had success in many areas and move it from *good* to *great*. She knew that grading practices driven by guiding policies was one of the areas in which she needed to improve.

Dr. Howe formed a grading task force in the fall of 2012 to first study possible changes to determining and reporting grades in Tri-Creek Schools. She asked me to serve as the group facilitator during the school year to help guide their study and discussions that would ultimately lead to making recommendations to the Tri-Creek

School Board. Dr. Howe wanted to ensure there was diversity in thought as well as perspective as we began to address issues that would impact the district in many ways.

The task force of about 20 people included parents, students, teachers, a sitting school board member, and individuals from the community at large. Survey data related to beliefs and opinions about grading were collected from all certificated members of the teaching staff, a large population of students, as well as members of the community. Several listening posts were held to allow any stakeholder in Tri-Creek Schools to have her or his thoughts heard as well as ask any specific questions. The task force convened in early September. The first few meetings involved studying the evidence from the surveys and listening posts and reviewing pertinent research evidence related to effective grading practices.

October

The task force decided to focus first on addressing issues related to grading practices at Lowell High School. Dr. Howe knew that grading changes at the high school would often have the greatest immediate impact on both teachers and students. She didn't charge the group, or me, to go after the low-hanging fruit. The task force concluded right away that there were two grading decisions that needed to be determined for Lowell High School:

1. **Weighted grades:** Move to using them or stay with the current system, which did not weight honors or AP courses.

2. **Valedictorian/salutatorian system**: Maintain the current GPA ranking system or move to a more high honors recognition.

Parameter Created: Incentivize Grades

The committee began by creating parameters for any recommendations that would eventually be made to the Tri-Creek School Board.

Parameter	Consideration
Consider the best interest of all Tri-Creek students	Board members, teachers, parents, and even students on the task force would at times be considering how decisions made would impact them individually, or from the perspective of one person or an anecdotal example. The task force would have to consider how its recommendations to the board would impact the vast majority of Lowell High School (Tri-Creek) students.

(Continued)

(Continued)

Parameter	Consideration
Incentivize grades	Grading decisions should promote challenging students to higher levels of effort, achievement, learning, and excellence. Grading policies and practices should not lead students to decide to take easier and less rigorous routes.
Embed a college- and career-ready mind-set	Preparing students for success in life beyond Lowell High School was a paramount consideration for the task force. Grading decisions needed to ensure students were receiving the type of feedback for learning and growth necessary to allow them to be successful long after Grade 12.

Weighted Grades

Lowell High School did not weight more rigorous courses, in terms of the GPA value, prior to the start of the 2012–2013 school year. Students received the same GPA weight for standard courses like English 12 as they did for more rigorous courses like Honors English 12 or AP English 12. Several task force members stated they had personally heard Lowell students mention they were trying to maintain a 4.0 GPA by not taking more rigorous classes. There was also no weight value or incentive for students taking AP courses to sit for AP exams. Students were opting out of these and other external assessments even when teacher input about their course work indicated these students would likely do very well. Not having a weighted grading system was creating a legion of Lowell High School students playing opossum with their GPAs.

Valedictorian or High Honors?

The task force decided that if embedding a mind-set of college and career readiness was a parameter for their decisions, the Tri-Creek/Lowell High School grading and honoring academic success system should align more tightly with those of universities. Any student earning a 4.0 was named valedictorian. These were students who had received all As from their freshman year through the first semester of their senior year (second-semester Grade 12 GPAs were not factored in). The previous school year, Lowell had several valedictorians. The perception was it had watered down its grading system and lowered expectations, but this was not at all the case. More truthfully, Lowell just had not increased incentives for students to attempt more rigor for fear of losing their 4.0 status since some of their peers might not. Weighted grades and the valedictorian decisions were parallel.

October–May

Authentic Meetings Over Time

I facilitated nine evening meetings with the task force between October and May. The need for multiple meetings was critical, as it allowed the group to have deep discussion and the ability to listen and reflect on opposing viewpoints related to any possible changes. The task force looked earnestly from multiple perspectives at what the impact would be for any decisions to be made.

The group focused first on determining whether and how weighted grades were going to be recommended. One evening the group used authentic examples, calculating the GPAs of current Lowell High School students who were taking AP or honors courses to see what their new or adjusted GPA would be with proposed changes in weighting grades. The group did this for multiple situations and examples to ensure an outlier didn't cloud the parameter of being in the best interest of all students.

Replicating the Desired State

Lowell High School students, the task force believed firmly, had the ability to achieve at much higher than current levels. The task force compared weighted grading formulas from high schools that were similar in size and demographics as well as those that had academic achievement levels that Lowell was striving for. They looked at schools meeting these criteria both locally and across the state before making any final decisions. The task force felt that replicating the practices those schools were implementing should be a strong consideration.

Decisions: Implementation Over Time

Weighted Grades

In May 2013, the task force recommended to the school board that weighted grades should be used for all AP and honors courses at Lowell High School. These would be for scholarship purposes only for the classes of 2014, 2015, and 2016 (the current ninth, tenth, and eleventh graders). Beginning with the class of 2017 (incoming freshman), weighted grades would apply to students' entire GPAs and all other purposes. AP courses would receive an additional 1.0 weight, while dual-credit courses and honors courses would get an added 0.5. Additionally, students must earn a grade of C or higher in the class to have the weight added to their GPA and transcripts.

Honors/Ranking System

Finally, whether to keep the current valediction/salutatorian honoring system was now on the table. The task force determined that if weighted grades were going to be recommended to the board, the following questions needed to be answered:

(Continued)

(Continued)

1. Should the honors system at Lowell High School encourage a mad-dash race, as many others school have, where students overextend themselves by taking too many rigorous courses only to keep up with a few specific peers?

2. Would some students still not take an AP or rigorous course, even with the weight to be added, fearing the increased rigor in the honors classes? Would they determine that playing it safe by taking regular classes was the better route for achieving a high GPA? (Thus back to the same problem the task force felt they currently had.)

The task force determined that some of these questions would need to be answered over time and that guidance counselors would play a critical role. They would need to be more intentional in their communication with parents and academically capable students about the benefits, academically as well as in terms of GPA weight, of taking honors and AP courses. The group's recommendation to the board was that starting with the class of 2015 (the following year's juniors), students would be recognized with the distinctions of summa cum laude, magna cum laude, and cum laude in addition to naming valedictorians and salutatorians for the next three years (June 2014, 2015, 2016). Students would need to meet both GPA and credit requirements for distinction. The classes of 2017 and beyond would no longer have valedictorian and salutatorian designations, only the honors distinctions.

The task force felt it was a simple decision to make the change occur over time as opposed to abruptly. First, school leaders would need time to engage in discussion and provide explanations with all stakeholders (parents, students, and the community). Lowell High School's tradition of the keynote speaker being the student whose GPA was the highest of everyone in his or her class could not be changed overnight. Also, and maybe more important, task force members felt that for the upcoming fall class of juniors and seniors, it would be totally unfair to change the rules of the game this late into it. A large number of students were in the running for these two distinct honors and had made course selection and other decisions based on. It simply would not be prudent to have the rules of the game change on them mid-stream.[1]

Lynne Haberlin, director of innovations in learning for Tri-Creek, who headed up the task force, said that the decisions were made "in an effort to have a system that would allow Lowell High School to honor more students who have worked hard and taken rigorous courses. It in no way waters down the challenges or rigor; if anything just the opposite. This now paves the way for other important policies and practices we hope to begin to study and implement in our grading system in the coming years" (quoted in Csepiga, 2013).

---

[1] Used with permission from Dr. Deb Howe of Tri Creek Schools.

CONCLUSION

Secondary schools, or any schools for that matter, embarking on making any significant changes in their grading systems need to determine their *grading givens* early in the process. This will prove to be essential in moving discussions and dialogue forward for effective changes to grading policy and practice. Each school must then determine key issues for possible change. Major topics could include whether to move to a standards-based reporting system, how homework will be included in the grade, or if traditions like the valedictorian race are in the best interest of their students. There are few wrong answers to these questions. Communicating early to all stakeholders and having well-established grading parameters can go a long way to making decisions that will lead to more effective grading in middle and high schools.

KEY IDEAS

1. Once individuals know what will not change, they may be much more amenable to discussion about what can and will.

2. Secondary schools would be well served by determining their grading givens before moving on to what will or might change.

3. Using letter grades versus standards-based report cards, determining how homework is calculated into grades, deciding how progress on non-academic skills will be reported, and discussing whether to keep the current student GPA ranking system are big issues all middle and high schools need to determine early in the process of changing grading policy and practice.

REFLECTION QUESTIONS

1. What are some of your school's grading givens? Why are they *givens?*

2. Where is your school related to the discussion of keeping the current letter grade system versus any form of a standards-based report card?

3. How is homework (use, grading, etc.) handled at your school? Are practices and policies consistently applied across classrooms?

Activity 8.2: Current Reality and Next Steps for Critical School or District Grading Decisions

Decision	Guiding questions	Answers or current reality	Long-term steps (4–9 months)
Decision 1: Letter grades vs. standards-based report cards or a hybrid	Do we have the interest, desire, and need to move to a standards-based reporting system?		
	What external evidence do we have (from neighboring districts)? What can we find out about what they are using?		
	If we are unsure, should we plan to study this in the coming year?		
	How will we determine capacity?		
	Would we consider a pilot?		
Decision 2: How much to include but also report to parents about student progress on non-academic skills	What is currently in place in our existing policy for including non-academic factors such as effort, work ethic, homework, etc.?		
	Do we cap the amount that homework can count toward grades?		

Decision	Guiding questions	Answers or current reality	Long-term steps (4–9 months)
	If not, should we? If yes, are we satisfied with the current cap?		
	If we have a cap, is it currently being consistently applied across classrooms?		
	How do we currently communicate student progress on non-academic skills? How much of these are currently being included in determining grades?		
	How might we begin to create a plan to better communicate student progress in these areas?		
Decision 3: Keeping valedictorian vs. moving to high honors	How can we incentivize more students to reach their highest potential?		
	What are other schools in our area or around the state that are like us doing?		
	What are other schools that have the academic success we aspire to have across the state doing?		

(Continued)

(Continued)

Decision	Guiding questions	Answers or current reality	Long-term steps (4–9 months)
	What does our community believe?		
	What do students believe?		
	If we were to move away from having one valedictorian, what might our system look like (e.g., cut-off GPAs)?		
	How would we determine who offers speeches at commencement?		
	If we move toward high honors, how should we phase it in for students who are in the middle of the game?		

Implementation

*Setting Up and Conducting
Action Research*

The truth shall set you free! We have all heard that phrase uttered—most of us many times. We all have experienced times when the truth hurt, maybe when we received honest bad news from someone that our performance in an area of our life was less than stellar. Whether the news is pleasant or not, finding out the truth is usually empowering.

International author and success coach Anthony Robins (1996), in his best-selling book and audio series *Personal Power II: The Driving Force,* says if we try something and it doesn't work, then we get an education. We succeed in life when we can make distinctions from these mistakes to know what to do differently next time. For a time, I, like many teachers, didn't want to try new grading practices in my classroom because I was afraid they might not work. I also, like many teachers, didn't want to try new grading practices in my classroom because I was afraid of the truth. That may be the way I was graded when I was a student, which led to the way I felt I should grade as a teacher, was wrong.

WHY ACTION RESEARCH

When we conduct experiments to find out the truth about something, there is a risk. The results might not validate our beliefs. At the same time, beliefs we have that might not be shared by others can be proven correct. Action research in teachers' classrooms needs to be a common practice.

The ability to gain insights as to what works and doesn't work is crucial for teachers to grow and develop. Action research into grading has not been as common in most middle and high school classrooms as it should. Two possible reasons for this are that teachers have perceptions that external investigations around grading don't apply to them and that they haven't been as intentional as they could be at being evaluators of their craft. Secondary schools where teachers get past these two issues can take a significant bite out of the gap in the grading research.

External Research Perception

Educational research for many teachers takes on two head-butting proverbs. For many busy, hardworking teachers, published research in education often lacks an element that's important to them: "It doesn't include *our* kids." Many of the numerous studies regarding effectiveness of grading generalize findings across entire populations (Metz & Page, 2002). When school or district leaders have made noncollaborative mandates justified from only *reading* about grading research, teachers have most often been unwilling to implement them with any level of fidelity. Many teachers disbelieve the conclusions from grading studies because they do not feel they are applicable to their own students. Teachers then, by and large, are unlikely to apply the research in the first place—mandate changes noncollaboratively, and they will be even less likely to consider it. Mertler (2014) tells us, "Because of this . . . there is a real need for the increased practice of teacher-initiated, classroom based action research" (p. 13).

The Need to Be Evaluators

In *Visible Learning for Teachers: Maximizing Impact on Learning,* Hattie (2012) introduces readers to the critical importance that adult beliefs about teaching and learning have an impact on student learning. He calls these *mind frames.* These ways of thinking truly guide teachers and leaders in the approaches they take to reach all students (p. 160).

Figure 9.1 highlights Hattie's nine mind frames and a description of each. The first mind frame points out the importance of teachers above all being evaluators—not evaluators of other teachers' classrooms or job performance, but constant evaluators of how their own actions are specifically impacting student learning. Hattie (2012) tells us that teachers must constantly be searching to better "know thy impact." He offers teachers questions they can ask to guide their development of the mind frame of becoming a better evaluator:

- How do I know that this (strategy) is working?
- How can I compare *this* with *that?*
- What is the merit and worth of this influence on learning?
- What is the magnitude of the effect?
- Where have I seen this practice installed where it has produced effective results (which would convince me and my colleagues of the magnitude of the effects)? (p. 161)

When secondary teachers conduct action research related to new or adjusted grading practices in their classrooms, they have an opportunity to answer many of the above questions and become better evaluators. Teachers can also use these questions to gauge how their existing grading practices are impacting student achievement.

Addressing Gaps in Research

Finally, when teachers are encouraged and expected to conduct their own investigations to look at how adjusted grading practices impact student learners, existing gaps in the grading literature get smaller.

Figure 9.1   Visible Learning Mind Frames

Mind frame	Description
I am an evaluator.	**Teachers understand their fundamental task is to evaluate the effect of their teaching on student learning and achievement.**
I am a change agent.	Teachers understand the greatest impact relates to them doing what is needed to impact achievement. They will innovate to do so.
I talk about learning not teaching.	Professional discussions are about learning not teaching.
I see assessment as feedback.	Assessments of students provide information first to the adults on the effectiveness of their impact.
I engage in dialogue not monologue.	Teachers listen to the students' learning (their questions, ideas, successes, challenges) as a primary mode for adjusting practice.
I enjoy challenge.	Teachers look forward to the task of meeting students' needs.
I develop positive relationships.	Teachers ensure students feel safe in making mistakes and learning from them.
I inform all of the language of learning.	Teachers develop a shared language of learning with their school community.
I see learning as hard work.	Teachers teach students the importance of concentrating, perseverance, and deliberate practice.

Source: Hattie (2012, pp. 159–165).

Secondary grading research has been too absent of teacher voices. This alone is one of the leading causes of pushback and ineffective implementation of grading changes in middle and high schools. School leaders must strongly consider teacher input when planning for any grading practice changes. Teachers must then be accountable for conducting action research on how new or adjusted grading practices are impacting student results. When teachers are also supported in conducting grading action research, they become better evaluators and schools more naturally close the evidence gap in grading. This provides a level of autonomy through experimentation that secondary teachers need as they embark on making changes in their grading practices.

Action Research Will Identify Skeptics and Cynics

Mandates or policy changes will never generate buy-in for changes in grading practices at the middle and high school levels. Even with action research, though, some teachers will still question the merit of nontraditional grading changes, even with solid evidence right in front of them, because of longstanding traditions of how grading has always been done.

Doug Reeves (2011b) talks about the need for school leaders to make sure they differentiate between skeptics and cynics in their buildings. He discusses that cynics never have enough proof and will challenge for unequivocal evidence that alternative policies, such as those related to grading practices, need to be perfect before being considered (p. 40). For example, if a school implemented an amnesty day that led to more than 60% of students who had been on the potential failure list now passing their classes, cynics would argue the amnesty day was ineffective because not every student passed. Furthermore, they'd argue, the practice should be abolished. Skeptics, on the contrary, might not be first in line to vote *yes, let's have another one.* They would, however, rationally observe first that this new grading practice did lead to less than 40% fewer failures. They might even say, "Let's try it again and see what happens."

Identifying skeptics and cynics can help school leaders mitigate pushback and ultimately help more teachers buy in to the new grading practices.

CONDUCTING AND MONITORING GRADING ACTION RESEARCH

When teachers are considering conducting action research, they need to remember a few simple steps to creating a plan: determine a problem to solve, determine the strategy you will use to attempt to solve that problem, determine the results you would expect to see if your problem was successfully solved, and then execute the plan. The simplicity here is intentional. I will outline each of these steps with guidance and examples. Once the plan has been executed, teachers will then need to determine if their problem has been solved and, if the strategy worked, if they should keep the strategy as is and replicate the plan, adjust it, or scrap it and start again. Specific questions can help guide teachers in making inferences after conducting their research as well.

The following sections discuss each step as well as questions to ask. See Appendix E for a chart of steps and questions at a glance.

Step 1: Determine the Practical Problem

The first step in conducting any effective action research project is determining a problem to solve. Teachers and administrators should not look at action research as a way to prove their hypothesis or disprove someone else's hypothesis regarding grading changes.

Researchers Vivian Robison and Mei Kuin Lai (2006), in their book *Practitioner Research for Educators: A Guide to Classrooms and Schools,* make specific mention of the importance of tailoring your action research to solve your problem (p. 17). Teachers face a myriad of problems in the classroom that adjusted or improved grading practices could begin to help solve or at least diminish. The examples in Figure 9.2 are all very common and practical problems that most middle and high school teachers deal with on a daily basis. They are categorized as being either academic or behavioral. Any of these would be a valid practical problem to begin the process of action research.

Figure 9.2   Practical Problems to Solve

Academic problems	Behavioral problems
Students failing the course	Students not participating
Students not completing assignments	Students not putting forth effort (only doing the minimum to get by)
Students not grasping key concepts and skills	Students missing work submission deadlines
Students not using feedback to learn or use when resubmitting work	Students not exceeding their potential

Activity 9.1: Determine a Practical Problem to Solve Through Improved Grading Practices

Practical problem(s) or situation(s) you are interested in solving through adjusted grading practices	Academic or behavioral
Example: Many students with outstanding assignments not completed	Academic
Example: Student engagement is very low	Behavioral

Step 2: Select a Strategy to Address the Problem

Once the practical problem has been selected, teachers individually or in teams discuss possible strategies for solving it. They must consider the nature of the problem as well as possible reasons for why it is occurring in the first place. This will better ensure alignment between the strategy and the problem itself. If teachers on a course team have been observing a great deal of apathy and low engagement that is leading to student failure, their strategy may be to include more relevant work tasks with an increase in student choice.

Test Theories

Robinson and Mai (2006, p. 19) remind us that the theories teachers have about the cause of a problem can go a long way in determining possible solutions. A group of teachers I worked with at Alton High School, in Alton, Illinois, were noticing that many of their failing students were applying themselves but were just not getting it. The teachers had believed for some time they needed to stop grading everything students completed. They decided as a professional learning community (PLC) to implement more informal ungraded assessments early in an upcoming unit. The teachers felt this would allow them to better use formative assessment approaches on early tasks and allow students to make as many errors as needed. These mistakes gave teachers a chance to provide more targeted feedback. Student failure significantly decreased compared to the previous unit.

Step 3: Determine Possible and Desired Outcomes

Next, teachers have to determine what would have to be true if the strategy were to be effective. As teachers determine what evidence would allow them to make accurate inferences about the effectiveness of strategies, they must look at both student outcomes and student actions.

Holistic and Relative Evidence Markers

When teachers have determined the practical problem they hope to solve and the strategies they will use to solve it, the next step is to determine what results they would expect to observe if their solution worked. Here, teachers are looking to set evidence markers. These are the observable measures they determine would be present if the problem was solved, or at least getting solved. Teachers can use evidence markers that are specific and holistic in their measurement (e.g., 100% of students passing the end-of-course essay) or relative measures (e.g., a decrease in the number of students missing more than one assignment). Figure 9.3 provides some examples of both holistic and relative measures.

Figure 9.3   Holistic and Relative Measures of Practical Grading Problems

Holistic	Relative
Less than 100% of students executing 100% effort	More students than expected failing courses
Less than 100% of students completing assignments	More students doing only the minimum to get by
Less than 100% of students meeting expected and reasonable deadlines for work submission	Fewer students than necessary not being engaged
Less than 100% of students participating in class (discussions, tasks, etc.)	Fewer students than necessary not exceeding their potential

Step 4: Make It Happ'n, Cap'n

Teachers and school leaders have asked me, "How do we make changes in grading practices?" My response is simple: Decide to. The word *decide* in its Latin root means "to cut off from." When we truly decide to do something, we literally sever any other option other than actually following through. The concept applies to this fourth step in the action research process. If teachers have determined a practical problem worth solving, the strategy they will implement, and what measurement of progress would need to look like if successful, then all that's left to do is fire up the engines and get the boat moving, Cap'n!

Vignette

Back at Westeast High School in the fall of 2013, English teachers were frustrated at the number of students who were either failing or just barely passing first-semester English 10. They determined one of the problems was that students were getting behind early in the semester and not able to catch up. Teachers attributed this in part to students being unaware, early on, what the expectations were for proficiency demonstration that would lead directly to the grades they would receive. Another dilemma they were facing was that several students were not applying themselves near the level they could and were simply doing enough to "play school" and earn grades like B−, C, and sometimes even D just to pass. Students were refusing to accept any challenges. Finally, the teacher team was concerned that perhaps students' grades were not reflecting congruence with the state-issued end-of-course assessment.

The team brainstormed several strategies to address these three issues. They determined one strategy that might help tackle all three was to implement a selection syllabus. This would provide students with the information to know all along where their grade was, and perhaps fewer students would procrastinate. Also, students would have to push themselves to higher levels of rigor to achieve high grades, and accurate weighting would make the grade they received more reflective of what they actually mastered. Finally, it would allow for some choice, which could address some of the apathy the teachers were noticing.

They invested time over the winter break to create and implement a selection syllabus for spring semester. They identified their critical standards for second semester and used these to create their syllabus, ensuring proper alignment of rigor and weight for all tasks and summative assessments. Finally, the teachers were intentional in providing a decent amount of student choice for more than half of the assignments. They collectively agreed to be open to student voice in offering other possible ways for students to demonstrate proficiency.

Importance of Determining Fidelity

Teachers must create clear expectations for what their strategy will look like when executed by multiple adults in action research settings. Far too often, strategies that are called the same thing in a collaborative setting are executed much differently once classroom doors are shut. Teachers must have a clear understanding and a concrete definition of what the strategies they agree on will look like when they are executing them.

If teachers executing the selection syllabus at Westeast, in the vignette, fail to ensure that they are all accurately weighting their assignments aligned to rigor levels, their results might lead them to inaccurate conclusions. For example, if assignments with lower rigor levels are overly weighted, and proficient students complete these with ease, some students may realize they have accumulated enough points for a high grade. There would be a high probability, based on the teachers' previous observations, that these students would likely shy away from other challenges. The English teachers might then infer the selection syllabus was not effective. That would not be the case necessarily because a true selection syllabus was actually not implemented.

MAKING QUALITY INFERENCES FROM ACTION RESEARCH

Action research of any kind should drive teachers' ability to make quality and accurate inferences from their results. There is a very good chance that more questions could be generated when teachers are finished. That is not a bad thing. *Re-search* means to search again. To go back and find clues about what you are looking for. When grading action research is finished, teachers will need to do that same thing. They do this by asking a series of three questions:

- Did it work? (And, by extension, was it working?)
- What actions should be replicated, adjusted, or deleted?
- Were (are) my grades truthful and reliable?

Question 1: Did it work?

The first question teachers want to ask is: Did my strategy solve my practical problem? This question implies two things:

1. There will or should be a definitive yes or no answer as to whether the strategy worked.

2. There was a defined stopping point at which to measure results.

Figure 9.4 Example of Action Research at Westeast High School

Practical problems	Strategy (adult action)	Fidelity of adult actions	Desired student outcomes
Higher than expected number of students failing English 10 Too many students not applying their best effort in achievement in English 10	Create and implement a selection syllabus for English 10	Teachers of English 10 will align priority Common Core standards to specific products and ensure accurate weight values based on importance of standards and rigor level. Teachers will provide students with a selection at the start of the semester and allow choice and flexibility in timelines for providing their evidence. Teachers will adhere to the selection point values for all assignments and engage in collaborative scoring of student work at least three times every month. They will also be intentional in guiding students to appropriate challenges related to certain assignments. Finally, teachers will welcome and honor and increase in student choice in assignments as long as rigor levels are not compromised.	**Measured Holistically** Total class failure will be reduced from 17% to 0 Students earning As or Bs will increase from 27% to 60% **Measured Relatively** More students will meet proficiency expectations: higher % of passing grades and more "high" grades (As and Bs) than in previous semesters. More students will apply themselves at high levels

In most middle and high schools, a stopping point to measure the impact of the strategy would occur at the end of a semester, when final grades are submitted.

The English 10 teachers at Westeast planned to look at their final results during their end-of-year PLC meeting that took place on the first of two teacher work days after the students left for the summer. Each teacher would present his or her results and share his or her take-aways, and then the team would determine some overarching inferences for possibly replicating, adjusting, or abandoning the selection syllabus. Each teacher would compare the number of students who passed and the overall grade distribution from the fall semester to the spring.

The evening before the meeting, one teacher, Sally, compiled her data and brought it to a meeting she was having with her principal, Rick (see Figure 9.5). She was very excited to show him these results prior to sharing with her peers the next day. Rick was delighted to see a decrease in students failing and the overall numbers of As and Bs increase from 44 students in the fall to 99 in the spring. He asked Sally if she would share this information and an overview of what a selection syllabus is at the final staff meeting in 2 days. She was so excited!

Figure 9.5   Sally's Results

	Adult action (measurable)	Student achievement results (measureable), Spring 2013
Sally (English 10 teacher at Westeast)	Implemented selection syllabus with fidelity	125/150 students passed (previous semester 115/150 students passed) +10 Overall grade distribution

Fall 2012	Spring 2013
A: 21	A: 57
B: 23	B: 42
C: 49	C: 22
D: 22	D: 4
F: 35	F: 25

Final English 10 PLC Course Meeting: Part 1

After Sally left the meeting with Rick, she was talking in the staff room with some teachers from other departments about her results and that Rick asked her if she would share all of this at the staff meeting. She talked about how she would outline her success and create some guidelines other people in different departments could use if they were interested in creating a selection syllabus for their class this fall.

John, known to be the most pessimistic person on the staff, was at another table and was fuming as he overheard the conversation. He rudely commented, "Great! So now I am going to have to change the way I grade and teach, and spend days on end this summer making a college syllabus for my high school class?!" Sally apologized to him and said she told Rick she'd be happy to do this, but also that it might not fit for everyone's class or subject matter.

John backed off a bit, but still added a few comments. He said he didn't really think 10 more students passing was a significant improvement from the fall semester. He told Sally she normally should expect more students to pass in the spring when they are more caught up in reading levels and finally start doing their homework. John stormed out, in his usually cynical manner. Sally began to feel a bit bad—not that John might feel he had to do more work now because of her, but because she was concerned maybe he was right. Maybe these results were to be expected. Sally wondered if 10 fewer failing grades was enough evidence for her to encourage others, even her English 10 PLC, to replicate the strategy the following school year.

The next day at her PLC course meeting, Sally showed her data on the screen for her peers. She was much less enthusiastic as she had been the day before. She started off saying, "I am not sure these numbers really tell us much changed in the students." Doug, a solid veteran on the team who'd heard about John's outburst at Sally, piped in right away. He brought up an important inference that Sally missed when she looked at her results. He said, "Sally, hold on—your use of the syllabus led to a much higher number of students earning As and Bs in your class, which alone should cause you to do backflips. Yeah, only 10 fewer students failed, but just look how many fewer Ds you had, too!"

The team all paused and noted the data point and Doug's inference. Doug reminded the team that one of the problems they were trying to address was that too many students were coasting by, applying just enough to get a passing grade and playing school. Sally chimed in and said, "Thank you, Doug. You're right! Most of my students (rolling her eyes a bit), with the exception of the 25, kept trying up until the final project and exam!" She snickered to herself and smiled, thinking, "To hell with John!"

The rest of the teachers all commented they saw significant drops in the number of students earning a D. Doug looked back at his data and realized he went from 18 Ds to 1 D. The selection syllabus had completely addressed and practically solved this problem.

Question 1A: Is it working?

Tom Guskey (Guskey, 2011; Guskey & Bailey, 2000, 2010) has routinely suggested that three key elements of any grade relate to product, process, and progress and are reported separately. (I hope that is starting to ring a bell!) Middle and high school teachers can use the third element, progress, as a guide for asking: Is the adjusted practice I am researching *working?*

Here, teachers are determining the effectiveness of their strategy on a relative basis. Sally can see that not every student received an A and mastered every course objective. She can see a noticeable increase in the number of students achieving at high levels with the number of As increasing from 21 to 57 and Bs from 23 to 42. Sally also saw an improvement in overall passing grades from her students since the fall semester. She had 10 more students earning credits and not needing to go through credit recovery. Here is where these relative numbers may leave additional clues as to the effectiveness of the strategy.

Doug helped Sally remember a critical question when determining inferences from action research results: Is it working? This allowed her to possibly see other results and impacts than if she had just stopped after asking the culminating question: Did it work? The significant reduction in D grades may very well indicate that the selection syllabus forced students to go beyond barely passing and demonstrate deeper levels of knowledge. This will likely be the main evidence marker that drives Sally and the rest of her English 10 PLC peers, and perhaps other teachers at Westeast, to consider replicating this strategy. Teachers may be more interested when looking at the data from their results with relative measures. It is unlikely, if not impossible, that 100% of students will earn As in a course the first time or not miss any assignments. Strategies that increase the number of students earning As or passing, or decrease the number of students missing work, are ones that should evoke effort in replacing strategy.

Here are some additional questions to help determine if a strategy is working:

- Did my students show expected growth?
- Did my students' grades depict a level of progress throughout the semester that I would expect based on how they arrived?
- Did more students earn passing or higher grades than in the absence of the strategy?
- Did more students' final grades provide a more accurate predictor related to an external measure than in previous semesters?
- Did more students also take more of an initiative in their own learning?
- Did more students make several attempts on assignments and tasks and apply the feedback I gave them appropriately?

Question 2: What actions should be replicated, adjusted, or deleted?

To effectively evaluate their action research, teachers must identify specific actions to replicate, adjust, or abandon for the next attempt. Teachers must use evidence in making the decisions to avoid guessing which strategies worked or didn't at the end of an action research cycle. Recall that as we were planning the action research, we defined what success would look like. This can be expanded even more with word pictures of success, either during the action plan phase or now, while evaluating what elements to keep, change, or forgo.

Create Word Pictures of Success

In PLC settings, teachers can determine examples of what effectiveness would look like if their strategies are successful. They need to create word pictures of success, which are the descriptions of student performance and behaviors teachers hope to see (Jones, 2014, p. 133). These can be measureable or holistic, such as increasing the number of students reaching academic performance levels (As and Bs). Teachers can also create success pictures of the student behaviors they hope to see more, which would be relative. Examples of these include an increase in student engagement, more students turning work in on time, and more students challenging themselves to work at harder levels.

Back to Mind Frames

When teachers are creating specific word pictures of success that would occur because of their strategies, they are utilizing two critical *Visible Learning* (Hattie, 2012) mind frames: teachers being evaluators and teachers seeing assessment as feedback to them. When teachers look at student results as an indication of how well they implemented a strategy and not just how the students did, they are using it as their own feedback. If the students aren't developing the skills they need to or showing the behaviors we would like to see, the teachers need to make adjustments. By default, they are then becoming better evaluators of their own performance. When teachers have a clear picture of the evidence they hope to see from students if their strategies are working, they have a better chance to accurately determine whether they should continue using the strategy or readjust their actions.

Teachers can come up with *if-then* statements to create a connection between their strategies and the word pictures of success they hope to observe. Here are some examples:

- If we ensure that our summative assessments are directly linked to external assessments, then the accuracy gap between grades and scores on external measures should decrease.
- If I create specific incentives for students to submit work early, then I will be able to provide better quality feedback and student performance will improve.
- If we create a solid and aligned selection syllabi to offer students multiple yet rigorous paths to proficiency, then we should see more students meeting their goals (earning higher and passing grades) and showing deeper levels of proficiency as well as more student ownership of their leaning.

- If I provide specific feedback (in the form of points) only for specific content objectives during the course of a unit, then proficiency for that specific skill should improve as should overall unit assessment scores.
- If we create a MEAEC system for students who get behind to get caught up soon rather than falling too far behind, then we should see increases in both achievement and motivation from all students.

Question 3: Were (are) my grades truthful and reliable?

A final task teachers must do when evaluating their grading action research is to determine if the change in grading practices has led to more truthfulness and reliability in their grades. Again, grades are truthful when they represent accurately how the students have mastered the academic standards of the class. Grades are reliable when teachers of like courses would administer the same grade for the same level of work.

Teachers also must look at how their grades correlate to external measures. Many secondary schools have state-issued end-of-course assessments. It is impossible to have all-inclusive reliability between the two because teachers will never know exactly what will be asked on these assessments. They certainly can make quality inferences, though. Teachers must apply grading practices that promote consistency between their grades and the scores on external assessments so they can provide "complementary rather than conflicting information" (Welsh & D'Agostino, 2009, p. 76).

Teachers need to ask a series of questions when looking at truthfulness and reliability. Here are some questions and checking tools to help guide this process.

1. Were my students' grades based on mastery demonstration of concepts and skills the same as those of students taught by other teachers of the same course?

Checking criteria: Grades should be determined primarily on school or district critical standards. Teachers should collaborate on the creation of any common task so it is aligned to the critical standards at the appropriate rigor level.

2. Did the students' grades correlate with external assessments?

Checking criteria: Teachers should compare all (or at least a subset) of student grades to some form of external assessment (district or school common assessment, end-of-course assessment, AP exam, Acuity, SMBC, PARCC, SAT, PLAN, etc.).

3. Would the students have had the same grades from the same quality of work in classrooms of my peers down the hall? (If not, then that's not fair and our grades are not reliable.)

Checking criteria: A consistent and scheduled (at least monthly) practice of collaborative scoring work and exchange of papers, assessments, and tasks/projects is essential.

Final English 10 PLC Course Meeting: Part 2

The end-of-year English 10 meeting continued after Sally presented. The team wanted to identify which practices and actions they should replicate and which needed possible adjustments in the fall.

Ali and Doug went next and co-presented their results. They work side by side and have been comparing data and doing action research on different practices for years. They each had approximately 125 students in their five classes. When they compared their results, they were both pleased with the number of students who received As and Bs. That was a huge initial indicator of success.

They also wanted to share with the team how they looked at their data to see if their final grades were aligned to their end-of-course assessment results. They would use the level of correlation as an evidence marker to determine if implementing the selection syllabus was successful. They both used the same syllabus and tasks. For whatever reason, Doug had a higher correlation to his grades on the end of course assessment than Ali did. This led the team into a discussion about what factors may have led to these differences in their grading and assessment practices.

Ali wondered if maybe she had been less demanding in the quality of evidence the students produced for proficient or even progressing work. Ali and

Figure 9.6   Doug and Ali's Results

	Adult action (measurable)	Student achievement results (measureable)
Doug	Implemented selection syllabus with fidelity	99 students with As and Bs 90 of these students earned an A or B on end-of-course assessment
Ali	Implemented selection syllabus with fidelity	101 students with As and Bs 71 of these students earned an A or B on end-of-course assessment

> *Doug both saw huge benefits from using the syllabus and agreed to continue its use in the fall. They planned to make one major adjustment in their practices: They would plan to do a lot more collaborative scoring in fall, at least once a week.*
>
> *(This example is authentic from a team of two chemistry teachers, who chose not to be named, from a high school in California.)*

STUDENT BAROMETERS

Teachers can use specific students as measures when conducting action research. While I was initially writing this chapter, America was steeped in the rhetoric of the 2012 election. For the first time in my life, I got the pollster phone call one evening. The man on the other end asked me if I knew there was a general election for president of the United States coming up November 5. (I played along for a few minutes as if I had not heard, before getting *the look* from my wife to stop messing with the man calling.) He asked if I had decided whom I was going to vote for or if I was leaning toward one candidate or another. Once I let him know who I was most likely going to vote for, he then asked me a series of demographic questions about the following:

- my sex
- my age
- my occupation
- my socioeconomic status

Obviously, not everyone in the Indianapolis metropolitan area received a call. The pollster was trying to gather *enough* data, or evidence markers, to help his party make the best inference possible for campaign decisions in Indianapolis. The demographic questions were to determine which groups were more likely to favor or not favor their candidate. I became a *barometer*—a sample reference point to be used to make an inference. Teachers can apply this same concept when implementing any strategy in secondary classrooms, specifically grading practices.

Determining Barometers

Middle and high school teachers, when setting up their action research, might consider determining a few student barometers. These are specific students who will be a gauge about whether your actions are working. Teachers select these students to monitor the impact because they feel they would be good representation of the new strategy's effectiveness. One reason for middle and high school teachers to select barometer students is because each teacher often has a case load typically of 100 to 150 students. To closely monitor every one for the effectiveness of the new strategy would add an immense amount of workload for the teachers. They can use barometers to focus on a few students as excellent measures of the effectiveness of the strategies being implemented and therefore not have to monitor the impact on every student at the same time. Teachers of course are still responsible for offering quality feedback and making determinations about effectiveness of practice and needed adjustments for all students, but these few will be more of a focus for a certain period of time.

The following are some criteria points to consider when selecting barometer students:

- comes to school consistently
- accepts feedback
- could be representative of other students having similar challenges OR are students whose success or failure should carry more weight

Westeast High School: Fall 2013

After Sally's presentation at the end-of-year staff meeting, there was a buzz around the staff. Several course PLCs got together over the summer to talk about their grading practices and to consider doing some action research. Principal Rick had informed the staff he would never mandate a specific grading practice be implemented in anyone's classroom. He would, however, expect teachers to be experimenting and conducting their own action research and use the quality of teacher reflections made from these as a large piece of evidence in their teacher evaluation.

The freshman at Westeast High School have their own wing devoted just to them and their teachers. Freshman teachers' PLCs are not organized around courses, but around the teachers who share the same students. This allows them to collaborate maybe less about specific content like the English 10 PLC was able to do, but more around building relationships and supporting students in other ways.

One of the PLCs, Team Titan, had three teachers who agreed to conduct action research around a specific grading practice they were implementing in their classrooms. They were, however, all a bit hesitant to implement any new strategy with all of their classes and students. One teacher, Jeff, commented, "What if it fails? Then I am behind and will lose all credibility with all students if I go back!" Another teacher, Mark, said, "I like to ease into new things. I'm worried it will be too hard for me to keep up if I do this with every class."

Rick met with the group and acknowledged their concern. He encouraged them to try the new strategy with at least one class this fall and to focus on a few students. This would allow them to not have to implement it in every class before they worked out some kinks. They could then monitor the impact of the strategy for more than just grades for a few students in that class. Rick also told them they could get a feel for the classes in which it might be the best to conduct their change in practice over the first month of the school year.

The three teachers determined that their practical problem was having too many first-semester freshmen failing core classes that were required for graduation. They also felt that this could be avoided if students didn't fail to hand in work or do so without missing deadlines. Finally, they felt that if the students get to at least a progressing level earlier during units, they wouldn't feel like they and the students were playing catch-up all semester.

Each teacher then selected her or his strategy. Then, they each considered what student behaviors would be indicators of the strategy working. Each had determined that her or his practical problem would be better measured relatively than holistically. Rick and the three teachers came up with some desired behavioral outcomes to look for as word pictures of potential success for all students:

1.   More work turned in

2.   Fewer delays in completing assignments without nagging

3.   Fewer errors on initial submissions

Next, all three teachers came up with three or four barometer students they felt would be great short- and long-term indictors of their strategy's success. They each considered students who would be good gauges for some of the pictures of potential success of the new strategies. They selected students who came to school every day, accepted feedback, and at times may struggle with the content but would show effort and make multiple attempts.

Each teacher committed to fidelity of implementation with the new grading practice and to monitor its impact on student achievement and behavior closely over the next few PLC meetings. They brought notes, comments, anecdotes, and student work to the next several PLC meetings specifically for their barometer students. In a sense, they were doing deep action research on a few specific students. Their plan can be seen in Figure 9.7.

Figure 9.7   PLC Teachers' Piloted Grading Changes

Teacher	Grading strategy	Barometer students	Reason for barometers	Student behavior pictures of successes	Pictures of success in student achievement
Jeff (Algebra)	MEAEC Practices	Joe D. Nick R. Kristen M.	These students get behind and struggle to get caught up, which leads to apathy. I hope this will get their heads above water and help them see the need to not give up.	Students will be more inclined to ask for time to get work in vs. just not doing it. More self-motivation and less need for constant prodding.	Better test scores on unit tests because they will be more proficient in problem solving and number sense skills from having to do the practice
Mark (Biology)	Selection syllabus	Sally Y. Helen D. Phil C.	All of these students are above grade level. I hope the selection syllabus will offer them some specific choices and ownership to go above and beyond standard.	More self-selecting their assignments from the provided choices that are more rigorous and challenging. Also, coming up with their own ideas to master standards above grade level.	Unit tests go from B to C+ to all As or at least B+ grades. Students attempt with success some of the college-level challenge problems I place at end of tests.
Bruce (Social Studies)	Early work incentives	Marc W. Brian D. Sam C.	These students are perpetually late with work but usually close to proficient. I hope early incentives will provide needed enticement to not procrastinate.	Fewer assignments late and at least one early deadline met by each student in next 2 weeks.	Improved scores on weekly quizzes and quarterly common assessments

Note: I adapted this authentic example from what several high school teachers in an Iowa high school did.

Piloting

By attempting a strategy with one class, and with an even smaller number of barometer students, teachers can experiment with new grading practices without overhauling to their entire system. The teachers in the example did exactly what Tom Guskey (2010, p. 24) strongly recommends, which is to pilot new grading practices before full implementation. This allows teachers to have their *change shrunk,* as Heath and Heath (2010) recommend. These teachers were less worried about trying the new practices because they didn't have to go all in early. Piloting new grading practices also allows teachers to do what many sustained great companies did, which is to fire BBs before they fire cannonballs (Collins, 2011). The teachers also created academic as well as behavioral word pictures of success.

Activity 9.2: Action Research Template

Practical problem I (we) are trying to solve	What does/would fidelity of the strategy look like? (Describe in detail.)	What are desired student outcomes (measurable)?	When will we measure these (assessment dates, PLC meetings for reviewing progress)?	What are pictures of success of student behaviors to monitor as progress toward success? (Is it working?)	Who are any barometer students? What are any specific pictures of success I will look for in their achievement or behavior?	How will we measure accuracy and fairness?

CONCLUSION

As mentioned in the Introduction, Chapter 1, and elsewhere throughout the book, one of the biggest reasons for possible lack of implementation of new and effective grading practices is the gap in the research (Webster, 2011). Teacher voice needs to be a primary consideration related to any adjustments in practice, specifically grading. By conducting your own classroom, department, or school grading practice research, not only will you determine what practices might work best for the students in your classroom, department, and school, but you are also likely to see great levels of increase in achievement both academically and behaviorally.

KEY IDEAS

1. There will always be cynics who are never satisfied with the evidence no matter how compelling it is. Grading practice changes and experiments need not wait for their approval.

2. Action research into grading practice implementation should be guided by specific questions to identify the practical problem and the best strategy to address it as well as definitions of success.

3. It is important to monitor fidelity of the adult action first, before looking at student results.

4. A strategy might be working even if desired results have not yet been achieved, and it's important to review these at regular intervals.

5. Barometer students are a great gauge to identify if strategies are working without having to implement an entirely new grading practice. (This would be an example of piloting.)

REFLECTION QUESTIONS

1. What is a question you have about grading practices and their impact on achievement in your school?

2. What current adult action/grading practice are you considering monitoring for implementation and effectiveness? (Which team/ department?)

3. What specific student outcomes will you monitor? What will be your interim dates and data points for possible adjustments?

4. How will you display/share results?

Appendixes

APPENDIX A: MONITORING GRADE INFLATION AND DEFLATION

Data for the past decade have indicated that both grade inflation and deflation are prevalent in our high schools. While Chapter 5 dealt with failure prevention strategies to avoid unnecessary grade deflation, monitoring grade inflation is just as important. ACT (2005) concludes that between 1991 and 2003 high school grades inflated by 12.5%. Many students who leave their high schools with diplomas arrive on campus or in workforce postsecondary settings lacking the skills necessary to succeed. Former West Virginia Governor Bob Wise (2008, p. 220) estimates that the United States would realize an additional $3.7 billion in reduced expenditures and increased earnings if more students graduating from high school were prepared for college and did not require remediation.

Using Internal and External Assessments as Monitoring Tools

Middle and high schools need to have a system in place for specific times during the year to monitor the accuracy of grade reporting and distribution. This can be accomplished at the district, school, or team/classroom level. Schools and districts must ensure that teacher grades complement and don't conflict with state or other external assessments (Guskey, 2009, p. 76). Schools can use data from external measures such as state tests, end-of-course assessments, SAT, ACT, PARCC, and Smarter Balanced assessments once they are fully implemented to determine if the grades teachers are reporting are aligned with external measures of students' mastery of specific academic standards.

Flood Light View

Districts can compare grade distribution to external assessment results by individual teachers' grades, by course, subject, or school to see how grades match. This type of analysis can offer districts and schools flood light views of how grades are aligning with student success on external measures. These are conducted only once or twice per year.

Figure A.1 shows a quick example of some data points that districts, schools, departments, teams, and individual teachers can use to monitor grade distribution and how it compares with internal and external assessments. It also shows the frequency with which they can and should be used to determine if the grades we are administering are what we would expect based on other assessments.

Flash Light Analysis

Schools can get a deeper view of how specific PLCs' or even individual classroom teachers' grades are aligning with external assessments. Benchmark assessments that measure the specific standards and objectives aligned with the school's curriculum can become a great quick gauge for monitoring both inflation and deflation across classrooms. NWEA, MAP, and Acuity are just a few of the assessments that are usually administered multiple times per year. These may be more useful than large-scale state or national assessments that occur usually only once a year. PLCs or other collaborative teacher teams can analyze how aligned their grade distribution is with internal measures.

Figure A.1   Flood Light Frequency of Grade Distribution Monitoring

Level	Comparison	Frequency
District	% of grades in English language arts and math to state-level (Common Core) assessments	Yearly
School	% of grades in any course that has an external or rigorous and aligned end-of-course assessment	Semester
School	% of grades in any course compared to quarterly benchmark assessments	Quarterly
School/teacher or team	Grade distribution based on gender, ethnicity, or socioeconomic status	Quarterly
Teacher or team	% of grades compared to unit assessments or other common summative assessments administered	Monthly (reporting period)

Figure A.2   Flash Light Frequency of Grade Distribution Monitoring

Task	Questions to ask	Dates to monitor data	Who is primarily responsible
Monitoring possible grade inflation and deflation by comparing grades to external assessment scores	How do we currently monitor? Do we know the results?		
	What could we use to compare (which assessments)?		
	How can we better know where we are in the next 18–24 months?		
Monitoring possible grade inflation or deflation based on gender, ethnicity, or socioeconomic grade distributions	Are the grade distributions between genders or between students of different ethnicities similar enough to what we would expect? (Have we seen trends over more than one semester?)		
	Are there disciplines, courses, and so on that have discrepancies that should drive questions?		
	Do we see discrepancies between socioeconomic status that should drive questions?		

Activity A.1: Individual Teacher Grade Distribution Analysis

Compare accuracy of grades to external measures such as national/state assessments, end-of-course assessments, SAT, and ACT for three teachers.

	Teacher 1			Teacher 2			Teacher 3	
Student 1	External assessment scores	Grades	Student 2	External assessment scores	Grades	Student 3	External assessment scores	Grades
	Progressing	B		Exemplary	A		Progressing	C
	Emergent	Credit recovery*		Proficient	D		Emergent	B
	Exemplary	B+		Progressing	Credit recovery		Proficient	A
	Proficient	B+		Emergent	Credit recovery		Emergent	C+
	Proficient	A		Proficient	A		Progressing	B+
	Emergent	C−		Proficient	C		Progressing	B−
	Emergent	Credit recovery		Proficient	C−		Progressing	A−
	Exemplary	A		Progressing	C		Proficient	A
	Progressing	B−		Proficient	Credit recovery		Emergent	B
	Proficient	B−		Exemplary	C		Progressing	B+
	Emergent	Credit recovery		Progressing	B		Proficient	A
	Progressing	B−		Proficient	C		Emergent	C+
	Exemplary	A		Emergent	C		Proficient	B
	Progressing	B		Exemplary	Credit recovery		Progressing	B
	Emergent	Credit recovery		Progressing	A		Emergent	B−
	Progressing	B		Proficient	B		Progressing	A−

Based on the three sets of students pulled from these teachers' classrooms and comparing final semester grades and state assessment scores, what inferences, hypotheses, and conclusions can you make?

---

*Credit recovery would indicate an "F" Grade.

Teacher 1

_____

_____

_____

_____

Teacher 2

_____

_____

_____

_____

Teacher 3

_____

_____

_____

_____

What questions do you have about the grading practices in all three of these classrooms?

_____

_____

_____

_____

_____

_____

_____

_____

_____

_____

_____

APPENDIX B: SUMMARY OF PRACTICAL GRADING EXAMPLES/STRATEGIES FOR DECREASING FAILURE

Strategy	SI²TE connection	Benefits	Potential implementation challenges	Possible provisions to put in place to address challenges
Early failure detection: Specific structure to monitor and intervene when students are in danger of failing a course	Support and intervention	• Provides school with system for being aware of potential course failures to have more time to prevent; also, can lead to making better inferences as to possible causes of student failure • Prevents students from getting so far behind that getting caught up is problematic, if not impossible • Focuses PLC discussion on probable reasons for possible failure to lead to specific prevention actions • Allows for multiple adults (teachers, counselors, etc.) to be involved based on the root cause of potential failure (e.g., attendance, not working, failure to grasp a concept)	• Disagreement by teachers of like courses regarding common measures of proficiency • When multiple possible reasons for failure are present, how to address specific root causes • Teams not submitting information in a timely manner to work as a functioning PLC	• Deadlines are well communicated to parents, department/team leads, and so on • Specific PLC time is scheduled to allow for analysis and action from early failure detection data

Strategy	SI²TE connection	Benefits	Potential implementation challenges	Possible provisions to put in place to address challenges
		• Often identifies teachers' most effective practices • Is an additional monitoring tool for grade inflation (if three of four biology teachers have 25% failure and one teacher has 0, the outlier, for whatever reason, will draw attention)		
MEAEC it happen: System is in place to ensure students have the opportunity and are expected to complete essential missed work shortly after it was assigned	Support and (early) intervention, time, evidence	• Students do not get behind in points or assignments • Ensures that the work teachers assign students is essential and linked to critical course objectives • Teachers can assign more significant work • Teachers are not faced with a huge number of makeup work requests during the final weeks of the semester • Students stay caught up during the unit of study in both work and content mastery	• Some educators believe that students will not do the work when it is assigned and will wait for the additional opportunity • Work is not targeted to critical course objectives	• Semester is well organized for how and when MEAEC practices will take place • PLC collaboration must be related to credible and targeted student work and essential tasks

(Continued)

(Continued)

Strategy	SI²TE connection	Benefits	Potential implementation challenges	Possible provisions to put in place to address challenges
Amnesty days: Announced or unannounced days when primary focus is to make up work, get additional support, and show proficiency with no penalty	Support and time, and evidence	• Students get caught up on specific work that was missed • Increased grades from accumulation of missing points • Increased proficiency in specific concepts and skills needed for future topics • Students will more likely persevere and put forth more effort because chance of potential failure has been reduced	• Potential for students to wait for amnesty and not put forth effort • Work for teacher to bring back old material for students (see MEAECs to address this challenge)	• Schedule amnesty days but perhaps do not announce them until day of • Host amnesty days by course, department, or discipline • Utilize PLC time early in the year to develop parallel assignments for students to reach mastery so teachers do not have to gather all older materials
Intentional use of homework: Homework is purposeful and provides the mechanism for practice and feedback; assignments are geared toward student skill level	Support and evidence	• Student work and practice are focused on their individual needs • Students see the connection between what they do at home as an extension of their classwork • Can create a focus and mechanism for collaboration in PLC meetings for sharing of potential homework based on a student's (or group of students') current mastery of skill	• Teachers having to give up autonomy of assignment administration and scoring • The need for multiple assignments vs. one size fits all • Students and parents seeing peers work on different assignments	• Each department makes guidelines that are created and adhered to based on the general makeup of the subject • Create guidelines that are implementable and able to be monitored for their effectiveness • Establish types of assignments that would be

Strategy	SI²TE connection	Benefits	Potential implementation challenges	Possible provisions to put in place to address challenges
				considered homework vs. classwork (homework should be set skill refinement or rehearsal)
Incentives for early work submission	Support and incentives and evidence	• Students and teachers focus more on incentive and feedback than on punishment and consequence • The feedback becomes the important focus, not the points coming off • Students are taught the value of early preparation and benefit vs. just the penalty for procrastination • Teachers often receive work in waves vs. all at once, making scoring and giving quality feedback a much easier task • Students learn to value teacher feedback and can become more proficient at using it to guide their own learning, making them more assessment capable	• Some students will still wait for the final deadline, and then some will still expect the same level of feedback • Students will often meet and exceed deadlines, demonstrating proficiency early; while a nice problem to have, teachers and PLCs will need to plan for this and have enrichment challenges ready for students going to the next level	• Prior to the start of a unit, PLCs prepare for and have specific enrichment ideas, lessons, or tasks for students who demonstrate proficiency early • Teachers in PLCs brainstorm specific lists of questions and other forms of feedback for students related to task feedback for novice learners, process feedback where there is some form of proficiency, and self-regulation for students demonstrating proficiency and mastery (See Chapter 7 for specific examples of feedback by courses)

(Continued)

(Continued)

Strategy	SI²TE connection	Benefits	Potential implementation challenges	Possible provisions to put in place to address challenges
Early final: Final is administered 1–2 weeks early. Proficient students are offered enrichment during the remaining time; specific targeted enrichment and remediation for key specific skills and concepts are offered to nonproficient students, who then retake the final exam.	Support and (early) intervention, incentives, and evidence	• Students actually receive feedback on their performance • Teachers don't stop their lives to grade 150 finals in 24 hours • Students may be motivated to learn content and material to earn the freedom that comes with early proficiency • Teachers have natural means to collaborate on plans, strategies, and ideas for differentiation after the final (both for how to remediate and for enrichment ideas and activities) • Students know exactly where their learning gaps are and can focus their studying • Students are motivated to strive for a higher grade after the first version of the exam is administered	• Communicating expectations to teachers and students can be difficult • Two versions of the final are needed to ensure reliability and prevent cheating • Teachers must have a specific plan for how to remediate/enrich for students after the first version of the final is administered	• Plan for students who are proficient • Specific priority standards (concepts and skills) to be placed on the final • Collaboration needs to take place for teachers to plan for both student groups

APPENDIX C: SUCCESSFUL CREDIT RECOVERY: MANY PATHS, ONE DESTINATION

As schools continue to experiment with and adjust existing credit recovery programs in an attempt to minimize dropouts and increase graduation rates, several factors and considerations can contribute to their success. Whether schools choose a traditional route, one based online or otherwise on technology, or a hybrid that combines the two, effective teaching will lead to effective student learning. Figure C.1 highlights some benefits and drawbacks of online versus traditional credit recovery settings.

Figure C.1   Traditional Versus Online Credit Recovery

Traditional (teacher-led) credit recovery		Online credit recovery
• Individual teaching and connections to students on a personal level—relationship building • Individual teaching for specific skill development and person-to-person feedback • Can be done before, after, or during school (e.g., study hall, advisory) • Individual plan(s) can be made for each student in each course based on skill proficiency needed, interest, and learning style	**Benefits**	• Students work at their own pace • Fewer teacher resources are needed to manage • Students work on their own time (before or after school, during study hall/free period) • Some programs allow for more natural differentiated learning • More students can be served at the same time (critical in schools with large need for credit recovery)
• More differentiated instruction needs to take place while students are present • Time-intensive for students who may need more acceleration to catch up • Cost of possible stipend to pay teachers as well as overload of teachers with already demanding schedules • Time and cost to set up and implement credit recovery settings • Fewer students can be served at one time.	**Potential drawbacks and considerations**	• Cost of purchasing or setting up the programs/courses • Time and input are needed to ensure courses are linked to (power) standards and proficiency indicators • Collaboratively scoring of student work is less likely; there is less reliability in grades and proficiency determination • Lessens ability to create and build individual learning plans • Fewer personal connections are made between students and teachers
Reflection question: What are some of your thoughts after reading about these benefits and drawbacks? Do any of them resonate with you and/or your schools setting? If so, how?		

If schools determine they are going to use an online setting for credit recovery, they must decide whether to purchase their courses or create them internally. Here are a couple of questions schools may need to consider when determining if they should purchase or create courses:

1. Is it more important to get started than to get it perfect?

2. What courses are most important to have right now? Do we want core areas (e.g., language arts, math) in place ASAP? If so, we might choose to purchase those instead of build them.

Figure C.2 highlights benefits and drawbacks of both.

Considerations for Success Online

Technology-based options for credit recovery have been expanding for the past decade and will continue to do so for some time. One of the overarching critiques of online learning for credit recovery is that there is the

Figure C.2   Created Versus Purchased Online Courses

Created online courses		Purchased online courses
• Can be set up to mirror traditional day school courses for consistency • Same assessments can be used as with traditional courses to ensure validity and reliability, and can be collaboratively scored by different teachers of the same course • Can ensure specific district power standards are the focus for assessments, proficiency, and completion of course	**Benefits**	• Instant setup; ready for students to use • One-stop shopping for core courses students need for graduation • Often linked to state or Common Core standards
• Time and internal cost to set up; not immediately ready for all students • Monitoring and maintaining courses (links, tasks, etc.) must be done consistently (manpower cost)	**Potential drawbacks and considerations**	• Initial cost for purchase and possible yearly cost for renewal • Potential that websites/links may not be updated or checked for consistency
Reflection question: What are some of your thoughts after reading about these benefits and drawbacks? Do any of them resonate with you and/or your schools setting? If so, how?		

risk of shuffling students out the door without the full value of a high school education. Schools and districts should not concern themselves with perceptions that lack facts. Schools should not ask themselves, "Is our online environment for credit recovery the same experience as a classroom?" but rather, "Does our online environment allow our students to demonstrate mastery of standards?" All students have unique learning needs and strengths. In many formal online learning situations, students have performed academically equally well as or better than students in more traditional instructional settings (Lemke, Coughlin, & Reifsneider, 2009, p. 32).

Teacher-Student Connection Critical

The most important influence on student learning in a school is that of the classroom teacher (Hattie, 2008). This does not change in an online setting. In their June 2008 report with the North American Council for Online Learning, Watson and Gemin mention that an effective predictor of student success in online settings is a high level of teacher involvement (p. 15). When schools simply purchase a slew of computers and courses because they are inexpensive in bulk, this most often leads to very low levels of teacher interaction. In these cases, schools are most likely to pass students because they are completing course requirements that are not always standards-based assignments. These settings can lead students to walk out having recovered their credit and learned little or nothing at all.

Effective classroom instruction and formative assessment are the cornerstones of student learning. Online environments are just that—learning environments. Notwithstanding any extraordinary circumstances, one would not and should not assume that effective teaching for effective learning would not still need to be part of the recipe. Credit recovery environments are filled with learners who are there because of some degree of lack of success. These learners need intervention as soon as an issue arises. Online learning settings are less geared for teachers to intervene quickly compared to traditional classrooms. Schools must plan to create online environments that have high levels of teacher interaction and intervention if they hope for successful online credit recovery implementation. This may mean a balance whereby students can complete some of the coursework at home, but there is an on-site requirement as well. The following are examples of successful online credit recovery settings that have tackled some of the key roadblocks to success.

Immediate Intervention

Pine Ridge High School, in Volusia County, Florida, has an Apex lab where any of the school's 2,200 students can work on courses needed to graduate (first time or recovery). Mrs. Feltner, who runs the program, gets an immediate email whenever students fail an online quiz, which allows her to intervene quickly. She feels that students who are struggling or are in a recovery situation are better served in an online lab where someone can step up and assist them right away. Students who are home with no one to help guide them will not receive the same level of support in developing or redeveloping critical skills (Trotter, 2008).

Effective Alignment and Personalization

Ector County, Texas, with a population of 26,000 students, uses a balance of paper-and-pencil and online models for credit recovery. Even the online courses that have been purchased are personalized. Ms. Rose Valderaz, the district's director of the Virtual High School, shares that part of the mission in the credit recovery program is to make sure students have learned enough of the skills and concepts they missed so they can succeed in the subsequent course.

Alignment and Losing Stigma

Two challenges schools face in implementing online credit recovery are having alignment between traditional classes and the online versions and the stigma that students taking these courses are earning substandard credits. Aldine Independent School District, serving 60,000 students outside of Houston, addressed both when it hired some of its master teachers to collaborate on creating curriculum for online credit recovery courses. When teachers from the district created the courses for online credit recovery, they provided immediate creditability for students earning credits in the online format. They then mandated that all students earning an online recovery credit pass an established and rigorous final exam. This would be beyond what some students who earned their credit as first-time learners had to do (Watson & Gemin, 2008, p. 8).

Pre-Assessments for Online Credit Recovery

Most students in credit recovery settings do not need to repeat the entire course they recently failed. Schools need to know which skills the students have mastered and which they are still missing—their on- and off-ramps, so to speak. In the Kentucky Virtual High School, students take an abridged version of the course they recently failed. Prior to starting a credit recovery class, students complete an informal diagnostic. Based on the evidence from these assessments, students are placed in either full or abridged courses. The school has also established cutoffs for recovery versus repeat. Students who score below 50% are not eligible for the credit recovery program. They need to take the entire course over and are not eligible for the abridged version (Blackboard, 2009, p. 6).

APPENDIX D: USING COMMON CORE SPEAKING AND LISTENING STANDARDS AS FEEDBACK AND GRADING TARGETS FOR STUDENT COLLABORATION AND PARTICIPATION

Many secondary schools are also starting to address collaboration as a method for grading more effectively. Collaboration is a key 21st century skill that all teachers and administrators can likely improve upon, and it is one students need to be college and career ready. CCSSI (English Language Arts & Literacy in History/Social Studies, Science, and Technical Subjects) states:

> To become college and career ready, students must have ample opportunities to take part in a variety of rich, structured conversations—as part of a whole class, in small groups, and with a partner—built around important content in various domains. Whatever their intended major or profession, high school graduates will depend heavily on their ability to listen attentively to others so that they are able to build on others' meritorious ideas while expressing their own clearly and persuasively. (p. 48)

The Common Core speaking and listening standards provide teachers with concrete targets to assess students and give feedback on essential collaboration skills. These are essential for students to develop to become college and career ready. The Common Core spiraling provides clear learning progressions for teachers to use for feedback, for student self-assessment and growth, and for potential criterion-based grading targets.

Figure D.1   Specific Speaking and Listening Standards Used in Creating the Student
Assessment Below

SL9-10.1a	**Come to discussions prepared, having read and researched material under study**; explicitly draw on that preparation by **referring to evidence from texts and other research on the topic** or issue to stimulate a thoughtful, well-reasoned exchange of ideas.
SL9-10.1b	**Work with peers to set rules for collegial discussions and decision-making** (e.g., informal consensus, taking votes on key issues, presentation of alternate views), **clear goals and deadlines, and individual roles as needed.**
SL9-10.1c	**Propel conversations by posing and responding to questions that relate the current discussion to broader themes** or larger ideas; **actively incorporate others into the discussion**; and clarify, verify, or challenge ideas and conclusions.
SL9-10.1d	**Respond thoughtfully to diverse perspectives, summarize points of agreement and disagreement,** and, when warranted, qualify or justify their own views and understanding and **make new connections in light of the evidence and reasoning presented.**

Figure D.2 Speaking and Listening Student Self-Assessment: Grade 9 Scoring Rubric

		Grading rubric (100 points)		
	Student-friendly success criteria (Students check ones met; teacher has veto rights)	I haven't been consistent in applying these strategies or haven't made sufficient effort to do so (0 points—checked off 3 or fewer) Practice/second-chance sessions on second Thursday of the month for second-chance time with teacher	I am continually demonstrating improvement on using and applying these strategies through practice and receiving feedback (15 points for 4 or 5 out of 7)	I regularly and successfully use these strategies (18 points for 6 or 7)
SL9-10.1a **Come to discussions prepared, having read and researched material under study**; explicitly draw on that preparation by **referring to evidence from texts and other research on the topic** or issue to stimulate a thoughtful, well-reasoned exchange of ideas.	I prepare for class or team discussions, having read and researched material assigned to the group or class			
	I explicitly refer to evidence from texts to make sure the discussion is rich and thoughtful			
SL.9-10.1b **Work with peers to set rules for collegial discussions and decision-making** (e.g., informal consensus, taking votes on key issues, presentation of alternate views), **clear goals and deadlines, and individual roles as needed.**	I help my peers create rules for discussion and ensure that I adhere to them			
	When necessary I support the group discussion by addressing norm violations that get in the way of group learning			

(Continued)

Figure D.2   (Continued)

SL.9-10.1c **Propel conversations by posing and responding to questions that relate the current discussion to broader themes** or larger ideas; **actively incorporate others into the discussion;** and clarify, verify, or challenge ideas and conclusions.	I help move the discussion forward by making sure my responses to the questions relate to the topic and bigger picture in a mature and focused approach			
SL9-10.1d **Respond thoughtfully to diverse perspectives, summarize points of agreement and disagreement,** and, when warranted, qualify or justify their own views and understanding and **make new connections in light of the evidence and reasoning presented.**	I comment back to peers by first summarizing their points (where we agree or disagree)			
		My point allotment for this 2-week cycle: _____/100 My Improvement Goal for the next 2 weeks is _____. I will specifically focus on _____ and seek help, coaching, and assistance from (my teacher) _____ and (peers) _____ and _____.		

APPENDIX E: EXAMPLE OF PLC/GRADE-LEVEL 100-DAY ACTION PLAN

To create an effective short-term (3- to 4-month or 100- to 120-day) action plan, in which your actions show dramatic improvements in achievement in one element of your school's grading practice adjustments or changes, the focus has to be on a few specific actions the teachers or PLC commit to and monitor.

SOME IMPORTANT POINTS TO CONSIDER

1. Determine what actions will have the greatest impact on student achievement. For example, if you have taken the time to have teachers really ensure that they have identified the most essential critical standards for targeted instruction and assessment, then you would already have the basis for creating a rigorous, accurate, and fair selection syllabus to offer students as a clear guide for earning specific and understood grades.

2. Decide on the essential high-impact actions your team will implement as well as committed deadlines for accomplishing tasks.

3. Determine future dates for monitoring grading change actions and their impact.

4. Update your project weekly or by some predetermined interval.

Example: High-impact actions that are to be employed in the plan to accomplish this goal:

1. Establish clear critical standards for 10th-grade language arts that are aligned with priorities for 11th and 12th grades.

2. Unwrap the essential and supporting standards to identify key concepts and skills as well as rigor levels.

3. Use text complexity as a gauge for helping students demonstrate mastery of concepts and skills, get through more difficult texts skills, maintain stamina, and see how they are acquiring points for the grade they are earning.

4. Create a specific structure for bimonthly meetings for the specific purpose of sharing success in student work as well as monitoring the behaviors of barometer students.

5. Create a specific structure, schedule, and protocol for collaborative scoring of student work.

6. Ensure that there are at least three rigorous common assessments to be administered across all four English 10 classrooms to monitor accuracy and fairness.

Figure E.1 Partially Completed Short-Term PLC Action Plan for Implementing a Selection Syllabus

Date	Actions	Primary responsibility	Evidence of success
August 1	English 10 teacher team starts a 100-day plan for building solid selection syllabus for students of English 10.		
August 5	English 10 teachers meet to decide specific priority standards that are the focus for the semester and unwrap to identify key concepts, skills, and rigor level. Team divides task as each teacher takes two of the eight priority standards and plans to bring detailed examples of possible assignments and tasks to meet standards, including different levels of text complexity.		
August 12	Team reconvenes to go over examples and agree on whether or not the activities, lessons, and possible student tasks meet the unwrapping targets.		
August 19	Team meets and drafts two versions of selection syllabus to implement in their classes this fall. Teachers are assigned the task over the next week to reflect on each and see which version is more aligned with current resources.		
August 26	Team agrees on both versions after revision to use with students this fall.		
August 30	Team agrees on point/weight value for task choices and grades that can be awarded for certain point accumulation by students.		
September 1	Students are given selection syllabus examples. Teachers gather input and comments to share at next PLC meeting about student reactions.		
September 8	Team divides to create drafts of the three common assessments. Teams of two bring the drafts for discussion and agreement on whether these are linked to the priorities of that 5-week period. (The team plans to have them administered at 5, 10, and 15 weeks to allow the last 3 weeks of the semester for intervention and enrichment were most needed.)		

Date	Actions	Primary responsibility	Evidence of success
September 15	Team brings first examples of student work for collaborative scoring.		
September 22	Team brings student work and anecdotes from barometer students for purposeful discussion.		
September 29	Team brings current grade distributions for monitoring. (Do some students need to be pulled off the selection syllabus because they are getting too far behind and have some forced choice?)		
October 4	Team brings common assessment 1 papers for collaborative scoring.		
October 8	Team has second meeting of week to share full results of common assessments to talk about any mid-course corrections that are needed.		
October 15	Team conducts collaborative walks in each other's classrooms focusing on specific strategies and student outcomes. (Teachers grade students based on speaking and listening standards.)		
October 22	Team debriefs on collaborative walks on speaking and listening assessments. Teachers address one specific student from each of their observations of peers' classroom to share the grade they would have given him or her.		
October 29	Team brings current grade distributions for monitoring. (Do some students need to be pulled off the selection syllabus because they are getting too far behind and have some forced choice?)		
November 4	Team brings common assessment 2 for collaborative scoring.		

APPENDIX F

AURORA PUBLIC SCHOOLS
HIGH SCHOOL STANDARDS-BASED REPORT CARD 2010-2011

Student: Jack Jones
Student ID: 12345678
Grade: 09

Gateway High School
1300 S. Sable Blvd.
Aurora, CO 80012

TERM	Q1		Q2		Q3		Q4	
Period	Absent	Tardy	Absent	Tardy	Absent	Tardy	Absent	Tardy
1	0	0	1	0				
2	0	1	1	0				
3	0	0	1	0				
4	0	0	1	0				
5	0	0	1	0				
6	0	0	1	0				
7	0	0	1	0				
8	0	0	1	0				

Attendance Summary

Academic Performance Level –Subject Areas	
NAME	**GRADE**
Demonstrates a thorough understanding of the grade level content and consistently applies the benchmarks, and/or concepts, and/or processes/procedures in a variety of contexts	A
Demonstrates understanding of the grade level content and applies the benchmarks, and/or concepts, and/or processes/procedures in a variety of contexts	B
Demonstrates understanding and application of most of the benchmarks, and/or concepts, and/or processes/procedures of the grade level content; needs teacher support to demonstrate proficiency	C
Demonstrates limited understanding and application of the benchmarks, and/or concepts, and/or processes/procedures of the grade level content; needs more instruction and/or practice to demonstrate proficiency	D
Rarely demonstrates understanding and ineffectively applies benchmarks, and/or concepts, and/or processes/procedures of the grade level content	R
Incomplete	I
No Evidence	N
Satisfactory for Pass/Fail courses	S
Unsatisfactory for Pass/Fail courses	U

Academic Performance Level –Work Habits	
NAME	**GRADE**
Consistently Meets	4
Frequently Meets	3
Sometimes Meets	2
Rarely Meets	1

Subject Areas				
COURSE	**Q1**	**Q2**	**Q3**	**Q 4**
HLA1012Q1 English 9 – Smith, A.	C			
HLA1012Q2 English 9 – Smith, A.		B		
STANDARDS/BENCHMARKS: 1 Read and understand a variety of materials 2 Write and speak for a variety of purposes and audiences 3 Use conventional grammar, usage, sentence structure, punctuation, capitalization, spelling 4 Apply thinking skills in many areas of literacy 5 Locate/select/use relevant information from a variety of sources 6 Read and recognize literature as a record of human experience COMMENTS: 1.1 Engages in reading increasingly complex text 1.3 Demonstrates increased stamina during reading 3.2 Demonstrates control over most basic standard conventions				
WORK HABITS:				
Effort - Perseveres and attempts quality work	4	4		
Engagement - Participates and listens	3	4		
Homework - Complete and on time	3	3		
Responsibility - Follows rules and directions; manages time; advocates for self	3	3		
COURSE:	**Q1**	**Q2**	**Q3**	**Q 4**
HSC3012Q1 Physical Science – Nelson, P	B			
HSC3012Q1 Physical Science – Nelson, P		B		

	Q1	Q2	Q3	Q 4

STANDARDS/BENCHMARKS:
  2.6 Energy transformations and heat loss
  2.8 Conservation of mass/energy can be measured and calculated
  2.9 Newton's Three Laws of Motion
  1.3 Identify major sources of error or uncertainty within an investigation
  5.3 Graphs/equations/models used to analyze systems with change/constancy				

COMMENTS:
  This is a test comment.
  All comments entered by teachers will appear here.				

WORK HABITS:				
Effort - Perseveres and attempts quality work	4	4		
Engagement - Participates and listens	3	4		
Homework - Complete and on time	3	3		
Responsibility - Follows rules and directions; manages time; advocates for self	3	3		
COURSE:	**Q1**	**Q2**	**Q3**	**Q 4**
HMA1010Q1 IntegratedAlgGeo1 – Davis, C	C			
HMA1010Q2 IntegratedAlgGeo1 – Davis, C		B		

STANDARDS/BENCHMARKS:
  2.2a Represents functional relationships using tables/graphs/equations
  2.1a Model linear real-world situations with equations/inequalities
  2.3a Solve problems using graphs, tables, and algebraic methods
  3.3a Fit curves to scatter plots to make predictions about the data				

COMMENTS:
  This is a test comment.
  All comments entered by teachers will appear here.				

WORK HABITS:				
Effort - Perseveres and attempts quality work	4	4		
Engagement - Participates and listens	3	4		
Homework - Complete and on time	3	3		
Responsibility - Follows rules and directions; manages time; advocates for self	3	3		
COURSE:	**Q1**	**Q2**	**Q3**	**Q 4**
HSS1011Q1 Geography – Cook, M	C			
HSS1011Q2 Geography – Cook, M		C		

STANDARDS/BENCHMARKS:
  5.1c How ideas in documents & Supreme Court rulings affect contemporary US
  5.1d How US political system has dealt w/ various constitutional crises				

COMMENTS:
  This is a test comment.
  All comments entered by teachers will appear here.				

WORK HABITS:				
Effort - Perseveres and attempts quality work	3	3		
Engagement - Participates and listens	2	3		
Homework - Complete and on time	3	3		
Responsibility - Follows rules and directions; manages time; advocates for self	2	3		
COURSE:	**Q1**	**Q2**	**Q3**	**Q 4**
HBT3030Q1 Word Processing – Allen, D	B			
HBT3030Q2 Word Processing – Allen, D		B		

COMMENTS:
  This is a test comment.
  All comments entered by teachers will appear here.				

WORK HABITS:				
Effort - Perseveres and attempts quality work	3	3		
Engagement - Participates and listens	2	3		
Homework - Complete and on time	3	3		
Responsibility - Follows rules and directions; manages time; advocates for self	2	3		
COURSE:	**Q1**	**Q2**	**Q3**	**Q 4**
HFL1012Q1 French 1 – Jones, B	B			
HFL1012Q2 French 1 – Jones, B		B		

COMMENTS:
  This is a test comment.
  All comments entered by teachers will appear here.				

WORK HABITS:				
Effort - Perseveres and attempts quality work	3	3		
Engagement - Participates and listens	2	3		
Homework - Complete and on time	3	3		
Responsibility - Follows rules and directions; manages time; advocates for self	2	3		

References

ACT. (2005). *Are high school grades inflated? Issues in college readiness.* Retrieved from https://www.act.org/research/policymakers/pdf/issues.pdf

ACT. (2010). *College and career readiness report.* Retrieved from http://www.act .org/research/policymakers/cccr11/pdf/ConditionofCollegeandCareer Readiness2011.pdf

Ainsworth, L. (2003). *Power standards: Identifying the standards that matter the most.* Englewood, CO: Advanced Learning Press.

Ainsworth, L. (2011). *Rigorous curriculum design: How to create curricular units of study that align standards, instruction, and assessment.* Englewood, CO: Advanced Learning Press.

Ainsworth, L., & Viegut, D. (2006). *Common formative assessments: How to connect standards-based instruction and assessment.* Thousand Oaks, CA: Corwin.

Allan, B. M., & Fryer, R. G. (2011). *The power and pitfalls of education incentives.* Washington, DC: Hamilton Project.

Allen, J. D. (2004). Grades as valid measures of academic achievement of class-room learning. *Clearing House: A Journal of Educational Strategies, Issues and Ideas, 78*(5), 218–223.

Allensworth, E. M., & Easton, J. Q. (2005). *The on-track indicator as a predictor of high school graduation.* Chicago, IL: University of Chicago. Retrieved from https://ccsr.uchicago.edu/sites/default/files/publications/p78.pdf

Allensworth, E., & Easton, J. (2007). What matters for staying on-track and graduating in Chicago Public High Schools: A close look at course grades, failures, and attendance in the freshman year. Chicago, IL: University of Chicago, Consortium on Chicago School Research. Retrieved from https:// ccsr.uchicago.edu/sites/default/files/publications/07%20What%20 Matters%20Final.pdf

American Educational Research Association. (2004). *Encyclopedia of Educational Research* (7th ed.). Macmillan Library Reference: Macmillan USA.

Amos, J. (2011, June 27). *Alliance president Bob Wise on CNN's Your Bottom Line.* Retrieved from http://all4ed.org/alliance-president-bob-wise-on-cnns-your-bottom-line/

Balfanz, R., Legters, N., & Jordan, W. (2004). *Catching up: Impact of the talent development ninth grade instructional interventions in reading and mathematics in high-poverty high schools.* Baltimore, MD: Johns Hopkins University, Center for Research on the Education of Students.

Bang, H., & Ross, S. (2009). *Volunteer motivation and satisfaction.* Retrieved from http://www.hrsm.sc.edu/jvem/v011n01/volunteermotivation.pdf

Blackboard®K-12 (2009, June). Credit recovery: Exploring answers to a national priority. Retrieved from https://www.blackboard.com/resources/k12/Bb_K12_WP_CreditRecovery.pdf

Blankstein, A. (2012). *Failure is not an option: 6 principles that advance student achievement in highly effective schools* (3rd ed.). Thousand Oaks, CA: Corwin.

Bolam, R., McMahon, A., Stoll, L., Thomas, S., & Wallace, M. (2005). *Creating and sustaining professional learning communities* (Research Report Number 637). London, UK: General Teaching Council for England, Department for Education and Skills.

Bowers, M. (2009, October 15). Norfolk superintendent seeking feedback for possible changes to grading policy. *Virginian-Pilot.* Retrieved from http://hamptonroads.com

Brookhart, S. (2011). *How to give effective feedback to your students.* Alexandria, VA: Association for Supervision and Curriculum Development.

Butler, R., & Nisan, M. (1986). Effects of no feedback, task-related comments, and grades on intrinsic motivation and performance. *Journal of Educational Psychology, 78,* 210—216.

Cahill, M., Lynch, J., & Hamilton, L. (2006). *Multiple pathways research and development: Summary findings and strategic solutions for overage, under-credited youth.* New York, NY: New York City Department of Education. Retrieved from http://schools.nyc.gov/NR/rdonlyres/B5EC6D1C-F88A-4610-8F0F-A14D63420115/0/FindingsofOMPG.pdf

Canady, R. L. (n.d.). *Grading practices that increase/decrease the odds for student success: General grading information packet.* Retrieved from http://www.schoolschedulingassociates.com/wp-content/uploads/canady/grading/Grading-Packet-10-11.pdf

Carey, T., & Carifio, J. (2012). The minimum grading controversy: Results of a quantitative study of seven years of grading data from an urban high school. *Educational Researcher, 41*(6), 201–208.

Carr, J., & B. Farr. (2000). Taking steps toward standards-based report cards. In E. Trumbull & B. Farr (Eds.), *Grading and reporting student progress in an age of standards* (pp. 185–208). Norwood, MS: Christopher Gordon.

Center for Public Education. (2012). *Credit recovery programs: Full report.* Received from http://www.centerforpubliceducation.org/Main-Menu/Staffingstudents/Credit-recovery-programs/Credit-recovery-programs-full-report.html

Chan, W. K., & Mauborgne, R. (2003, January). Fair process: Managing in the knowledge economy. *Harvard Business Review.* Retrieved from http://hbr.org

Cognard, A. M. (1996). *The case for weighting grades and waiving classes for gifted and talented high school students.* Storrs: University of Connecticut, National Research Center on the Gifted and Talented. Retrieved from http://www.gifted.uconn.edu/nrcgt/reports/rm96226/rm96226.pdf

Collins, J. (2001). *Good to great: Why some companies make the leap . . . and others don't.* New York, NY: Harper Business.

Collins, J. (2011). *Great by choice: Uncertainty, chaos, and luck-why some thrive despite them all.* New York, NY: HarperBusiness.

Colvin, G. (2005, July 25). America isn't ready (Here's what to do about it). *Fortune.* Retrieved from http://archive.fortune.com/magazines/fortune/fortune_archive/2005/07/25/8266603/index.htm

Common Core State Standards Initiative. (2014a). *English language arts standards: Anchor standards: College and career readiness: Anchor standards for reading.* Retrieved from http://www.corestandards.org/ELA-Literacy/CCRA/R

Common Core State Standards Initiative. (2014b). *English language arts standards: Speaking and listening: Grade 9–10.* Retrieved from http://www.corestandards.org/ELA-Literacy/SL/9-10/

Common Core State Standards Initiative. (2014c). *Standards for mathematical practice.* Retrieved from http://www.corestandards.org/Math/Practice

Common Core State Standards Initiative. (n.d.). *Common Core State Standards for English language arts and literacy in history/social studies, science, and technical subjects: Appendix B: Text exemplars and sample performance tasks.* Retrieved from http://www.corestandards.org/assets/Appendix_B.pdf

Conley, D. T. (2000, April). *Who is proficient? The relationship between proficiency scores and grades.* Paper presented at the Annual Meeting of the American Educational Research Association, New Orleans, LA.

Cooper, H. (1989). A synthesis of research on homework. *Educational Leadership, 47*(3), 85–91.

Cooper, H. (2006). *The battle over homework: Common ground for administrators, teachers, and parents* (3rd ed.). Thousand Oaks, CA: Corwin.

Cooper, H., Robinson, J. C. & Patall, E. A. (2006). Does homework improve academic achievement? A synthesis of research, 1987–2003. *Review of Educational Research, 76,* 1–62.

Cooper, H., Valentine, J., Charlton, K., & Melson, A. (2003). The effects of modified school calendars on student achievement and on school and community attitudes. *Review of Educational Research, 73*(1), 1–52.

Cox, R. (2009). "It was just that I was afraid": Promoting success by addressing students' fear of failure. *Community College Review, 37*(1), 52–80.

Csepiga, M. (2013). Tri-Creek School Board approves changes affecting valedictorians, weighted grades. *NW Indiana Times.* Retrieved from http://www.nwitimes.com

Csikszentmihalyi, M. (1990). *Flow: The psychology of optimal experience.* New York, NY. HarperPerennial.

Darling-Hammond, L. (2006). Assessing teacher education: The usefulness of multiple measures for assessing program outcomes. *Journal of Teacher Education, 57*(2), 120–138.

Darling-Hammond, L. (2010). *The flat world and education: How America's commitment to equity will determine our future.* New York, NY: Teachers College Press.

Des Moines Public Schools. (2015). *DMPS Secondary Grading Practices.* Des Moines, IA: Author. Retrieved from http://grading.dmschools.org/uploads /1/0/4/8/10487804/dmps_grading_handbook_14-15.pdf

Donnegan, B. (2008). The linchpin year. *Educational Leadership, 65*(8), 54–57.

Drews, T., & Giles, P. (2002). Liberal arts degrees and the labour market. *Perspectives on Labour and Income, 13,* 27–33.

DuFour, R., Dufour, R., Eaker, R., & Karhanek, G. (2004). *Whatever it takes: How professional learning communities respond when kids don't learn.* Bloomington, IN: Solution Tree Press.

Duncan, C. R., Noonan, B., Simon, M., Tierney, R., Forgette-Giroux, R., & Hachey, K. (2009). *Comparing grading practices between secondary mathematics teachers in Ontario and Saskatchewan.* Retrieved from http://www.mea.uottawa.ca/ documents/CSSE-2009-RD.pdf

EngageNY. (2012). *Common Core shifts.* Retrieved from https://www.engageny .org/resource/common-core-shifts

ESPN. (2010). *Joyce tops survey; players nix replay.* Retrieved from http://sports .espn.go.com/mlb/news/story?id=5281467

Evans, W., Oates, W., & Schuab, R. (1992). Measuring peer group effects: A study of teenage behavior. *Journal of Political Economy, 100,* 966–991.

Fergus, M. A. (2008). Some area high schools rethink valedictorian's role in graduation, but student speakers remain. *Chicago Tribune.* Retrieved from http://articles.chicagotribune.com

Fisher, D., Frey, N., & Pumpian, I. (2011). No penalties for practice. *Educational Leadership, 69*(3), 46–51.

Fontana Unified School Board. (2011). *Secondary Grading Policy.* Fontana, CA: Author. Retrieved from http://www.fusd.net/district/schsupport/secondary/ grading%20policy.pdf

Friedman, S. (1998, April). Grading teachers' grading policies. *NASSP Bulletin,* pp. 77–83.

Fryer, R. G., Levitt, S. D., List, J., & Sadoff, S. (2010). *Enhancing the efficacy of teacher incentives through loss aversion: A field experiment* (Working Paper 18237). Cambridge, MA: National Bureau of Economic Research. Retrieved from http://rady.ucsd.edu/docs/faculty/Fryer_et_al_Teacher_Incentives_ NBER_WP18237_2012.pdf

Gainey, D. D., & Webb, L. D. (1998). *The education leader's role in change: How to proceed.* Reston, VA: National Association of Secondary School Principals.

Gillespie, M., Kim, B., Oswald, F., Ramsay, L., & Schmitt, N. (2002). *Biodata and situational judgment inventories as measures of college success: Developing and pilot testing phases.* New York, NY: College Board.

Godfrey, K. E. (2011). *Investigating grade inflation and non-equivalence* (Research Report 2011–2). New York, NY: College Board.

Goodson, I., & Hargreaves, A. (1996). *Teachers' professional lives.* Washington, DC: Falmer Press.

Green, K., & Emerson, W. A. (2007). A new framework for grading. *Journal of Assessment and Evaluation in Higher Education, 32,* 495–511.

Greene, J. P., & Winters, M. A. (2007). Revisiting grade retention: An evaluation of Florida's test-based promotion policy. *Education and Finance Policy, 2,* 319–340.

Griswold, P. A. (1993). Beliefs and inferences about grading elicited form student performance sketches. *Educational Assessment, 1*(4), 311–328.

Guskey, T. R. (Ed.). (1996). *Communicating student learning: ASCD year book 1996.* Alexandria, VA: Association for Supervision and Curriculum Development.

Guskey, T. (2011). Stability and change in high school grades. *NASSP Bulletin, 95*(2), 85–98.

Guskey, T., & Bailey, J. (2000). *Developing grading and reporting systems for student learning.* Thousand Oaks, CA: Corwin.

Guskey, T., & Bailey, J. (2010). *Developing standards-based report cards.* Thousand Oaks, CA: Corwin.

Guthrie, J. W. (Ed.). (2002). *Encyclopedia of education.* New York: Macmillan.

Gwynne, S. C. (1992). The long haul. *Time, 140*(13), 34–38.

Hanover Research. (2011). *Effective grading practices in the middle school and high school environments.* Washington, DC: Author. Retrieved from http://www.apsva.us/cms/lib2/va01000586/centricity/domain/63/hanover_research_–_effective_grading_practices_in_the_middle_school_and_high_school_environments.pdf

Hanover Research. (2013). *Replacing "zero" grading at the secondary level.* Washington, DC: Author. Retrieved from http://dumais.us/newtown/blog/wp-content/uploads/2013/08/Hanover_ReplacingZeroGrading.pdf

Hattie, J. (2008). *Visible learning: A synthesis of over 800 meta-analysis related to achievement.* New York, NY: Routledge.

Hattie, J. (2012). *Visible learning for teachers: Maximizing impact on learning.* New York, NY: Routledge.

Heath, C., & Heath, D. (2010). *Switch: How to change things when change is hard.* New York, NY. Broadway Books.

Heflebower, T., Hoegh, J., & Warrick, P. (2014). *A school leader's guide to standard based grading.* Bloomington, IN: Marzano Research Laboratory.

Henderson, N. (2013). Havens of resilience. *Educational Leadership, 71*(1), 22–27.

Holmes, C. T. (1989). Grade-level retention effects: A meta-analysis of research studies. In L. A. Shepard & M. L. Smith (Eds.), *Flunking grades: Research and policies on retention* (16–33). Philadelphia, PA: Falmer Press.

Howe, B. (Superintendent, Tri Creek Schools). Lowell: IN (personal interview, 2014).

Indiana Department of Education. (2014). *Science.* Retrieved from http://www.doe.in.gov/standards/science

Jacob, B., & Lefgren, L. (2007). The effect of grade retention on high school completion (Working Paper No. 13514). Cambridge, MA: National Bureau of Economic Research. Retrieved from http://www.nber.org/papers/w13514

Jones, B. R. (2014). *The focus model: Systematic school improvement for all schools.* Thousand Oaks, CA: Corwin.

Jumper, T. J., Executive Director of Educator Quality and Leadership. Mason City High School, Mason City: IA (personal interview, 2014).

Jussim, L., & Eccles, J. (1992). Teacher expectations I: Construction and reflection of student achievement. *Journal of Personality and Social Psychology, 63,* 947–961.

Kahneman, D. (2011). *Thinking, fast and slow.* New York, NY. Farrarr, Straus and Giroux.

Kessels, U., Warner, L. M., Holle, J., & Hannover, B. (2008). Threat to identity through positive feedback about academic performance. *Zeitschrift fur Entwicklungspsychologie und Padogogische Psychologie, 40*(1), 22–31.

Kim, W. C., & Mauborgne, R. (2003). Tipping point leadership. *Harvard Business Review, 81,* 60–69.

Kirschenbaum, A., Simon, S., & Napier, R. (1971). *Wad-ja-get? The grading game in American education.* New York, NY: Hart.

Kluger A., & DeNisi A. (1998). Feedback interventions: Toward the understanding of a double edged sword. *Current Directions in Psychological Science, 7*(3), 67–72.

Kurutz, R. D. (2013). Many high schools in W.Pa. move away from naming single valedictorian. *Triblive.com.* Retrieved from http://triblive.com/news/alle gheny/4097048–74/class-students-valedictorian#ixzz3BmvkWvGx

Lang, D. (2007). Class rank, GPA, and valedictorians: How high schools rank students. *American Secondary Education, 35*(2), 36–48.

Lemke, C., Coughlin, E., & Reifsneider, D. (2009). *Technology in schools: What the research says: An update.* Culver City, CA: Cisco.

Lavy, V., & Schlosser, A. (2007). *Mechanisms and impacts of gender peer effects at school* (NBER Working Paper No. 13292). Retrieved from http://www.nber .org/papers/w13292

Major League Baseball. (2013). *Official baseball rules.* Retrieved from http://mlb .mlb.com/mlb/downloads/y2013/official_baseball_rules.pdf

Mansell, W. (2009, September 23). Research reveals teaching's holy grail. *Times Educational Supplement.* Retrieved from https://www.tes.co.uk

Martindale, S. (2012). School principal alters grades without teacher's consent. *Orange County Register.* Retrieved from http://www.ocregister.com

Marzano, R. (2006). *Classroom assessment and grading that work.* Alexandria, VA: Association for Supervision and Curriculum Development.

Marzano, R. (2007). *The art and science of teaching.* Alexandria, VA: Association for Supervision and Curriculum Development.

Marzano, R., Pickering, D., & Pollock, J. (2001). *Classroom instruction that works: Research-based strategies for increasing student achievement.* Alexandria, VA: Association for Supervision and Curriculum Development.

Matthews, J. (2013, December 15). D.C. teacher quits over grading, disruption. *Washington Post.* Retrieved from http://www.washingtonpost.com

Maxwell, L. (2013, February 4). Texas district goes door to door to find dropouts. *Education Week.* Retrieved from http://www.edweek.org

Merriam-Webster. (2014a). *Develop.* Retrieved from http://www.merriam-web ster.com/dictionary/develop

Merriam-Webster. (2014b). *Policy.* Retrieved from http://www.merriam-webster .com/dictionary/policy

Mertler, C. (2014). *Action research: Improving schools and empowering educators.* Thousand Oaks, CA: Sage.

Metropolitan School District of Wayne Township. (2015). *Grading Scale.* Indianapolis, IN: Author. Retrieved from http://www.wayne.k12.in.us/district/grading-scale.asp

Metz, M. H., & Page, R. N. (2002). The uses of practitioner research and status issues in educational research: Reply to Gary Anderson. *Educational Researcher, 31*(7), 26–27.

Middleton, W. (1933). Some general trends in grading procedure. *Education, 54*(1), 5–10.

Minnema, E. (2007). *An investigation of data driven practices at the high school level* (Unpublished doctoral dissertation). University of Minnesota, Minneapolis.

Mosher, F. (2011). *The role of learning progressions in standards-based education reform* (CPRE Policy Brief #RB-52). Philadelphia: University of Pennsylvania, Graduate School of Education. Retrieved from http://www.cpre.org/role-learning-progressions-standards-based-education-reform

Nagel, D. (2008). Giving high school students more time. *Principal Leadership, 8*(7), 29–31.

Nagel, D. (2010). Built-in remediation. *Educational Leadership, 68*(2), 66–67.

National Association for College Admission Counseling. (2013). *State of college admission report.* Retrieved from http://www.nacacnet.org/research/Publications Resources/Marketplace/research/Pages/StateofCollegeAdmission.aspx

National High School Center. (n.d.). *Early warning system high school tool.* Retrieved from http://www.betterhighschools.org/EWSTool.aspx

Nield, R. C., & Balfanz, R. (2006). Unfulfilled promise: The dimensions and characteristics of Philadelphia's dropout crisis, 2000–2005. Retrieved from http://www.csos.jhu.edu/new/Neild_Balfanz_06.pdf

O'Connor, K. (2009). *How to grade for learning, K–12* (3rd ed.). Thousand Oaks, CA: Corwin.

O'Connor, K. (2010). *A repair kit for grading: Fifteen fixes for broken grades* (2nd ed.). Boston, MA. Pearson Education.

Orfield, G. (2004). *Dropouts in America: Confronting the graduation rate crisis.* Boston, MA: Harvard Education Press.

Page, E. B. (1958). Teacher comments and student performance: A seventy-four classroom experiment in school motivation. *Journal of Educational Psychology, 49*(4), 173–181.

Paluska, M. (2013). Henry County schools superintendent dodges questions about grade changes. *CBS46.* Retrieved from http://www.cbs46.com

Pape, L., & Wicks, M. (2012). *National standards for quality online programs.* Vienna, VA: International Association for K–12 Online Learning.

Parker, S. (2013, June 26). *Fed up teachers refuse to teach summer school in Texas.* Retrieved from http://www.takepart.com/article/2013/06/26/summer-school-dallas-no-teachers

Patall, E. A., Cooper, H., & Robinson, J. C. (2008). The effects of choice on intrinsic motivation and related outcomes: a meta-analysis of research findings. *Psychology Bulletin, 134,* 270–300.

Pauly, M., (2009). *One principal's self-study: Facilitating collaborative analysis of student work to inform teaching and learning* (Doctoral dissertation). Available from ProQuest Dissertations and Theses database. (UMI No. 3372099)

Perkins-Gough, D. (2013). The significance of grit: A conversation with Angela Lee Duckworth. *Educational Leadership, 71*(1),

Pink, D. (2011). *Drive: The surprising truth about what motivates us.* New York, NY: Penguin Group.

Pink, D. (2012). *To sell is human: The surprising truth about moving others.* New York, NY: Riverhead Books.

Popham, W. J. (2008). *Transformative assessment.* Alexandria, VA: Association for Supervision and Curriculum Development.

Purdue University. (2014). *Academic regulations and procedures: Grades and grade reports.* Retrieved from http://www.purdue.edu/studentregulations/regula tions_procedures/grades.html

Qualia, R. & Corso, M. (2014). *Student voice: The instrument of change.* Thousand Oaks, CA: Corwin.

Raznov, G. B. (1987). *High school teachers' needs, attitudes, and actions in response to comprehensive change: The standardized curriculum policy of the School District of Philadelphia.* Retrieved from http://repository.upenn.edu/dissertations/AAI8714114

Reeves, D. (2004). The case against the zero. *Phi Delta Kappan, 86,* 324–325.

Reeves, D. (2008). Leading to change/effective grading practices. *Educational Leadership, 65*(5), 85–87.

Reeves, D. (2009). *Leading change in your school: How to conquer myths, build commitment, and get results.* Alexandria, VA: Association for Supervision and Curriculum Development

Reeves, D. (2011a). *Elements of grading: A guide to effective practice.* Bloomington, IN: Solution Tree Press.

Reeves, D. (2011b). Skeptics and cynics. *American School Board Journal, 198*(10), 40.

Reeves, D. (2012, July). The ketchup solution. *American School Board Journal,* pp. 35–36.

Robbins, A. (1996). *Anthony Robbins' personal power II: The driving force!* (Audio CD). Robbins Research International.

Robelen, E. (2010, June 29). Texas judge says no to minimum-grading policy. *Education Week.* Retrieved from http://blogs.edweek.org

Robinson, V., & Lei, M. K. (2006). *Practitioner research for educators: A guide to improving classrooms and schools.* Thousand Oaks, CA: Corwin.

Roderick, M., & Camburn, C. (1999). Risk and Recovery from course failure in the early years of high school. *American Educational Research Journal, 36,* 303–343.

Rose, S. (2012). *Third grade reading policies.* Denver, CO: Education Commission of the States. Retrieved from http://www.ecs.org/clearinghouse/01/03/47/10347.pdf

Rose, S. & Schimke, K. (2012). *Third grade literacy policies: Identification, intervention, retention.* Retrieved from http://files.eric.ed.gov/fulltext/ED535949.pdf

Rosenthal, R., & Jacobson, L. (2003). *Pygmalion in the classroom: Teacher expectation and pupils' intellectual development.* Wales, UK: Crown House.

Rubie-Davies, C. (2008). Teacher expectations. In T. Good (Ed.), *21st century education: A reference handbook* (pp. 254–265). Thousand Oaks, CA: Sage.

Sadler, P., & Tai, R. (2007). Weighting for recognition: Accounting for advanced placement and honors courses when calculating high school grade point average. *NASSP Bulletin, 91*(1), 5–32.

Sarasota County School Board. (2015). *Middle School Student Progression Plan (Grades 6–8)*. Sarasota, FL: Author. Retrieved from http://www.sarasota-countyschools.net/WorkArea/DownloadAsset.aspx?id=22332

Schmidt, A. (2007). High-school students aim higher without learning more, federal studies find. *Chronicle of Higher Education, 53*(27), A32.

Schmoker, M. (2006). *Results now: How we can achieve unprecedented improvements in teaching and learning.* Alexandria, VA: Association for Supervision and Curriculum Development.

Schneider, M. (2010). *Finishing the first lap: The cost of first-year student attrition in America's four-year colleges and universities.* Washington, DC: American Institutes of Research.

Shannon, G. S., & Bylsma, P. (2007). *Nine characteristics of high-performing schools: A research based resource for schools and districts to assist with improving student learning* (2nd Ed.). Olympia, WA: Office of Superintendent of Public Instruction.

Shedd, J. (2003). The history of the student credit hour. *New Directions for Higher Education, 2003*(122), 5–12.

Simmons, K., & Sutter, D. (2005). WSR-88D radar, tornado warnings, and tornado casualties. *Weather and Forecasting, 20,* 301–310. Retrieved from http://www.nssl.noaa.gov/users/brooks/public_html/feda/papers/simmonssutter.pdf

Smith, M. (Principal, North High School), Van Der Wall, J. (School Improvement Coordinator, North High School), & Vukovich, M. (Associate Principal, North High School). Des Moines: IA (personal interview, 2014).

Southwell, S. (2013). Updated: Some LISD parents upset over draft middle school grading policy. *Lewisville Texan Journal.* Retrieved from http://lewisvilletexan.com

St. George, D. (2014, March 10). Math exam failure persists in Montgomery, even as efforts are underway to help. *Washington Post.* Retrieved from http://www.washingtonpost.com

St. Louis Board of Education. (2012). *Draft promotion and retention policy and regulation 2012–2013.* Retrieved from http://www.slps.org/cms/lib03/MO01001157/Centricity/Domain/3688/Proposed%20Promotion%20and%20Retention%20Policy.pdf

Starch, D., & Elliott, E. C. (1913). Reliability of the grading of high school work in mathematics. *School Review, 21,* 254–259.

Stiggins, R. (2005). *Student-involved assessment for learning* (4th ed.). Boston, MA. Pearson/Merrill Prentice Hall.

Stiggins, R. J., Arter, J. A., Chappuis, J., & Chappuis, S. (2004). *Classroom assessment FOR student learning: Doing it right—using it well.* Portland, OR: ETS Assessment Training Institute.

Stiggins, R., & Chappuis, J. (2011). *An introduction to student-involved assessment for learning* (6th ed.). Boston, MA: Pearson.

Stoll, L., Bolam, R., McMahon, A., Wallace, M., & Thomas, S. (2006). Professional learning communities: A review of the literature. *Journal of Educational Change, 7,* 221–258.

Stutz, T. (2010, November 26). School districts drop fight over truth-in-grading law. *Dallas Morning News.* Retrieved from http://www.dallasnews.com

Sum, A., Khatiwada, I., & McLaughlin, J. (with Palma, S). (2009). *The consequences of dropping out of high school: Joblessness and jailing for high school dropouts and the high cost for taxpayers.* Boston, MA: Northeastern University, Center for Labor Market Studies. Retrieved from http://www.northeastern.edu/clms/wp-content/uploads/The_Consequences_of_Dropping_Out_of_High_School.pdf

Symonds, W. C., Schwartz, R., & Ferguson, R. (2011). *Pathways to prosperity: Meeting the challenge of preparing young Americans for the 21st century.* Cambridge, MA: Harvard University Graduate School of Education, Pathways to Prosperity Project. Retrieved from http://dash.harvard.edu/bitstream/handle/1/4740480/Pathways_to_Prosperity_Feb2011-1.pdf?sequence=1

Tan, S. (2013, June 17). Buffalo graduation rates sank to 47 percent in 2012. *Buffalo News.* Retrieved from http://www.buffalonews.com

Texas AFT. (2012, November 27). *New pre-filed legislation: Banning grade inflation.* Retrieved from http://www.texasaft.org/new-pre-filed-legislation-banning-grade-inflation/#sthash.mfcvGl19.dpuf

Tierney, R. (2011). *Insights into fairness in classroom assessment: Experienced English teachers share practical wisdom.* Retrieved from https://www.academia.edu/1157097/Insights_into_Fairness_in_Classroom_Assessment_Experienced_English_Teachers_Share_their_Practical_Wisdom

Tomlinson, C. A., & Imbeau, M. B. (2013). *Leading and managing a differentiated classroom.* Alexandria, VA: Association for Supervision and Curriculum Development.

Trotter, A. (2008, May 19). Online options for "credit recovery" widen. *Education Week.* Retrieved from http://www.edweek.org

Truog, A. L., & Friedman, S. J. (1996, April). Evaluating high school teachers' written grading policies from a measurement perspective. Paper presented at the annual meeting of the National Council on Measurement in Education, New York.

Valedictorian, you're retired. (2012, August 20). *Chicago Tribune.* Retrieved from http://www.chicagotribune.com

Vatterott, C. (2009). *Rethinking homework: Best practices that support diverse needs.* Alexandria, VA: Association for Supervision and Curriculum Development.

Viadero, D. (2009). Turnover in principalship focus of research. *Education Week.* Retrieved from http://www.edweek.org

Vickers, J. (2000). Justice and truth in grades and their averages. *Research in Higher Education, 41*(2), 141–164.

Wang, A. (2012). Some schools removing valedictorian title: Districts break tradition, honor more students. *Azcentral.com.* Retrieved from http://www.azcentral.com/news/articles/2012/04/26/20120426valedictorian-title-erased.html

Watson, J., & Gemin, B. (2008, June). Promising practices in online learning for at-risk students and credit recovery. North American Council For Online Learning. Retrieved from http://www.k12hsn.org/files/research/Online_Learning/NACOL_CreditRecovery_PromisingPractices.pdf

Webster, K. L. (2011). *High school grading practices: Teacher leaders reflections, insights, and recommendations.* Ann Arbor, MI: ProQuest.

Welsh, M. E., & D'Agostino, J. (2009). Fostering consistency between standards-based grades and large-scale assessment results. In T. R. Guskey (Ed.), *Practical solutions for serious problems in standards-based grading* (pp. 75–104). Thousand Oaks, CA: Corwin.

Wiggins, G., McTighe, G., & McTighe, J. (1998). *Understanding by design.* Alexandria, VA: Association for Supervision and Curriculum Design.

Wise, B. (2008). *Raising the grade.* San Francisco, CA: Jossey-Bass.

Wormell, 8i, R. (2006). *Fair isn't always equal: Assessing and grading in the differentiated classroom.* Portland, ME. National Middle School Association.

Yazzie-Mintz, E. (2010). *Charting the path from engagement to achievement: A report on the 2009 High School Survey of Student Engagement.* Bloomington, IN: Indiana University, Center for Evaluation and Education Policy. Retrieved from http://ceep.indiana.edu/hssse/images/HSSSE_2010_Report.pdf

Zehr, M. A. (2012, March 23). Districts embracing online credit-recovery options. *Education Week.* Retrieved from http://www.edweek.org

Zoeckler, L. (2005). *Moral dimensions of grading in high school English* (Doctoral dissertation, Indiana University). Retrieved from https://scholarworks.iu.edu/dspace/bitstream/handle/2022/7144/umi-indiana-1163.pdf?sequence=1

Index

A SAGE Company

Corwin is committed to improving education for all learners by publishing books and other professional development resources for those serving the field of PreK–12 education. By providing practical, hands-on materials, Corwin continues to carry out the promise of its motto: **"Helping Educators Do Their Work Better."**